Labour Law in Finland

Labour Law in Finland

Antti Johannes Suviranta†
Jaana Tuulikki Paanetoja

This book was originally published as a monograph in the International Encyclopaedia of Laws/Labour Law and Industrial Relations.

Founding Editor: Roger Blanpain
General Editor: Frank Hendrickx
Volume Editor: Frank Hendrickx

Wolters Kluwer

Published by:
Kluwer Law International B.V.
PO Box 316
2400 AH Alphen aan den Rijn
The Netherlands
E-mail: lrs-sales@wolterskluwer.com
Website: www.wolterskluwer.com/en/solutions/kluwerlawinternational

Sold and distributed by:
Wolters Kluwer Legal & Regulatory U.S.
920 Links Avenue
Landisville, PA 17538
United States of America
E-mail: customer.service@wolterskluwer.com

ISBN 978-94-035-3476-3

e-Book: ISBN 978-94-035-3906-5
web-PDF: ISBN 978-94-035-3916-4

This title is available on www.kluwerlawonline.com

The Authors

Antti Johannes Suviranta was born on 30 November 1923. After service with the Finnish Army during World War II, he studied law at the University of Helsinki, Finland, graduating in 1948. He continued with postgraduate studies at Helsinki and Harvard Law School, earning a Master's from Harvard in 1952 and a doctorate from Helsinki in 1963. While engaged in his degree work, he served as a clerk and deputy for a district judge, as an official of the university administration in Helsinki, and as a civil servant with the Finnish Ministry of Finance. In 1962, he became acting professor of Labour law at the University of Helsinki, holding that position until his permanent appointment to the chair in 1967. In 1968 he served as an auxiliary justice at the Supreme Administrative Court of Finland. In 1970, he became president of the Finnish Labour Court, first on a part-time basis, but serving full-time from 1971 to 1982, on leave of absence from the University. From 1973 to 1979, he was also chairman of the Finnish Labour Council. From 1982 until his retirement in 1993, he was president (chief justice) of the Supreme Administrative Court. His other service includes engagement as the chairman, member or secretary of several government commissions, in particular on taxation, administrative procedure and labour legislation.

Chief Justice Suviranta authored several books and a number of articles, mainly on tax, labour and administrative law. He lectured in several countries. He was chairman of the Finnish Labour Law Society from 1974 to 1982 and a member of the Executive Committee of the International Society for Labour Law and Social Security from 1970 to 1985. From 1984 to 1993, he was a member of the Committee of Experts of the International Labour Organization on the Application of Conventions and Recommendations, and from 1990 to 1998, a member of the European Commission for Democracy through Law (the Venice Commission). From 1977 to 1979, he was chairman of the Finnish Lawyers' Association, and from 1986 to 1989, president of the International Association of Supreme Administrative Jurisdictions. In 1973 he was inducted into the Finnish Academy of Science and Letters, in 1989, he became a working member of the Society for Finnish Literature, and in 1994 an associate member of the International Academy of Comparative Law. Dr Suviranta passed away on 30 March 2008.

The Authors

Jaana Tuulikki Paanetoja was born on 16 October 1964. She studied law at the University of Helsinki, receiving her LLM in 1988, LLLic in 1992 and LLD in 2013. She completed training on the bench from 1989 to 1990. From 1990 to 1992, she was a researcher in a project financed by the Academy of Finland and, from 1992 to 1995, Assistant Professor of Labour Law at the University of Helsinki, working in that capacity until her permanent appointment as Secretary of the Labour Council in 1996.

From October 2013 to July 2016, Dr Paanetoja was on leave of absence from her position with the Labour Council to work as a Professor of Labour and Social Law at the University of Lapland. She is an Adjunct Professor of Labour and Social Law at the University of Lapland and an Adjunct Professor of Labour Law at the University of Eastern Finland and at the University of Helsinki.

In 2005, she also graduated from the University of Applied Science in Hämeenlinna and had teacher education. She was a part-time (neutral) member of the Civil Service Board from 1999 to 30 November 2013, when the Board was wound up. She has been a part-time (neutral) judge in the Labour Court. Paanetoja is the author of several books and articles on labour and social law. She has also participated in legislative work; for example, from 1990 to 1993 as secretary of the tripartite committee, which prepared a proposal on the Act on Working Hours (1990–1993) and the committee which clarified the application of the Act on Working Hours (1999–2000). She was also a member of a committee which remodelled the legislation on occupational safety and health exemptions and the Labour Council. In 2018, she was appointed to investigate as neutral expert harassment and other inappropriate treatment in the film and theatre industry and in 2019 to investigate the reform of the social service promoting access to employment and rehabilitative work activities for people with intellectual and other disabilities.

Table of Contents

List of Abbreviations

Akava	Confederation of Unions for Academic Professionals in Finland
EU	European Union
EEC	European Economic Community
EEA	European Economic Area
ICFTU	International Confederation of Free Trade Unions
ILO	International Labour Organization
IOE	International Organization of Employers
LS	International Labour Office, *Legislative Series*
LTK	*Liiketyönantajain Keskusliitto* (Employers' Confederation of Service Industries; from 1995 PT, *see below*)
PT	*Palvelutyönantajat ry* (Employers' Confederation of Service Industries; until 1995 LTK, PT merged with TT in 2005 to become EK)
SAJ	*Suomen Ammattijärjestö* (Finnish Trade Union Confederation; 1907 to 1930 and 1960 to 1969)
SAK	*Suomen Ammattiyhdistysten Keskusliitto*, since 1969 Suomen *Ammattiliittojen Keskusjärjestö* (Central Organization of Finnish Trade Unions; from 1930)
STK	*Suomen Työnantajain Keskuslitto* (Finnish Employers' Confederation); merged in 1993 with TT and 2005 with EK
STTK	*Suomen Teknisten Toimihenkilöjärjestöjen Keskusliitto* (Confederation of Technical Employee Organizations in Finland); from 1993 *Toimihenkilökeskusjärjestö STTK* (Finnish Confederation of Salaried Employees STTK), at the moment *STTK*
TT	*Teollisuuden ja Työnantajain Keskusliitto* (Confederation of Finnish Industry and Employers, from 2005 EK *Elinkeinoelämän keskusliitto*, Confederation of Finnish Industries)

List of Abbreviations

TVK	*Toimihenkilö- ja Virkamiesjärjestöjen Keskusliitto* (Confederation of Salaried Employees; until 1992)
WFTU	World Federation of Trade Unions

Foreword

The previous updated edition of this work described Finnish labour law as it stood in 2016. Since then, some main labour laws have been totally rewritten or individual provisions have been amended as a result of national developments or the influence of EU law. The present monograph takes these developments into account. The structure of the work has remained almost the same as that of the original.

Introduction

Chapter 1. General Background

§1. GEOGRAPHY AND POPULATION

I. The Country

1. Finland is, next to Iceland, the northernmost independent country in the world. It lies in northern Europe stretching from the 60th to the 70th northern latitude, or from the Baltic Sea to near the Arctic Ocean. Finland covers an area of 303,891 square kilometres of land and 34,544 square kilometres of inland waters. It has some 1,100 kilometres of coastline on the Gulf of Finland and the Gulf of Bothnia, and 2,582 kilometres of land frontier with Sweden, Norway and Russia.

2. Finland was christianized during the twelfth and thirteenth centuries and became an integral part of the Kingdom of Sweden. As a result of war defeats, parts of Finland were ceded to Russia in 1721 and 1743 and the whole country in 1809, when Finland became an autonomous Grand Duchy within the Russian Empire. Finland retained its old laws and even the Swedish Constitution of 1772 and 1789, the Emperor of Russia replaced the King of Sweden as the Grand Duke of Finland. In 1917, Finland became an independent republic. As a result of World War II, parts of Finland comprising about 12% of its area were ceded to the Soviet Union. The inhabitants of those areas, however, moved – without being forced to do so – to the remaining parts of the country and were settled there.

II. The People

3. By population, Finland is a small country. The population reached 5.4 million in 2013. By the end of 2021, it had 5,548,241 inhabitants (men: 2.743,000 and women 2.805,000). The percentage of people of 65 and over was 6.7 in 1950, 14.6 in 1997, and 23 in 2021. The corresponding percentages for children (under 15) are 30% in 1950, 18.7% in 1997, 16.3% in 2015 and 15.4% in 2021.

4. The population of Finland is culturally, racially and religiously fairly homogenous. Culturally Finland is a part of the Scandinavian (Nordic) sphere, and as in the other Scandinavian countries, the Lutheran church is predominant, comprising 66.6% of the population. The members of the Greek Orthodox church amount to

1.1% and the members of all other registered denominations also to 1.8% of the population, while 30.6% of the population are outside the registered religious communities or the community is unknown. Linguistically there are two national languages with equal rights, Finnish and Swedish. The Swedish-speaking minority comprised 8.6% of the population in 1950, 5.7% in 1994, 5.3% in 2013 and 5.2% in 2021. The decline is due to a smaller birth rate and larger emigration among the Swedish-speaking population. The Sámi (Lapps) and the Roma (gypsies) can be regarded as minorities not only linguistically (Sámi-speaking: 0.04%) but also culturally and possibly even in a racial sense. The linguistic and cultural rights of the Sámi (as an indigenous people) and the Roma are specifically protected by the Constitution.

§2. Political and Legal System

I. Constitution

5. The old Swedish constitutional enactments of 1772 and 1789 were in 1919 replaced with a new republican constitution, the Form of Government Act, which guarantees the fundamental rights of the citizens and determines the main principles of the organization and powers of the three branches of the State. Mainly for historical reasons, however, the organization and procedures of the legislative branch are to a large extent embodied in another constitutional enactment, the Parliament Act, 1928. The 1928 Act was, however, mainly a consolidation of the Parliament Act, 1906, and its amendments. By the 1906 Act, the old four-estate legislature (nobles, clergy, burghers and peasants) dating back to the fifteenth century was replaced with a unicameral legislature elected with an equal and universal suffrage of all adult men and women. The constitutional provisions on fundamental rights were modernized in 1955, augmented with new provisions on economic, social, cultural and environmental rights, and extended to cover everyone within the jurisdiction of Finland and not only Finnish citizens. After several years of preparation, a new Constitution of Finland, to consolidate the Form of Government Act (the 1995 provisions on fundamental rights included), the fundamental provisions of the Parliament Act, and two more constitutional enactments, was adopted by Parliament in February 1999. Under the constitutional procedure, the new Constitution was passed by the new Parliament, elected at the general elections of March 1999 and signed by the President of the Republic on 11 June 1999. The Constitution took effect on 1 March 2000.

6. Legislative power is exercised by the Parliament and the President of the Republic. The President has, however, a suspensive veto right only: his veto can be overruled by the Parliament at its next session. Special procedures with qualified majorities are required for constitutional amendments. Parliament is elected for a term of four years, but the President of the Republic may, upon proposal of the Prime Minister, order new general elections before the expiry of the four-year term. The President is elected by the people for a term of six years in Finland, and he may be re-elected, but for one consecutive term only. The executive power is exercised by him and the Cabinet, appointed by him, but required to enjoy the confidence of the Parliament. Judicial power is in the hands of independent tribunals. The new Constitution of Finland enhanced the position of Parliament and the Prime Minister in comparison with the President of the Republic. The Prime Minister is elected by Parliament, and the other ministers are appointed by the President as proposed by the Prime Minister. The President may still return an Act adopted by Parliament for reconsideration, but Parliament needs no longer wait until its next session for the reconsideration.

7. Finland was administratively subdivided into provinces until the end of 2009, with each headed by a governor appointed by the President. The Province of Åland (Aaland Islands), comprising one-half of 1% of the entire population, enjoys self-government with an elected provincial legislature and an executive board. The provinces were further subdivided into municipalities (communes) with locally elected organs and the power to tax persons with a domicile or a piece of real property within the borders of the municipality. Several administrative tasks originally belonging to the provinces have since been transferred to other units of state administration, namely, municipalities, nineteen in total, and their regional federations. Several other regional units of various sectors of the state administration were merged in 2010 into fifteen Economic Development, Transport and Environment Centres and to regional state administrative agencies. There are six of these, and the equivalent authority in the Åland Islands is the State Department of Åland. Where occupational safety is concerned, the agencies are tasked with overseeing compliance with the employment legislation. In addition, they are responsible for investigating serious accidents in the workplace, determining the causes of occupational and work-related diseases and measures to prevent these, carrying out product control and participating in proceedings relating to labour offences.

The organization of public healthcare, social welfare and rescue services will be reformed in Finland and the responsibility for organizing these services will be transferred from municipalities to well-being services counties from the beginning of 2023. Under the reform, a total of twenty-one self-governing well-being services counties will be established. In addition, the City of Helsinki will be responsible for organising health, social and rescue services within its own area.

Finland is a member of the Nordic Council, an organ elected by the Scandinavian legislatures (the Parliaments of Denmark, Finland, Iceland, Norway and Sweden as well as the provincial legislatures of Åland in Finland and the Faeroe Islands and Greenland in Denmark). The Nordic Council has, however, no supranational powers; it can make recommendations only. In 1989, Finland joined the Council of Europe and acceded to the European Convention on Human Rights, and as of 1 January 1995, Finland has been a member of the European Union (EU). From the very beginning, on 1 January 1999, Finland joined the European Monetary Union (EMU). Finland applied for membership in North Atlantic Treaty Organization on 17 May 2022.

II. Finnish Politics

8. The spectrum of political parties in the country has varied somewhat in the post-war years. In Table 1 are the results of the general elections in 1987, 1991, 1995 and 1999.

Table 1 Results of Finnish General Elections

	1987	*1991*	*1995*	*1999*
National Coalition Party (moderate conservatives)	53	40	39	46
Christian League of Finland	5	8	7	10
Liberal Party	–	1	–	–
Progressive Finnish Party (neoliberals)	–	–	2	–
Centre Party of Finland (with agrarian traditions)	40	55	44	48
Swedish People's Party in Finland (non-socialist language party)	12	11	11	11
Coalition of Åland	1	1	1	1
True Finns' Party (until 1995 Finnish Rural Party, a breakaway group from the Centre Party)	9	7	1	1
Reform Group (a breakaway group from the Progressive Finnish Party)	–	–	–	1
Green League	4	10	9	11
Ecological Party	–	–	1	–
Social Democratic Party of Finland	56	48	63	51
Left Wing Alliance (until 1987 Democratic League of the People of Finland)	20	19	22	20
Total	200	200	200	200

The list runs approximately from right to left politically, but does not aspire to describe all the nuances. One clear distinction to note, however, is that all parties except the Greens, the Ecological Party and the last two on the list, the Social Democrats and the People's Democrats, along with their successors, are non-socialists. For many post-war decades, the country was governed mainly by coalition cabinets, formed around the Centre Party and, later, the Social Democrats. These parties worked in partnership with the small parties in the centre (Swedes – including Ålanders – and, earlier, Liberals) and, occasionally, the People's Democrats, the Rural Party, or the (moderate) Conservatives. Beginning with the elections of 1987, the political colours of the coalitions have fluctuated: first came the

Blue-Red Cabinet (Social Democrats, Conservatives, Swedes and the Rural Party), from 1991 the Blue-Green Cabinet (Centre Party, Conservatives, Swedes and the Christian League) and from 1995 to 1999 two 'rainbow cabinets' (Social Democrats, Conservatives, the Left Wing Alliance, Swedes and Greens).

The 2015 parliamentary elections saw the Centre Party rise to become the country's largest. The True Finns maintained the considerable support that the party had gained between 2007 and 2011 elections and became a government party in 2015 for the first time in its history. The National Coalition Party received more votes than the True Finns but ended up third in the final tally of seats in Parliament. The outcome for the fourth largest party, the Social Democrats, was poor. Voter turnout in the elections was 66.9%.

The following is the distribution of seats in Parliament following the 2015 elections: Centre Party, 49 seats; True Finns, 38; National Coalition Party, 37; Social Democrats, 34; Green League, 15; Left Wing Alliance 12; Swedish People's Party in Finland, 9, and the Christian Democrats, 5. The Centre Party, True Finns and National Coalition Party had formed the government, which was led by Prime Minister Juha Sipilä (Centre Party).

In 2019, Social Democrats (The Social Democratic Party of Finland) received 17.7% of the votes, Finns Party 17.5%, National Coalition Party 17%, Centre Party 13.8%, Green League 11.5%, Left Wing Party 8.2%, Swedish People's Party in Finland 4.5%, the Christian Democrats 3.9% and others 6%. The voting percentage of Finnish citizens living in Finland was 72.1, 2 percentage points higher than in the previous Parliamentary elections.

The following is the distribution of seats in Parliament following the 2019 elections: Social Democrats 40, Finns Party 39, National Coalition Part 38, Centre Party 31, Green League 20, Left Wing Alliance 10, Swedish People's Party in Finland 9 and the Christian Democrats 5.

All parties' support remained under 20% for the first time in 2019 and the differences between the three biggest parties were small. The Social Democrats gained a total of 546,471 votes, the Finns Party 538,805 and the National Coalition Party 523,957 votes. The Blue Reform that separated from the Finns Party gained 1.0% of all votes cast. Groups outside the Parliamentary parties increased their support from the previous elections.

The Social Democrats, The Centre Party, Green League, The Left Wing Alliance and The Swedish People's Party formed the government, which was led first by Prime Minister Antti Rinne (Social Democrats). Rinne resigned after half a year and Prime Minister Sanna Marin (Social Democrats) continued on the basis of the same government programme (Inclusive and competent Finland – a socially, economically and ecologically sustainable society).

III. The Law

9. The development of the inherited Swedish law began gradually in the 1860s; but the main models for this development were – and largely still are – sought from Sweden. In addition to this, outright borrowing. Finland has been an active partner in the Scandinavian legislative cooperation in various fields of private law since the

1920s. The significance of this cooperation has, however, diminished during the last decades, mainly because it has been regarded, especially in Sweden, as too slow a method for law reforms. Some legal differences between Finland and the other Scandinavian countries stem from the fact that the predominant influence of German legal science continued in Finland for longer than elsewhere in Scandinavia. Like the other Scandinavian countries, Finland is a country of mainly statutory but not systematically codified law. As a consequence, the interpretation of statutory provisions by courts and their expounding and systematization by legal scholars are more important than the creation of new judge or scholar-made legal rules. Statutory provisions are generally interpreted less literally than, e.g., in England but more literally than, e.g., in Sweden. Now, the conventions of the Council of Europe, the treaties, directives and regulations of the EU, and the case law of the Strasbourg and Luxembourg Courts constitute new elements, which influence the domestic legislation, the practice of courts and administrative authorities, and the science of law as well as legal life in general.

§3. The Economy

I. General

10. Finland has been characterized as a national economy based on wood. Forests are in fact the foremost natural resource of Finland. Of the land area, forest land comprises 75.5% and agricultural land 9.0%. The remaining part consists mainly of hills, swamps, etc., in addition to the small part required for building lots, streets, railways, etc. Due to soil and weather conditions, it is not feasible to enlarge the area of agricultural land. However, small fields not suitable for mechanized agriculture are gradually being turned over to forestry. Due to changing economic circumstances, especially under the agricultural policies of the EU, this development is now extending to other kinds of agricultural land. Weather is, however, an inhibiting factor in forestry, too. Due to a short growing season and a low summer temperature, the trees grow slowly especially in northern Finland, where it takes about 120 years for a tree to reach cutting age. Finland has some hydroelectric power (12.2% of total energy consumption in 1950 and 10.1% in 1995; during the same period, the share of firewood went down from 33% to 2.7%) and mineral resources (mainly chromium, zinc, sulphur and limestone) but no coal, oil or natural gas.

11. Finland has been a predominantly agricultural country. As late as 1950, 46% of the economically active population was engaged in agriculture, forestry and fishing. The exports consisted mainly of wood products (pulp, paper and sawn goods), while the other manufactures (textiles, metals, etc.) were mainly produced for home consumption. Due to war reparations, to be paid in kind, Finland had to develop its engineering industry in particular. Later on, other branches, especially high technology (electronics and mobile phones) followed suit, while other, especially labour-intensive fields (textiles, shoes, etc.) have suffered in competition with low-wage countries. Meanwhile, the mechanization of agriculture has led to a steep decline in the agricultural population. Finland has been a country of smallholdings, owned by their cultivators, although agricultural units have to a considerable extent been combined, diminishing the number of farms, from 331,000 in 1959 to 155,000 in 1996. The development is, however, shown more clearly by the fact that permanently hired help is nowadays employed by very few farms and that the number of family members working on the farm has also decreased considerably. Concurrently, smallholders' possibilities of earning additional income from forest work have also diminished, as work in forests has also been mechanized and the nature of employment in forest work has been shifting from seasonal to permanent.

Foreign trade has always been an important factor in the economy of Finland. In 1997, the exports amounted to 34.2% of the gross national product. Before joining the EU on 1 January 1995, Finland was a member of the European Free Trade Association (EFTA), and it had free trade agreements with the European Economic Community (EEC) as well as the Soviet Union and many of the other CMEA (the Council for Mutual Economic Assistance, Comecon) countries, and later, with the Baltic States. From 1 January 1994, Finland belonged to the European Economic Area (EEA) – and as a member of the EU, it still forms part of it. The five important international trading partners in 2015 were Germany, Sweden, Russia, The Netherlands and China. In 2020 (the second quarter of the year), the combined exports of goods and services decreased by 18% relative to the corresponding quarter of the previous year. International trade, or exports and imports, fell in both goods and services. Twenty-eight percent less services were exported and twenty-two percent less services were imported than in the previous year. Europe's share of Finland's exports was sixty-six per cent. Finland is very sensitive to fluctuations in terms of trade. A rise in import prices or a drop in the demand for export products easily leads to a steep rise either in the foreign debt, as in 1975 (when the net foreign debt amounted to 20.5% of the gross national product, as contrasted to 2.4% in 1960 or 9.2% in 1970) or in unemployment, as in 1977 and 1978, or in both, as during the unprecedented depression of the early 1990s (with net foreign debt of 54% in 1994 and still 43% in 1997), to which the collapse of Soviet trade and the recession in the West contributed together with domestic factors.

12. Finland has a mixed economy in the sense that, while private ownership is predominant, there is also a considerable public sector, and some important enterprises are co-owned by the State – either as a majority or a minority shareholder – and by private interests. Public ownership is not, however, a result of any nationalizations. Many enterprises – such as the main line railways as well as the most important mines and hydroelectric plants – have from the very beginning been in public ownership, while others have been bought by the State, in many cases, in order to prevent their total collapse in economic difficulties. At present, public ownership is being diminished by way of privatization, mainly by selling shares in State-owned companies to private investors. Foreign investments to Finland have mainly consisted of credits to Finnish enterprises (often guaranteed by the Finnish government); direct investments by means of subsidiaries in Finland were relatively scarce, except in the 'standard fields' of oil distribution, electronic data processing, etc. Multinational corporations thus had less significance in Finland than in most countries of Western Europe. The fairly restrictive Act on the Right of Aliens and Certain Corporations to Own and Possess Real Property and Company Shares, 1939, was, however, repealed as of 1 January 1993, and the very few remaining restrictions no longer apply to aliens but to persons domiciled abroad. A considerable number of Finnish industrial companies and their individual plants have in recent years been sold to foreign owners, and foreign companies have also established new subsidiaries in Finland. (Correspondingly, Finnish companies have a growing number of subsidiaries abroad.) The interest of foreign institutional investors in Finnish securities has increased sharply, enlarging the share of foreign ownership in the company shares quoted at the Helsinki Stock Exchange from 19% in 1993 to 53% in 1997.

13. By the standard measure of gross national product per person, Finland was EUR 37,615 in 2014 and EUR 45,644 in 2021. In terms of quality of life, Finland's rating might not be as high. Housing is made expensive by the severe climate, and in life expectancy of the adult population, Finland ranks after many countries with a lower rating in the gross national product contest.

II. Labour Force and Employment

14. In 1960, 1976, 1985 and 1998, the working-age (in 1960, 15 years and over, in later years, 15 to 74 years) population was composed (*see* Table 2).

Table 2 Population Composition (000)

	1960	*1976*	*1985*	*1998*
The labour force	2,128	2,244	2,600	2,507
Homemakers	350	242	131	109
Students, servicemen in the armed forces, prisoners, etc. (fit to work)	189	393	354	379
Disabled or retired	418	625	625	883
Total	3,085	3,531	3,710	3,878

The decrease in the number of homemakers (or housewives) can also be seen in the fact that the rate of economically active women was increasing in the age group of 25 to 64, reaching its peak in the 1980s. Correspondingly, the vast increase in full-time education and the much improved old age and disability benefits are seen in the facts that the rate of economic activity has as a rule been decreasing in all age groups of men and earlier in the youngest and oldest age groups, in recent years in all age groups, of women. Table 3 shows the rate of economic activity of both sexes in the different age groups, i.e., the number of those economically active as percentages of the whole population in the age and sex group.

Table 3 Economic Activity by Gender

	1950		1985		1998	
Age	Men (%)	Women (%)	Men (%)	Women (%)	Men (%)	Women (%)
15 to 24	82.5	59.0	55.0	54.9	46.7	44.9
25 to 44	96.9	58.4	95.0	87.0	91.8	82.5
45 to 64	94.1	54.8	74.4	69.5	70.7	67.6
65 and over	56.7	20.6	10.6	4.8	6.0	1.7
15 and over	89.6	53.4	74.6	65.8	68.4	61.0

15. In the years 1959 to 1975, the yearly average number of unemployed varied between 25,000 and 63,000, or between 1.2% and 2.9% of the labour force, except that in 1968 there were 85,000 unemployed, or 3.9% of the labour force. In 1976 and 1977, unemployment rose rapidly, reaching 196,700, or 9.1% of the labour force in February 1978. From 1979 to 1986, the number of unemployed fluctuated between 114,000 and 138,000, or between 4.7% and 5.5% of the labour force, but then fell gradually to 80,000 or 3.1%, in 1989. A steep rise followed, reaching its peak of 408,000 or 16.6%, in 1994. Thereafter, unemployment has been slowly decreasing (314,000 or 12.7%, in 1997). In 1960, 1974 (still a normal year), 1985 (a normalized year) and 1998 (with slowly decreasing unemployment), the number of employed by branches of activity (*see* Table 4).

Table 4 Employed Persons by Branch of Activity (000)

	1960	1974	1985	1998
Primary:				
– forestry and log floating	143	59	52	24
– agriculture	618	303	228	121
Secondary:				
– construction of buildings	119	126	137	108
– other construction	78	61	41	33
– mining, manufacturing, electricity, gas and water	470	613	597	476
Tertiary:				
– trade, financing and insurance	229	449	447	589
– transport, storage and communications	138	154	186	170
– services	304	464	749	701
Total	2,099	2,229	2,437	2,222

In June 2016, the labour force was about 2,558,000. It was 33,000 persons less than one year earlier. The employment rate (15 to 64 years) was 72%. Finland had 264,000 unemployed persons and the unemployment rate was 9.3%.

In 2021, the labour force was 2,595,000. Finland had 187,000 unemployed persons and 1,340,000 persons outside the labour market. The unemployment rate was 6.7%.

Chapter 2. Definitions and Notions

§1. Industrial Relations

16. The study in Finland of labour questions with the methods of social sciences has its roots in the German *Sozialpolitik* of the late nineteenth century. Especially since World War II, research in this field has been most closely related to the Anglo-American study of industrial relations. Research on industrial relations has especially been conducted within two main academic fields, sociology and social policy, but in later years, interest in this subject has also been shown by scholars in economics, business management, and political science. Besides the more or less 'positivistic' Anglo-American tradition, there were some attempts at least to treat this subject with Marxian methods.

§2. Labour Law

I. The Notion and Its Development

17. Labour law as an independent branch of law and legal science is in Finland of recent origin. There were studies on various parts of what is now called labour law, but these parts were not considered to constitute an integrated whole. Various kinds of legal relationships between employers and employees (masters and servants) were studied within the law of obligations (contracts) and thus within the realm of private law. The legal regulation of hours of work and occupational safety and health, however, were together with other aspects of the legal regulation of business activities referred to the branch of public law called economic law, also treating such subjects as land partition, land reform, and water law. Meanwhile, the subject of *Arbeitsrecht* had taken shape in Germany. Finland was not slow to follow suit. The contractual and protective aspects of the law concerned with labour relationships were gradually united to form a common subdivision of economic law, and even the term 'labour law' had already been used first in the early 1910s, although the denominations 'workers' legislation' and 'labour legislation' were in general use superseded by it only in the 1930s. This evolution was completed in the 1950s, when labour law was commonly regarded as an independent branch of the law and no longer a mere subdivision of economic law.

18. The unity of labour law is, in Finnish legal writing, seen in the fact that the spheres of application of the important statutes in the field – contractual as well as protective – are defined in identical terms. In Chapter 1, section 1, subsection 1 of the Employment Contracts Act from 2001 employment contract is defined as a contract whereby one party, the employee, undertakes to perform work for the other party, the employer, under his direction and supervision in return for wages or other remuneration. A similar definition, or a reference to this definition, is met in the other statutes. It can be seen that this definition also includes definitions for the three central notions of the labour law: the employer (for whom work shall be performed under his direction and supervision and in return for remuneration), the employee (who shall perform work for another under the latter's direction and supervision and in return for remuneration), and the employment relationship (the legal relationship between an employer and an employee). There has been some controversy as to whether the definition of labour law should be based on the notion of employment relationship (and thus to define labour law as the branch of law relating to the employment relationship or, within the purposes of this relationship, to the parties thereto) or on the notion of employee (leading to defining labour law as the branch of law relating to the employee in his relationship to the employer). As even the latter approach does not treat the employee as an isolated being but in his relationship with his employer, the difference between the two approaches is more in emphasis than in points of fact.

II. System

19. The old distinction between the private law and the public law elements in labour law is still seen in the traditional systematics of Finnish labour law. Traditionally, the main subdivisions of labour law are the following:

(1) General Principles: This is the introduction to labour law, defining such notions as those described in the preceding paragraph.

(2) Employment Terms: This field treats the reciprocal rights and duties, essentially of a private-law character, of employers and employees. There is a further subdivision in accord with the various sources from which these rights and duties are derived. Consequently, we speak of (a) the Law of (individual) Employment Contracts; (b) the Law of Collective Agreements; and (c) the Law of Cooperation Within Undertakings.

(3) Employee Protection: This concerns the rules of law aimed at the protection of the employees with regard to their life, health, working capacity, development, and other elements of welfare. The main subdivisions are (a) Working Time Regulation; and (b) Annual Leave; and (c) Occupational Safety and Health. The rules of employee protection are mainly of a public law character, but many of them contain a private-law core. This entails that although the observance of the various statutes in this field is officially supervised, and violators are prosecuted, employees have independent rights to the benefits granted them by the statutes, and may themselves sue their employers to recover any benefits due to them.

(4) Employees' Social Security: The purpose of the rules of law in this area is to ameliorate and repair the effects of various dangers which affect employees. Accordingly, the main subdivisions are: (a) Workmen's Compensation (for occupational accidents, injuries and diseases); (b) Unemployment Insurance; and (c) Employees' Pensions. As the scope of labour law is defined with the aid of the notion of employment relationship (or employee position), such branches of social security as national pensions, sickness insurance, etc., are outside labour law, since their coverage is not defined by means of the notion of employment relationship (or employee position). It should be noted that a part of the labour legislation is applicable also to civil servants. However, as

this *Encyclopaedia* is not concerned with social security, even those parts of social security which are in Finland referred to as labour law remain outside the scope of this monograph.

(5) Labour Disputes and Placement: These areas are traditionally treated as a separate subdivision of labour law, consisting of (a) Labour Disputes and Conciliation; and (b) Placement and Vocational Guidance.

20. As shown, the distinction between individual and collective labour law has not been a main dividing line in Finnish systematics, nor are Finnish systematics in other respects identical to the general framework of this Encyclopaedia. In the systematics of some more recent textbooks, however, the distinction between individual and collective labour law has been given a more prominent place. In this monograph, the Encyclopaedia's general framework is followed.

§3. Employment Relationship (Employee Position)

I. The Five Characteristics and Their Significance

21. The conceptual framework governing the regulation of employment contracts and employment relations varies from country to country. For example, Finland has enacted the Employment Contracts Act as the basic law governing employment relationships,[1] with the Act providing the legal definition of an employment relationship and thereby of an employment contract. The Act also has provisions on the conclusion and duration of an employment contract, the rights and obligations of the employer and employee, transfer of undertakings, lay-offs and the termination of an employment contract (giving of notice and cancellation). In addition to the Employment Contracts Act, Finland has a range of other employment laws, such as the Working Time Act and Annual Holidays Act, the Occupational Safety and Health Act, the Collective Agreements Act, the Act on the Protection of Privacy in Working Life, the Act on Cooperation within Undertakings, the Employees Pensions Act and the Unemployment Security Act. The scope of application of all these Acts is in one way or another linked to the definition of an employment relationship laid down in the Employment Contracts Act.

Whether an employment relationship exists is assessed, and the line between an employment relationship and activities falling outside of it is drawn, by examining whether the definition of the scope of application of an employment contract set out in Chapter 1, section 1, subsection 1 of the Employment Contracts Act is actually fulfilled in performing work.

22. Traditionally, the view has been taken that the essential criteria that must be met for an employment relationship to exist are the same as for an employment contract. An employment relationship exists if one worker or more than one together have committed themselves personally to perform work under the direction and

1. The Act currently in force dates from 2001. Its predecessors were the Employment Contract Acts of 1970 and 1922.

supervision of an employer for remuneration. All of these individual or basic criteria for an employment relationship must be fulfilled in reality when the work is performed for an employment relationship to exist:

(a) The threshold for fulfilling the contract criterion required of an employment relationship is low. An employment contract can be concluded orally, in writing or electronically (telefax or e-mail). It can also come into being tacitly through the work being done without any express arrangements having been made for its performance. In such cases, the worker begins doing the work and the employer permits its performance.
(b) In an employment relationship, the work must be performed for another person, that is, an employer (criterion of work being done for another person). Work in the sense of the Employment Contracts Acts encompasses all human behaviour or activity which has economic significance. This could involve active, passive, mental or physical behaviour. The requirement of performing work for another means that the benefit resulting from the work must accrue to the employer. The employee benefits from his or her work in the form of remuneration, which is paid in exchange for the benefit that the employer gains from the worker's efforts. For example, a traditional case of work being done for oneself is that done by a shareholder in a general partnership or a partner in a decedent's estate where this is based on no more than the person's status as a shareholder in the company or as a partner in an undistributed estate.
(c) The criterion of remuneration must also be met for an employment relationship to be created. In other words, the person performing the work must receive wages or some other form of compensation. A work-related legal relationship may, however, be an employment relationship even if no agreement has been made on compensation. The Employment Contracts Act states in Chapter 1, section 1, subsection 2 that the Act is to be applied even if no agreement has been made regarding compensation; however, it is not applicable if the circumstances under which the work is done indicate that the parties' intention has been that the work be done without compensation. Compensation may take the form of any payment or performance which has economic value to its recipient. Thus, remuneration may be money, a payment in kind or a combination of the two. Reciprocal performance of work is also considered remuneration. In addition, the fact that the cloakroom attendant in a restaurant may receive tips from customers has fulfilled the criterion of remuneration. The opportunity to receive teaching has in some cases also been considered sufficient remuneration for purposes of the Act.
(d) A key element of an employment relationship is that a certain individual commits him or herself to performing the work personally (personal performance criterion). The personal obligation to perform the work entails that no one other than a human being may have the status of 'worker'.
(e) According to the Employment Contracts Act, the worker must perform the work under the direction and supervision of the employer (direction criterion). What the direction and supervision are to consist of are not specified in the Act but the elements of the criterion are relatively well-established in the legal literature and case law. Nevertheless, the factors determining whether the criterion

has been met vary from case to case. 'Direction of the employer' refers to the employer's right before commencement and during the performance of the work to determine where, how and when the work is done. 'Supervision' means the employer's right to monitor that the worker observes the instructions given regarding performance of the work. The criterion is somewhat problematic in practice because the employer is not required in concrete and specific terms to direct and supervise the worker's work. The position of the parties to an employment contract must be such as to allow the employer, should he or she so desire, to undertake actions geared to direction and supervision; in other words, no concrete direction and supervision are required. Direction and supervision take the form of, among other actions, setting deadlines for the performance of work or reminding workers that the work has to be done.

Precisely because of this legal definition of an employment relationship, difficulties in drawing the line between an employment relationship and other forms of working are not nowadays as common as they have been earlier in Finland. Another factor possibly reducing the number of disputes is the long-established practice in the labour market. However, the new features, such as digitalization, may cause an increased need for interpretations. For example, The Labour Council has already given two opinions on Appwork (food delivery).

Often it becomes clear on the basis of a single criterion whether or not an employment relationship has been created. Ambiguities and disagreements regarding the nature of the legal relationship under which work has been performed frequently appear only after an employment relationship has ended. The actions brought tend to involve pay and the payment of various forms of compensation. Most often, the situation is one in which the party who has performed the work demands outstanding remuneration, such as holiday or working time pay, based on a relationship that he or she considered to be an employment relationship. The remuneration will not have been paid while the party worked for the employer because at the time the work was not seen – at least not by the employer – as being done as part of an employment relationship but rather, in the majority of cases, was viewed as work done by an independent entrepreneur.

For the most part, disagreement arises regarding the distinction between the work of a worker and of an independent entrepreneur. The decision as to whether an employment relationship exists is ultimately made by a general court.

23. Where difficulties arise in distinguishing between work done under an employment relationship and other work, such as the work of an independent entrepreneur, disputes can generally be described as difficult. Although 'employment relationship' has a legally defined and precise set of criteria, it often becomes necessary after examining the individual criteria for an employment relationship to assess as a whole all of the facts that have been brought to bear in the case. Such an assessment may be required because the individual criteria may each be met regardless of whether the work is done as part of an employment relationship or as an independent entrepreneur. Where the individual criteria for an employment relationship are fulfilled, this does not necessarily – when detached from the context as a whole – provide a solution; an assessment of the situation as a whole is required.

No such comprehensive assessment of the case is necessary, however, if one of the individual criteria, for example, that requiring a binding contract between the parties has not been met.

A comprehensive assessment takes into account all of the facts that have been brought to bear in the case. It is necessary to distinguish between an employment relationship and the legal relationships in which the individual criteria for an employment relationship are fulfilled but which nevertheless differ from an employment relationship in a manner indicating that they can be deemed to fall outside the scope of protection afforded by employment legislation. It is thus not the case that resort must be had to a comprehensive assessment whenever it has to be determined whether an employment relationship exists. However, a comprehensive assessment is the means of last resort for making that determination. Ultimately, the decision on the existence of an employment relationship, that is, on whether a party in fact had the status of 'worker', is made in stages. First, an examination is made of the individual criteria and only when this has been done does it become necessary to assess the legal relationship as a whole. The law contains no provisions for making a comprehensive assessment but it has become the established approach in practice. It has also been accepted in legislative drafting and in research.

A comprehensive assessment of a worker's status is just that: it is an examination of all of the facts pertaining to the contractual relation under which the work is done and a determination on that basis of whether an employment relationship exists. However, the factors figuring in the assessment are individual because the decision being made always involves a single case. Employment laws have for the most part been enacted to protect workers. Accordingly, it is important that a court be able to identify the person who is the object of protection, that is, a worker in an employment relationship. In a comprehensive assessment, efforts are made to do so by examining the circumstances under which the work is done. The question to be answered is whether it is possible to determine from the circumstances whether the party performing work is in need of protection or not. In addition, the assessment can take into account the terms of the employment contract and the parties' own conceptions of their status. These two factors may influence the assessment of the legal nature of the relationship only if the parties have complied with those terms and conceptions. It should be pointed out, however, that only a proven joint purpose and actions according to that purpose may in practice be considered in the assessment. This being the case, a contract pertaining to work, the terms of the contract and the parties' conceptions must in practice always be examined together with the actual circumstances.

24. Some of the work fulfilling the criteria for an employment relationship may nevertheless fall outside the scope of application of the Employment Contracts Act based on the demarcation set out in the Act. According to Chapter 1, section 2 of the Act, it is not applied to ordinary voluntary non-vocational activities, for example, in sports clubs, youth associations, parishes and patient associations, where no wages are paid for the work (the scope of application of the Occupational Safety and Health Act is broad and the Act is applied in these cases as well); to those employment relationships or service obligations that are subject to public law (e.g., central and local government posts); or to contracts for work to be performed that are governed by separate provisions in the law. For example, the Act does not apply to seamen.

II. Supplementary Provisions

25. The employer's right to direct and supervise the work is not deemed to be precluded merely on the ground that the work is to be carried out at the employee's home or another place of his own choice. And where an employee makes use of machines or other implements of his own in his work, the mere fact that the share of such implements in the operation is greater than the share of his personal effort is not deemed to preclude the contract from being considered an employment contract.

III. Width of the Notion

26. The provisions just reviewed might show that the notion of employment relationship (or employee position) is wide in Finland. There is also extensive jurisprudence and literature to the same effect.

What is known as the principle of mandatory application of labour legislation prescribes that the Employment Contracts Act and, by extension, other labour legislation, must be applied to every employment relationship fulfilling the criteria for such a relationship regardless of other contracts and other agreements. The requirement for mandatory application is that the legislator has not excluded the type of employment in question from the scope of the relevant Act. Mandatory application is not a legal principle proper, but rather a consequence of the mandatory nature of the provisions setting out the scope of application of the Acts.

IV. Scope of Statutes

27. As a rule, labour legislation is applicable the first time an employee begins to perform the work on the basis of the contract concluded with the employer. Application ceases when the work is no longer being done. Some labour legislation may, however, be applied even before an employment relationship is created through an employment contract, that is, immediately after the contract on the work being done has been concluded. Which of the foregoing applies is determined from the wording of the relevant provision. For example, Chapter 7, section 1 of the Employment Contracts Act provides that 'an employment contract' may be terminated and Chapter 8, section 1 that an 'employment contract' may be cancelled. In the latter case, it is sufficient that the parties to the contract have committed themselves in the form of a contract to do the work. It is not necessary for the work to have begun as set out in the contract. There are, however, provisions in certain labour laws whose application is expressly linked to the work begun or to the duration of the employment relationship.

Chapter 3. Historical Background

§1. Individual Employment Relationships

28. Mercantilism inherited from the Swedish era and supplemented with Russian bureaucracy continued in Finland for much longer than in the central regions of Europe. Employment conditions in urban trades were regulated by guild ordinances, factory ordinances, mines ordinances, and several other statutes given for different groups of trades. It was only in the Trades Act of 1868 that the guild system was abolished. This Act, and still more its successor of 1879, was based on liberal principles. Among other rules, these Acts contained provisions on employment contracts in all urban trades. These provisions were based on the principle of the freedom of contract, but not in an extremist way. In an agricultural country, the bulk of hired work was not, however, performed in urban trades but in agriculture and domestic work. In these fields, employment relations continued to be regulated in a more traditional manner; the last Servants' Act was enacted in 1865 and remained in force until 1922. In addition, seafarers had legal rules of their own in the Skippers' Act from the Swedish era and then in the Maritime Act of 1873.

29. Emerging industrialization and the growing political power of the Left – especially after the introduction of equal suffrage and unicameral legislature in 1906 – gave rise to efforts to renew the legislation concerning individual employment contracts. An official report for a comprehensive Employment Contracts Bill, based, *inter alia*, on the Belgian act on employment contracts of 1900 and the abortive Swedish reports on the same subject of 1900 and 1901, was presented in 1908. After several further rounds of preparation, an Employment Contracts Act was finally enacted in 1922, replacing the Servants' Act of 1865 and the provisions on employment contracts in the Trades Act of 1879, but extending far beyond the scope of these two acts, to cover in principle all kinds of employment relationships. Seafarers continued, however, to have rules of their own; the provisions on employment relations in the Maritime Act of 1873 were succeeded by the consecutive Seamen's Acts of 1924, 1955, 1978 and 2011 (Seafarers' Employment Contracts Act). For apprentices, provisions deviating in some respects from the Employment Contracts Act were given in the successive Apprenticeships Acts of 1923 and 1967, replaced in 1992 by a new Act on Education by Apprenticeships, which in turn was superseded by the provisions on apprenticeship education in the comprehensive Vocational Education Act, 1998 which was repealed in 1999 and the provisions of the vocational education were moved to Professional Education Act. The Employment Contracts Act itself was in 1970 replaced by a new Act with the same name, developing the old Act in many details and introducing some new principles, such as non-discrimination and statutory protection against unfounded dismissals. Job security and non-discrimination have been further developed in subsequent legislation. In 2015 the Non-Discrimination Act came into force and the provision of discrimination on Employment Contracts Act was moved into it. In 1995, a tripartite Government commission was instituted with the task of preparing a thorough revision of the Employment Contracts Act, 1970. The new Employment Contracts Act came into force in 2001.

§2. EMPLOYEE PROTECTION

30. Provisions to protect employees against various dangers have never been totally lacking in Finnish legislation. Even the individual Trades Acts of 1868 and 1879 contained provisions restricting, *inter alia*, the employment of children under 12, the hours of work of children under 15, and the night work of young persons under 18, and Finland was the first country to prohibit the manufacture and sale of matches containing white phosphorus in 1872. In lack of effective supervision, the protective provisions in the Trades Acts, were, however, in many cases disregarded in spite of the penalties involved. Therefore, the real beginning of a more comprehensive employee protection was the Act for the Protection of Factory Workers of 1889. This Act laid down the fundamental duties of a factory owner to take care of the safety and healthiness of the workplace. Restrictions on the employment, hours of work and night work of children and young persons were tightened, and the first industrial inspectors were installed, with powers not only to inspect factories and institute prosecutions for violations but also to order the factory owners to remove defects within a fixed time.

31. Beginning with an Act of 1914, the provisions of the 1889 Act have gradually been replaced with consecutive new statutes, expanding the principles of the older Act in many respects to: cover more and more and finally virtually all working places, enlarge the employers' duties and to specify them more in detail, enlarge the industrial inspection, and make the inspectors' powers more effective. Regulation of working time was extended to adult male and female employees in 1908 as regards work in bakeries, and in 1917, a statutory working day of eight hours was introduced as a fairly general measure. In the newer statutes, employees are no longer regarded solely as persons to be protected by others; gradually, they have been given both rights and duties regarding the safety work at the workplace without, however, diminishing the ultimate responsibility of the employer for the safety and healthiness of the work and working environment.

§3. TRADE UNION FREEDOM

32. In the era of the guild system, in other words, until 1868, it was forbidden and punishable for journeymen and other employees to associate for the furthering of their interests. After that time, there were no legal restrictions aimed specifically at curtailling trade union freedom. However, the freedom of association in general hardly existed at that time. Since 1849, no associations could be founded without Government approval, and such approvals were at times granted very restrictively. These restrictive practices were also applied to workingmen's associations when the labour movement reached Finland during the last decades of the nineteenth century. These restrictions were not, however, applied with a view to furthering the employers' interests but in order to combat revolutionary tendencies feared by the Russian authorities. In spite of these restrictions, the first local trade unions were founded during the 1880s and their first national federations during the last years of the century.

33. As a result of defeat in the Russo-Japanese War, 1904–1905, the Russian authorities were forced to undertake a certain liberalization in Finland. Among the liberalization measures, the freedom of association was enacted in 1906 as a constitutional right of citizens. There were no separate provisions for trade unions, but like other associations, trade unions could now be founded without any need for a Government authorization. One of the first associations to make use of the new constitutional freedom of association was the Finnish Trade Union Confederation (SAJ), founded in 1907. Towards the last years of the Russian era, and especially during World War I, the Russian authorities, however, again tried to curtail the freedom of association despite its constitutional protection.

34. In 1919, an Associations Act was enacted with more detailed provisions concerning associations under the constitutional protection. The fundamental provisions of the 1906 Act were included without alterations in the Finnish Constitution, also enacted in 1919. In addition to these constitutional provisions and the provisions of the Associations Act, concerning all associations, provisions to protect the freedom of association in employment were included in the Employment Contracts Act, 1922. According to these provisions, it was unlawful and punishable for an employer or his representative to prevent an employee from belonging to or joining a lawful association. It was also unlawful and punishable for an employee to interfere with his employer or a fellow worker in the same way. A contract whereby either party binds himself not to belong to an association was declared to be null and void. In spite of all these provisions, one of the results of the 1918 civil war was that in the years to come, trade unions – which to a large extent were Communist dominated and often preferred political activities to the immediate furthering of their members' interests – were seen with great suspicion by the authorities and the employers alike. Many employers in fact preferred to hire unorganized employees and even fired organized ones, without having to fear any legal counter measures. The SAJ and several national unions (federations) were dissolved by court order for subversive activities in 1930. And in 1931, an Act to Protect Labour Peace was passed with provisions prescribing punishments for, e.g., forcing an employer or an employee to join an association, to withdraw from an association, to take part in a strike, or to make amends for having acted as a strikebreaker or for having employed strikebreakers.

35. Already in 1930, before the old confederation was dissolved, a new Central Organization of Finnish Trade Unions (SAK), under Social Democrat auspices, was founded and began to gain the confidence of society. It lasted, however, until World War II before the most important employers' organizations were prepared to accept the trade unions on an equal footing. Agreements to this effect were concluded between the Central Organization of the Finnish Trade Unions and the Finnish Employers' Confederation (STK) in 1940, 1944 and 1946, and the Act to Protect Labour Peace was repealed in 1945. The protection of trade union freedom was further enhanced by the Shop Steward Agreement, 1969, by the corresponding agreements concluded with the organizations of white-collar employees, and by the provisions of the present Employment Contracts Act 1970, prohibiting discrimination, giving the shop stewards special protection against dismissals, entitling them to perform their duties in the employers' time, and allowing the employees to use the employer's premises for their meetings (outside working hours). In 1989, the Associations Act 1919 was replaced by a new Associations Act. In the new Act, the freedom of association is, in contrast to earlier legislation, the same for foreigners as for Finnish citizens. In connection with the constitutional reform concerning fundamental rights in 1995, the constitutional protection of the freedom of association was also extended to foreigners and redefined in some other respects.

§4. Collective Labour Relations

I. Negotiations and Agreements

36. The first recorded strike in 1491 was conducted with success by longshoremen in Turku in support of their wage demands against Hanseatic merchants. As the first industrial action with organizational background, the strike conducted by a typographers' glee club in 1872 is usually mentioned, and in 1890, the typographers' local union in Helsinki forced a wage agreement by means of a strike. An industry-wide agreement in the typographical industry was concluded in 1900. Other industries followed the typographers, and in the decade before World War I it seemed as if Finland would little by little follow the other Scandinavian countries in spreading collective agreements to all wage-earners. However, in the years of mutual distrust after the civil war in 1918, collective agreements fell largely into disuse. Only in the typographical industry has the system of industry-wide agreements continued without interruptions until the present day. In other fields, some sporadic local agreements were concluded now and then, but in general, there were no formal relations between employers and organized labour. This did not signify that organized labour would not have had any influence on employment conditions: strikes were numerous and solid and often they ended with an informal promise from the employers to observe certain minimum conditions for the time being.

After the organized employers and organized labour in 1940 agreed to accept each other as equals, and after the war had ended in 1945 and 1946, collective agreements were concluded for blue-collar employees in all major industries. For the white-collar (salaried) employees, there was no such overnight development, but gradually the collective agreements have reached a very broad coverage even here. The coverage for the collective agreements has also been broadened as regards the subject matter covered. Many of the first agreements of 1945 and 1946 only contained fundamental provisions on wages and a few other questions. Gradually, the provisions regarding these questions have become more and more extensive and detailed, and more and more questions, such as annual holidays, sick pay, maternity leave, travelling costs, etc., have been covered. In addition to the ordinary collective agreements, the STK (succeeded in 1993 by the Confederation of Industry and Employers) and the SAK have concluded general agreements on such questions which can better be regulated by inter-industry agreements and which need not be re-examined as often as the intra-industry agreements are renewed. The agreement of 1940, by which the confederations recognized each other, was a declaration of principles only; but the general agreements of 1944 and 1946 already contained fundamental provisions to be observed by the industry-wide organizations and their members; most of the provisions in the 1946 agreement remained in force until 1997. Since the mid-1960s, the confederations have supplemented the fundamental agreement of 1946 with general agreements aimed to regulate specific questions, such as the general introduction of the forty-hour week (1965), protection against unwarranted dismissals (1966), holiday pay (1967), occupational safety (1968), shop stewards (1969), communications within undertakings (1970), cooperation within undertakings (1981), etc. Several of these agreements have been replaced or amended with subsequent agreements. In 1997, the fundamental agreement of 1946 as well as most of the specialized general agreements were finally replaced by a new comprehensive General Agreement. This was amended in 2001. Some fields, e.g., the Metal Trades, however, remained outside the scope of the new comprehensive agreement and have instead made arrangements of their own. A general agreement, corresponding to the fundamental agreements of 1944 and 1946, was concluded in 1970 between the Employers' Confederation of Service Industries and the SAK. The confederations of white-collar employees as well as the Employers' Confederation of Service Industries have in many cases become parties to the same specific general agreements with the STK and the SAK, or they have similar agreements of their own. However, the confederations of white-collar employees have not concluded permanent general agreements corresponding to the fundamental agreements of 1944 and 1946. Until 1994 they instead had confederation-wide master agreements for each agreement round containing material corresponding as well to the contents of the said fundamental agreements as to many of the provisions in the industry-wide agreements of blue-collar employees. The Confederation of Finnish industries laid off the confederation-level agreements in 2017.

At the moment, The Finnish Forest Industries Federation is in the process of withdrawing from collective bargaining, and terms of employment will be negotiated at company- and/or product-line level. The Finnish Forest Industries Federation is responsible for the currently valid collective agreements until their expiry (at the latest until the end of 2022). There have also been changes in the field of technology industries. The activities of Technology Industries of Finland have been divided in 2021 between two separate associations. Technology Industries of Finland gave up national collective bargaining activities and the responsibility for national collective agreements has been transferred to a new employers' association (Teknologiateollisuuden työnantajat ry). The new association has started its operations and cooperates closely with Technology Industries of Finland.

The objective of the change has been to further improve the conditions for workplace bargaining. The new organizational structure offers companies two alternative ways for collective bargaining: a national or company-specific collective agreement.

37. For the first collective agreements, there was no legislative basis. The 1908 report for an Employment Contracts Bill contained a chapter on collective agreements; but in the continued preparation, the two subjects were separated, and a separate Collective Agreements Act – based largely on Hugo Sinzheimer's draft for a German Collective Agreements Act, never realized in its home country – was enacted in 1924 (although it was seen that in the prevailing circumstances the significance of the new act would remain rather small). To cope with the expected rise of the agreement system, a modernized version was prepared, and a new Collective Agreements Act was passed in 1946. The new act was accompanied by a Labour Court Act, following the Scandinavian model in instituting a specialized tripartite court for legal disputes concerning collective agreements. Under the 1924 act, collective agreement disputes had belonged to the jurisdiction of ordinary courts, although in practice, the agreements often contained an arbitration clause substituting arbitration for suits at ordinary courts. In 1974, a new Labour Court Act was enacted, mainly to improve the Court's procedure, which already, under the 1946 act, was very modern in comparison with the actual procedure at the ordinary Finnish courts. Several, mostly technical changes came into force from the beginning of 2017 at the same time with a new Court Act. After several futile attempts to modernize the Collective Agreements Act, some provisions in this act were amended in 1984 and 1986. In these amendments, the surveillance duty of the agreement parties was defined more in detail, the maximum amounts of the compensatory fines (civil penalties) for violations of duties based on collective agreements were increased so as to restore partially their original real value, and the applicability of these remedies was extended to certain violations not previously covered.

II. Mediation

38. According to the Trades Act, 1879, mediation in labour disputes was entrusted to the councils of the local Trades Societies (compulsory associations in each town for merchants, industrialists and artisans) augmented for this purpose with employee representatives, comprising one-third of the augmented council. However, this system fell into discredit and disuse, and mediation was instead conducted on an ad hoc basis by factory inspectors and other State officials. The mediation system was put on a statutory basis in 1925 with an Act on Conciliation in Collective Labour Disputes. Under this Act, there were several part-time district conciliators, and special conciliators and mediation boards could be appointed when needed. There was, however, no duty for the parties to take part in any conciliation procedures or even to give advance information of strikes and lock-outs, and the possibilities for the conciliators to offer their services without having been asked to do so were very limited. These defects were mended with the next Act on Conciliation in Labour Disputes, 1946, making it a duty for the parties to give advance notice of strikes and lock-outs to the conciliators and to the opposite party of at least two weeks, obliging the parties to appear before the conciliator upon demand, entitling the conciliators to act on their own initiative, and entitling the Ministry of Social Affairs to postpone an intended strike or lock-out in certain cases with another period of two weeks. The system has been further developed by the present Act on Mediation in Labour Disputes, 1962, under which there are one (or two) full-time National Conciliation Officers in addition to the part-time district conciliators and the occasional special conciliators and mediation boards. At the moment, there is one full-time National Conciliator and five part-time conciliators. The National Conciliator is an impartial public servant. The National Conciliator's Office is an independent central government agency, which comes under the Ministry of Employment and the Economy. The agency is headed by the National Conciliator.

III. Shop Rules

39. In the 1920s and 1930s, the organized employers defended their reluctance to conclude collective agreements, *inter alia*, with the argument that not only is the labour legislation in Finland more extensive and detailed than in the other Scandinavian countries but employment conditions are also regulated in detail in the shop rules. In the Trades Act, 1879, shop rules were regarded as a part of the employment contracts of the employees: the employer had the power to draw up the rules, and if they had been drawn up in the language of the employees, they were binding upon them after the lapse of the period of notice to be observed in the employment relationships. As a companion statute to the Employment Contracts Act, 1922, a separate Shop Rules Act was enacted, giving the shop rules a more collective, two-sided and officially controlled nature. The shop rules remained to be drafted by the employer, but in manufacturing, all employers except the very smallest became not only entitled but also obliged to draft shop rules, which had to contain stipulations concerning certain enumerated matters. The draft rules were to be presented to the employees for their opinion, which had to be sent to the authorities together with the employer's draft, although the employer's draft had to be confirmed except if it was at variance with the law or contained unfair stipulations. With the advent of the collective agreements, the shop rules have lost much of their significance. The Shop Rules Act, 1922, was repealed by the Cooperation Within Undertakings Act, under which shop rules were adopted by the employer and the employees' representatives in common and no official approval was any longer needed. In the Cooperation Within Undertakings Act (2007) there were only a few provisions of shop rules. In the present Cooperation Within Undertaking Act (2022), there are no provisions for shop rules.

Chapter 4. The Role of Government in Labour Law and Industrial Relations

40. In Finland, the role of the Government in labour relations has traditionally been fairly large in comparison with its Scandinavian neighbours and many other countries in Western Europe. However, the influence of the Government is seen more in detailed – and complicated – labour legislation than in administrative interference in the day-to-day conduct of individual and collective labour relations; even the detailed and complicated legal provisions are less a product of official inventiveness than a result of compromises between the conflicting demands and aspirations of employer and employee organizations. The two Government departments which had the main responsibility for the administration of labour matters were, until 1989, the Ministry of Labour and the Ministry of Social Affairs and Health. The Ministry of Labour was a specialized agency for employment questions, while the broad and varied competence of the Ministry of Social Affairs and Health was only partially concerned with labour matters. In 1989, the Finnish name of the Ministry of Labour was changed from *työvoimaministeriö* to *työministeriö*, and the tasks of the Ministry of Social Affairs and Health in labour-related matters were transferred to it. The Ministry became responsible for unemployment allowance matters. The responsibilities of the Ministry increased in 1997 with refugee and asylum seeker matters, as well as migration matters. In connection with the establishment of the Ministry of Employment and the Economy (*työ- ja elinkeinoministeriö*), matters related to refugees, asylum seekers and migration were transferred to the Ministry of the Interior. In 1997, the matters concerning labour protection were, however, transferred back to the Ministry of Social Affairs and Health. Incomes policy has been conducted more or less on an ad hoc basis under the auspices of the Prime Minister's Office. The Ministry of Employment and the Economy began its work on 1 January 2008. The Government Programme of Prime Minister Matti Vanhanen's second Cabinet, dated 19 April 2007, included the decision that the new Ministry of Employment and the Economy would 'assume responsibility for the duties of the existing Ministry of Trade and Industry, the tasks of the Ministry of Labour, excluding migration and integration matters, and the functions of the Department for Development of Regions and Public Administration of the Ministry of the Interior, excluding the Regional and Local Administration Unit'.

§1. Manpower Administration

41. The main responsibilities of the Ministry of Employment and the Economy in employment matters are employment policy, placement, and vocational guidance. Public employment and business services (known, based on the Finnish acronym, as TE services) are services for employers and job seekers provided by a local administrative agency that reports to the Ministry of Employment and the Economy. The services are designed to best address clients' needs in keeping with a three-pronged model focusing on finding employment for job seekers in a timely manner, improving the availability of trained labour and ensuring a favourable environment for businesses.

I. Employment Policy

42. According to a constitutional amendment of 1972, it rested upon the Government to provide work for every Finnish citizen when needed, except as far as an Act of Parliament contained exceptions to this duty. As shown in the economic survey, it was not possible for the Government to live up to the obligations of this constitutional provision. In connection with the constitutional reform concerning fundamental rights (this ineffectual duty to provide work was replaced with a duty for the public powers to promote employment and to strive to guarantee everyone the right to work. Employment policy was described more in detail in the Employment Act, 1987. According to this Act, the Government was supposed to achieve full employment, which ensures the livelihood of the citizens and is based on the performance of productive work, promoting a steady and regionally balanced development with regard to economy, employment and other societal aspects. The Act further included provisions on the different methods to achieve full employment, combat unemployment and prevent shortage of manpower, such as general economic policy, public works (to be planned in advance and conducted by the National Government and the municipalities), vocational training for the unemployed, etc. If neither work nor training could be provided, an unemployment benefit was as a rule paid to those unemployed who were not entitled to benefit from unemployment insurance for the period in question.

II. Manpower Services

43. The current Act on public employment and business service came into force in January 2013. As a public employment and business service, the employment and economic development office, the customer service centre of the employment and economic development administration, and the centre for economic development, transport and the environment distribute information and give advice on: (1) vacant positions and job seeking, (2) labour force availability and acquisition, (3) training opportunities and other possibilities for skills development, (4) the labour market, occupational sectors, and occupations, (5) starting up of business activities and opportunities for developing them and (6) services, subsidies, and compensations provided for implementing change security.

44. The Nordic labour market service model entered into force on 2 May 2022. In the model, jobseekers apply for work on their own initiative and receive support for the process from the TE Office or from municipalities participating in the local government pilots to promote employment. Each jobseeker's need for services and prospects to apply for work is assessed individually. Jobseekers still have to apply for work in order to receive unemployment benefits. What is new is that, as a rule, jobseekers must apply for four job opportunities per month. Active jobseekers have already done this before. If the jobseeker's skills to look for work or to be employed are found to be lacking, the jobseeker gets access to services quicker.

Sanctions related to unemployment benefit are staggered. In the first case of forgetfulness or neglect, a jobseeker receives a reminder, which does not affect the payment of unemployment benefits. If a jobseeker repeatedly neglects their employment plan, the sanctions become more severe.

A. *Job seeking*

45. An individual client's job seeking starts on the day when he/she requests it electronically in the online service intended for the purpose, or personally at the employment and economic development office, and when he/she is registered as a jobseeker in the customer data system of the employment and economic development office. The employment and economic development authorities may accept a request presented by other means, too.

46. A new customer service model aims to provide jobseekers with more individualized and adequate support in job seeking.

47. The TE Office or the local government pilot will arrange an initial interview for a jobseeker, if possible, within five working days of the start of the job search. Interviews are mainly organized at the office of the TE Office or the local government pilot, but they can also be arranged in some other way due to, for example, an inordinately long trip to the relevant office. Alternatively, the TE Office or the local government pilot will organize a supplementary job search discussion in which an employment plan will be drawn up for him/her. However, the initial interview must be arranged without delay thereafter.

In the initial interview, a jobseeker's situation will be analysed and an employment plan will be prepared. In the interview what kind of jobs could be applied for or whether the jobseeker needs to acquire training or change fields will also be discussed. The aim is for jobseekers to find employment as quickly as possible.

48. Each jobseeker is subjected to an individual service need assessment, which primarily charts the jobseeker's capacity to find employment in the open labour market. An expert at the TE Office or the local government pilot will prepare jobseekers with a personal employment plan with the aim of finding employment quickly. The employment plan specifies the goals of the job search, how the jobseeker will promote his/her employment, what services he/she needs, and how he/she will manage matters in the future with the TE Office or the local government pilot. The implementation of the employment plan is monitored in job search discussions.

B. *Vocational Guidance and Career Planning*

49. Employment and economic development authorities may offer vocational guidance and career planning to support individual clients in making career choices, vocational development, placement in working life, and lifelong learning. With the client's consent, appropriate psychological assessment methods may be used in order to assess an individual client's vocational and career options, competence, and suitability, if necessary.

§2. Administration Concerning Individual Employment Relations and Labour Protection

50. In 1973, a separate National Labour Protection Board was created to head the newly reshaped Labour Protection Administration. The ministries – originally the Ministry of Social Affairs and Health, from 1989 the Ministry of Labour – were thereafter mainly concerned with legislative questions: the drafting of bills to be presented to Parliament as well as the preparation of ordinances and regulations to be adopted by virtue of powers given in legislation. However, the National Labour Protection Board and the administration under it dealt with matters concerning individual employers, employees, working sites, etc. In 1993, the National Labour Protection Board was, however, suppressed and its tasks transferred to the new Labour Protection Division of the Ministry of Labour, which accordingly thereafter headed the Labour Protection Administration. The transfer of labour protection matters back to the Ministry of Social Affairs and Health in 1997 included the transfer of the Labour Protection Division to that Ministry. In addition to individual matters, it rests with the Labour Protection Administration to take care of the planning and development of employee protection, to conduct research and training in the field and to give advice and guidance relating to the application of labour protection provisions. The Labour Protection Administration is in the Labour Protection Administration Act declared to be independent when performing its supervision duties (in order to comply with the International Labour Organization (ILO) Labour Inspection Convention, 1947 (No. 81). This provision was intended to imply that the Minister and the Secretary General of the Ministry of Social Affairs and Health have no authority to give the Labour Protection Division or the administration under it instructions concerning such matters. Due to defects in legislative drafting, this intention did not, however, materialize in all respects. Besides the Labour Protection Administration, there are within the area of individual employment relations and labour protection some other organs with specific tasks. A New Act on Occupational Safety and Health Enforcement and Cooperation on Occupational Safety and Health at Workplaces was enacted in 2006.

I. The Labour Protection Administration

A. *Organization*

51. In the Act on Occupational Safety and Health Enforcement and Cooperation on Occupational Safety and Health at Workplaces, the tasks of the occupational safety and health authorities are defined to inspect workplaces and other locations of supervision and take other actions required by legislation. Occupational safety and health authorities shall in their enforcement activities promote cooperation between employers and employees.

52. The Labour Protection Administration includes six regional state administrative agencies and centres for economic development, transport and the environment. Where occupational safety is concerned, the agencies are tasked with overseeing compliance with the employment legislation. In addition, they are responsible for investigating serious accidents in the workplace, determining the causes of occupational and work-related diseases and measures to prevent these, carrying out product control and participating in proceedings relating to labour offences. The actual fieldwork is carried out by inspectors.

B. *Inspections*

53. Workplace inspections shall be carried out as frequently and efficiently as is necessary for effective enforcement. Especially effective inspection actions shall be targeted in workplaces where there are serious risks to life or health. Inspections must, when necessary, be carried out at all hours of the day when work is done. An inspection, or any other enforcement action taken to investigate the matter, shall be carried out without delay if occupational safety and health authorities have been notified of a suspicion that a provision to be enforced by occupational safety and health authorities is being breached at the workplace or whenever the employer, the occupational safety and health representative or the occupational safety and health committee, or a corresponding cooperation body, so requires, if the circumstances mentioned in the request or notice give cause for it.

54. An inspector is empowered to enter any workplace as well as any other place where he has good reason to suppose that work is done. He may also enter any other premises, such as canteens, washrooms, etc., which have been made available by the employer for the employees in accordance with labour protection provisions. He can, either in the presence of witnesses or alone, interrogate any persons working in the mentioned places or obtain any necessary information from them. He has an extensive right to see the employer's documents, registers, plans, drawings, etc., to obtain copies of them, to take samples, after informing the employer of the matter, of raw materials or other materials used at the workplace, or of products manufactured or used at the workplace, for a separate analysis or investigation (a current price must be paid for a sample, unless its value is insignificant), to take photographs and to obtain information from the employer orally and in writing; all this in so far as is necessary for the purposes of the inspection. All inspections shall be carried out in such a way that the aims of labour protection are assured without any unnecessary disturbance of the activities at the workplace. Any trade secrets of the employer as well as any information relating to the health, etc., of the employees must not be revealed by the inspector except in so far as it is necessary for police investigations or other similar purposes. The name of any person giving information concerning defects or shortcomings at a workplace shall likewise be kept secret.

If an inspection is carried out in consequence of such information, this fact shall not be revealed to the employer or his representative. Inspectors must, on request, prove their powers for carrying out inspections by a certificate issued by the occupational safety and health authority.

C. Securing Compliance

55. When an inspector finds defects or shortcomings at a workplace, his normal procedure is to discuss the matter with the employer and to give appropriate instructions for the defects or shortcomings to be rectified or remedied. If an employer does not fulfil the obligations imposed on him by provisions to be enforced by occupational safety and health authorities,[2] the inspector must issue to the employer written advice to eliminate or remedy the non-complying conditions. In some cases, instead of written advice, the inspector will issue an improvement notice obliging the employer to eliminate or remedy the non-complying conditions. Likewise, the inspector may issue an improvement notice if the employer does not follow written advice. In the written advice and improvement notice, the inspector will specify the provisions to be applied and the defects that have been observed as to compliance with them. In an improvement notice, the time limit must be specified within which the employer must make the conditions comply, if this is not immediately possible. The inspector shall oversee that the employer has followed the improvement notice within the specified time limit. If the necessary measures have not been taken, the inspector shall without delay submit the matter to occupational safety and health authorities. If the inspector notices that issuing written advice or an improvement notice will obviously not lead to remedying or eliminating the non-complying conditions or the matter brooks no delay, the inspector may submit the matter to occupational safety and health authorities without issuing written advice or an improvement notice.

56. Occupational safety and health authorities may oblige an employer to remedy or eliminate non-complying conditions within a specified time limit. When setting a time limit, the authorities must take into account the time limit previously set in the improvement notice. Occupational safety and health authorities may, as a sanction for an obligation impose a default fine or threat that the non-complying conditions will be ordered to be remedied or eliminated at the defaulter's expense or the concerned activity will be stopped. Occupational safety and health authorities may in their decision order that the decision shall be observed despite appeal. If a defect or shortcoming at the workplace causes a risk to the life or health of an employee, the competent occupational safety and health authority may prohibit the use of a machine, work equipment or other technical device, a product or a work method or the continuation of work until the non-complying conditions have been remedied or eliminated. The occupational safety and health authority may order a

2. This means the office of an occupational safety and health inspectorate acting as a district authority under the Ministry of Social Affairs and Health; as regards the control of product safety and the related procedure.

default fine as a sanction for the prohibition notice. The inspector may promptly issue the prohibition notice as a temporary prohibition notice if the risk to life or health is immediate. A temporary prohibition notice must be complied with immediately. The inspector shall without delay submit the matter to occupational safety and health authorities. Before making a binding decision, the occupational safety and health authority shall, in addition to what is provided on hearing a party in the Administrative Procedure Act, allow the competent occupational safety and health representative an opportunity to be heard. A copy of the decision shall be given to the representative free of charge.

57. Orders given by occupational safety and health authorities may be appealed to a (regional) Administrative Court. A further appeal can be taken to the Supreme Administrative Court upon leave of that Court. Leave can, however, only be granted if a precedent is needed. It is natural that the methods just described for securing compliance are mainly in use as regards occupational safety and health. If provisions on hours of work and annual holidays are not complied with, the next step after advice is given to the employer – or, in the case of more severe violations, the very first step – is normally to prosecute the employer for the violation.

II. The Labour Council

58. The Labour Council, established in 1946, is a special authority operating in connection with the Ministry of Employment and the Economy and exercising independent decision-making power, and the purpose of its establishment was to create an expert body enjoying the trust of the labour-market parties, which could as quickly and uniformly as possible handle application issues of labour legislation relating to working hours, annual leave, the use of children and the young for work and certain other application issues of Acts relating to labour protection including certain enacted applications concerning cooperation Acts. The composition of the Labour Council is tripartite. It has at least nine members appointed by the government for three years at a time. The members – except the Chairman – have two deputy members. The Chairman and the member with a degree in law are appointed from among people familiar with the tasks of a judge and who cannot be considered to represent either employer or employee interests. Besides them, the Labour Council has an independent member who has a relevant university degree and is familiar with labour protection issues and who is appointed on the basis of the opinion of the labour protection administration. Six members are appointed on the basis of opinions issued by the labour-market parties. Three of them represent the employers and another three the employees. When appointing these members and their deputies, attention must be paid to the power relations in the labour-market organization, and to the Labour Council having expertise from different branches. Irrespective of its tripartite nature, all the members and deputy members of the Labour Council shall operate subject to public liability. The Labour Council handles and issues opinions on matters of interpretation and application relating to the Working Hours Act, the Act on Young Employers, the Annual Leave Act as well as the Act on Occupational Safety and Health. But the Labour Council also handles issues relating to the scope of application of the Act on Cooperation within Undertakings and the Act on Cooperation within Finnish and Community-wide Groups of Undertakings. As the term 'opinions' suggests, the opinions are not legally binding, but in practice, for example, courts have usually decided cases in accordance with the opinions issued by the Labour Council.

59. The Labour Council also processes appeals against decisions concerning some derogation permits by Regional State Administrative Agencies (aluehallintovirasto (AVI) in Finnish). Appeals against a decision concerning a claim for correction issued by the Labour Council should be addressed to the Labour Court. Since 1 January 2016, there has been only one Regional State Administrative Agency which decides the permits (AVI Southwestern Finland).

A decision may be submitted to the Labour Council for reconsideration of an appeal taken by a party – the applicant, or in some cases, a shop steward or other representative of the employees.

III. The Institute for Occupational Health and the Institute for Health and Welfare

60. The Finnish Institute of Occupational Health (FIOH) operates under the Ministry of Social Affairs and Health and specializes in well-being at work, research, advisory services and training. It was formerly administered by a private (although Governmentsubsidized) foundation. It is administered by bodies in which organs and organizations holding central positions in the development of labour protection are represented. The Institute is a research and service institution for scientific, educational, publication, information, diagnostic, medical, and other similar activities in labour protection and occupational health.

61. The Finnish Institute for Health and Welfare (THL) studies, monitors, and develops measures to promote the well-being and health of the population in Finland. It gathers and produces information based on research and register data. It also provides expertise and solutions to support decision-making. It serves various parties: the government, municipal and provincial decision-makers, actors in the social welfare and health sector, organizations, the research community and the public.

§3. Administration Relating to Collective Labour Relations

62. Apart from legislative, budgetary and similar matters, handled directly by the Ministry of Employment and the Economy, official action relating to collective labour relations mainly consists of mediation in labour disputes. Mediation is, however, conducted in an independent manner by the official conciliators, the only functions for the Ministry being to decide questions concerning deferments of strikes and lock-outs (for not more than two weeks) and the appointments of ad hoc conciliators and conciliation boards for particular cases.

I. Mediation in Labour Disputes

63. According to the Act on Mediation in Labour Disputes, there are one (or two) full-time National Conciliation Officers, appointed by the President of the Republic for four years at a time. There are also six part-time conciliators, appointed by the Council of State (the National Cabinet) for a period of three years. An ad hoc conciliator or a conciliation board may be appointed for a particular conciliation duty by the Ministry of Employment and the Economy. As this rarely happens and as the most important collective agreements are industry-wide, the National Conciliation Officers have a key position in the mediation system. Apart from actual conciliation work, they have to cooperate in other ways with the employers' and employees' organizations, endeavouring to further the relationships between employers and employees and their organizations.

64. A party intending to commence a strike or lock-out has to give notice to the opposite party, and also to the office of the National Conciliation Officers (or, as regards a local conflict, to one of the part-time conciliators) at least fourteen days beforehand. If a labour dispute is intended to give rise to a work stoppage or the extension of the same that is considered, in the light of its scope or the nature of the sector involved, to affect essential functions of society or to prejudice the general interest to a considerable extent, the Ministry of Employment and the Economy may, at the proposal of the conciliator or conciliation board involved, and with the object of reserving sufficient time for mediation, prohibit the projected stoppage or its extension or commencement for a maximum of fourteen days from the announced date of its commencement. As there is no compulsory arbitration, it is lawful to begin the proclaimed stoppage after the expiration of the period of notice and its possible extension by the Ministry provided that the stoppage is not contrary to the terms of the peace obligation based on a collective agreement then in force. The duty to give notice of an intended strike or lock-out and the power of the Ministry to defer it for a fortnight only refer to work stoppages in connection with labour disputes. This means that political demonstrations and solidarity actions without any selfish purpose do not require any notice and cannot be deferred by the Ministry. (The confederations of employers and employees have, however, in 1993 signed a declaration that they and their member federations will inform the National Conciliation Officer and the appropriate federation of employers or employees four days in advance of any work stoppage with a political or solidarity motive. A similar clause – not a mere declaration – has been included in the General Agreement of 1997 making the duty to inform, however, dependent 'on the possibilities'.) This is also the case, under an amendment of 1986, as regards conflicts belonging to the jurisdiction of the Labour Court or of arbitrators, that is, in essence, conflicts violating the peace obligation under the Collective Agreements Act.

65. The Mediation Act contains detailed instructions for mediation procedure. As soon as the competent conciliator has received the notice mentioned in the preceding paragraph, he or she shall take such measures as he deems appropriate to settle the dispute. He may also act upon his own initiative whenever he becomes aware of a labour dispute which endangers industrial peace. The parties are obliged to attend negotiations convened by the conciliator and shall supply such information as the conciliator deems necessary, to be kept secret by the conciliator if so requested by the party supplying it. After making himself thoroughly conversant with all matters relating to the dispute, the conciliator will endeavour to induce the parties to determine the matters in dispute precisely and to restrict them to as few issues as possible. He will then seek to bring about a compromise based mainly on the parties' own demands and proposals, suggesting such concessions and adjustments as appear appropriate and fair. If he fails to settle the dispute by negotiation, he may – but need not – present a draft settlement to the parties, recommending them to accept it within a short time limit, fixed by him. If a settlement is not reached, the conciliator shall consider whether and in which manner the proceedings should be continued. (In practice, new discussions may be conducted immediately to modify the proposed settlement, or the industrial action threatened with may commence, the conciliator following the situation and calling the parties to new negations after some days or a couple of weeks.)

66. The services of the official conciliators are subsidiary in the sense that the parties may agree upon a person or body to mediate in a dispute or even to settle it. In such a case, the parties should notify the office of the National Conciliation Officers of the fact, and the official conciliators may not take any steps to mediate in the dispute unless it appears that the private procedure will not bring about a settlement. If a dispute concerning an existing collective agreement falls within the competence of the Labour Court or arbitrators, the provisions of the Mediation Act are not applicable to the dispute. In such a case, the conciliator shall clarify the situation to the parties. He is not obliged to try to mediate in such a dispute, nor are the parties obliged to take part in any mediation procedures. Whether the conciliator is in such a case free, as he used to be, to offer his services (to be accepted or rejected by the parties), seems unclear under the amendment of 1986. In fact, the amended provision has not prevented the National Conciliation Officer from offering his 'good services' or the parties from using them, even though such cases have been rare.

II. Income Policy

67. A comprehensive incomes policy conducted under this name is a fairly new phenomenon in Finland. However, control of prices and wages during various periods has had similar aims. The wartime control of prices and wages continued in Finland until the beginning of 1956, although the controls were breached considerably in the post-war years, the trade unions pushing through wage rises in excess of the real economic possibilities, with inflationary consequences. When the controls were lifted in 1956, agricultural prices were immediately raised, and when a trade union demand for either a compensatory wage rise or a restoration of the earlier level of agricultural prices was rejected, the wage demand was put through by means of a nineteen-day general strike, the first and only one since 1917. The wage rise once more resulted in price increases, inflation, economic stagnation, and a heavy devaluation in 1957. Despite initial success and continuing efforts towards a stabilization policy, wages continued to rise somewhat faster than the production during the following decade, resulting in a 4% to 5% yearly inflation and finally a new 24% devaluation in 1967.

68. The expression 'incomes policy' was first met in the preparations connected with the 1967 devaluation. The Finnish economy of that period was characterized by an extensive use of index linkages. In the existing collective agreements, most of them concluded in 1965 for three years, wages and salaries were tied to the cost-of-living index, and so were many other long-term obligations, such as bank deposits, bonds and loans, both with regard to capital and to interest. It was seen that the price and wage rises after the devaluation would lead to a rapidly ascending inflationary spiral. In this situation, the trade union confederations were prepared to abstain from the wage increases due to the rise of the index from the beginning of 1968, with the condition, however, that most of the other index linkages in society would also be abolished. Such an agreement was in fact reached between the Government and the organizations of the employers, employees, agricultural producers, municipalities, etc., and legislation was enacted to ban index clauses in future contracts and to remove the effects of such clauses in existing contracts as far as future index changes were concerned; an exception was constituted for the index linkages of pensions, alimonies, insurances and some similar obligations. It was also agreed in the same context that the wage increases for 1969 would be very moderate. A similar agreement was concluded in 1970.

69. For these years, the incomes policy was a success – indeed too much of a success in the sense that the economic upswing resulted in a shortage of skilled labour, a wage drift in metal-working and some other industries, and the impossibility of being able to reach an incomes agreement for 1971 without substantial wage increases surpassing again the real possibilities of the economy. The development was accentuated during the following years, resulting in a 15% to 19% yearly inflation in 1973, 1974 and 1975. Despite the inflation, it was still thought during these years that the world economic crisis would bypass Finland doing little harm; but a rapidly deteriorating balance of payments led in 1976 and subsequent years to grave unemployment and to an exhaustion of Government resources. In this situation, the organizations were again prepared to agree to a more restrained incomes policy, the restraint reaching its culmination in December 1977, when an agreement was reached to postpone, for some months, the wage increases due according to existing agreements in March and September 1978. This meant a culmination in another sense, too: the agreement was not adhered to by two confederations of white-collar employees, the Confederation of Salaried Employees (TVK) and the Confederation of Technical Employee Organizations in Finland (STTK), but for the first time, the effects of the agreement 'concluded between the most representative confederations' were by an Act of Parliament extended to the whole labour market. The two confederations acquiesced in the situation; but when after some weeks Finland felt forced to make another devaluation (of about 7%, but making about 15% together with two small devaluations in 1977), the employees' 'most representative confederation' itself, the SAK, felt itself bound to declare that the agreement policy had lost its credibility and to push through a partial withdrawal of the deferment of the wage increases. The solutions of incomes policy were during this period very comprehensive, bearing also upon agricultural and other prices, rents, taxes, interest rates, pensions, holidays, unemployment benefits, maternity leave, etc. To give effect to the agreements, legislation was needed as regards, e.g., taxes, rents and price controls. In the early and middle 1980s incomes policy continued in a similar manner, although the solutions were not as comprehensive as during the preceding decade. The financial boom ('casino economy') of the late 1980s once more brought about wage increases which widely surpassed the real long-run possibilities of the national economy.

70. The 'casino economy' ended in 1991 in the worst depression since the 1890s, with unemployment rates approaching 20% and public and private foreign debt increasing rapidly. Now the incomes policy has to face new challenges. Earlier, incomes policy had been said to aim 'at the maintenance of an economic balance and at the furthering of economic growth and the growth of real earnings'. It is true that the economic situation had at times led the negotiating parties to agree on a zero growth of nominal wages (entailing a diminution of real earnings) or on a postponement of wage increases, based on existing agreements. But in autumn 1991, the aim of the Government (and, of course, of the employer organizations) was to push through a swift cut of even nominal wages. This proposal was opposed vehemently by the employee organizations, but after several weeks of futile negotiations, a proposal for an incomes policy solution, entailing a smaller (in most cases a 3%) cut of nominal wages and salaries was reluctantly accepted by the confederations on both sides. However, the ensuing negotiations to put the master agreement into effect on the federation level lasted for several more weeks, as the same trade union leaders who as members of the boards of the confederations had voted for the acceptance of the proposal were, as chairmen of their federations, very reluctant to persuade their own federations to follow the master agreement. Meanwhile, the pressure in the money market on the Finnish currency became too severe, and the bank of Finland and the Government were forced to devaluate the Finnish Mark by about 14%. After the devaluation, it was impossible to conclude any collective agreements on the basis of the master agreement. In the still worsening economic situation, the confederations were, however, prepared to accept a new master agreement, based on a zero growth of nominal wages and salaries; and this agreement was also in general adopted the federation level.

71. The recession and peak unemployment continued for the next couple of years. The employers began to advocate decentralized bargaining, the era of consensus was said to be over, and wage increases were few. The analysts were in 1994 still of the opinion that with an unemployment rate of 19%, wages could not rise. The export industries were, however, already moving rapidly upwards and were not able to resist substantial wage demands, while the upward trend did not extend to home market industries and services, where no wage increases worth mentioning could be pushed through; and because of the huge outlays caused by the unemployment, governmental and municipal employees had to accept solutions implying salary cuts in fact if not in form. In 1995 the economic situation was still very much the same, even though the unemployment was slowly diminishing. On the one hand, it was clear that the employees of the export industries were again ready and able to extract themselves a part of the proceeds of the continuing boom within their branches, and on the other that other employees were not any more ready to content themselves with an inferior position but would force through substantial increases without regard to the economic situation of their employers and the whole country. Incomes policy was once more needed; and after very complicated negotiations a solution for the next two years could in September 1995 be reached. The trade unions accepted wage rises which in their members' eyes were very modest even though they in fact increased the economic gap between the active population and persons depending on pensions, unemployment benefits, etc.

72. Economic development from upto 2008 was fairly favourable, with one exception: despite an encouraging increase in the number of employed persons, the downward trend in unemployment has continued to be rather modest. In addition, Finland planned to join the EMU from its outset. To prevent the favourable economic and financial climate, which was also badly needed for a more rapid improvement in the employment situation and for the fulfilment of the conditions for joining the EMU, from being endangered by too big and too uneven wage rises, incomes policy was once more resorted to in 1997. After some weeks of hectic negotiations, a solution for the next two years (from 1 January 1998 to 15 January 2000) was finally accepted in December 1997. Only some minor fields, such as physicians, judges, ships' officers and municipal firemen, remained outside the agreement, and were consequently as a rule bound by their old collective agreements until the close of the then-current agreement period, in most cases, 31 January 1998. Eventually, agreements were concluded for these minor fields, too, albeit in two cases – firemen in early 1998 and air controllers in early 1999 – only after long strikes. Since 2008 the unemployment rate has increased. The unemployment rate in March 2017 was 9.6%.

73. In connection with the installation of the First Rainbow Cabinet in 1995, the confederations of employers and employees had issued at the initiative of the Prime Minister a Declaration of Intent, supporting the economic policies of the new Cabinet. At the installation of the Second Rainbow Cabinet in 1999, the confederations published a similar declaration, referring especially to the absolute necessity to keep inflation down, since it is impossible for a member of EMU to resort to devaluation as a solution to economic difficulties. On 27 September 1999, the Board of the SAK decided that the organization will not participate in negotiations for a comprehensive incomes solution because ten of its member federations, mostly within the manufacturing industries, had announced that they were striving towards independent collective bargaining at the federation level.

74. To lead the various rounds of incomes policy, an ad hoc Incomes Policy Officer was as a rule appointed on each occasion, although for most of the first rounds the appointee was the same person, Mr Keijo Liinamaa, then the Secretary General of the Ministry of Manpower and a former and later National Conciliation

Officer. After the death of Mr Liinamaa in 1980, income negotiations were for several rounds conducted by Mr Matti Pekkanen, Managing Director of the Federation of Wood Processing Industry (not an employers' federation). The controversial round of 1991 was led by one of Finland's top politicians, Mr Kalevi Sorsa (a former Prime Minister and Speaker of the Parliament) as an Incomes Policy Officer, while the solutions of 1995 and 1997 were the result of negotiations led more directly by the Government and its Prime Minister, represented in the negotiations primarily by Mr Raimo Sailas, Secretary General of the Ministry of Finance.

75. At the moment, Russia's war in Ukraine is weakening the outlook for the Finnish economy and pushing up inflation. As a result of the war, foreign trade with Russia is collapsing, and higher uncertainty and inflation are undermining the prospects for consumption and investment.

76. According to the Bank of Finland articles on the economy, Finland's economy was growing well before the war started, and this will serve as a good foundation for the year's growth overall. The Finnish economy is projected to grow by 1.7% in 2022, but growth will slow to 0.5% in 2023 due to the impacts of the war

77. The Government Programme of the current Prime Minister, Sanna Marin, aims to increase well-being and prosperity. This means ecologically and socially sustainable economic growth, high employment and sustainable public finances, as well as a level of stability in the economy would enable unforeseen impacts on people's well-being to be avoided.

Chapter 5. Sources of Labour Law

§1. The Constitution

78. As already mentioned, the Finnish Constitution of 1919 was from 1 March 2000 replaced by a new Constitution, finally adopted in 1999. According to an original provision in the chapter of the Constitution of 1919 on the fundamental rights of the citizens ('Bill of Rights'), the labour of the citizens was placed under the special protection of the State. In 1972, this constitutional provision was augmented with a clause on the duty of the State to provide work. In connection with the constitutional reform concerning fundamental rights in 1995, the whole provision was, however, replaced with an entire section (section 18 in the 1999 Constitution) on rights connected with work and labour. This section begins with a provision stating that everyone has the right under law to acquire his living through work, occupation or trade of his own choice, and that the public powers shall take care of the protection of manpower. It is, furthermore, a duty of the public powers to promote employment and to strive to guarantee everyone the right to work. The right to education for employment is regulated by an Act of Parliament. It is in addition a constitutional right of everyone not to be dismissed from work without reasons stipulated in an Act of Parliament.

79. Except for the provision on job security, the constitutional provisions just discussed mainly imply tasks for the public powers and no enforceable rights for individuals. The original 1919 provision making the labour of the citizens one of their constitutionally protected rights, was, however, already seen to signify that the Constitution treats this right on an equal footing with other fundamental rights, especially property rights, and in a clash between these fundamental rights it has been regarded as possible to restrict property rights in the interests of labour protection in a manner which otherwise would not have been permissible under the Constitution. This equality of labour rights certainly has not been impaired by the new provisions. It does not, however, entail the supremacy of labour rights over property rights. In particular, it is difficult to interfere with existing contractual relationships. Thus, when holiday rights of employees are improved, the improved provisions are regularly made applicable to existing employment relationships only after the lapse of the period of notice from the effective date of the new legislation. If this method is not practicable, and especially when the rights of the employees shall be interfered with and recourse, therefore, cannot be had to the provision on the labour of every one, the Finnish method of 'exceptions to the Constitution' (corresponding roughly to the *Verfassungsdurchbrechungen* of the Weimar Republic but practised in Finland since the last decades of the nineteenth century) is used. This means that a provision deviating from the Constitution can be adopted observing the procedure for constitutional amendments (requiring either a majority of five-sixths of the votes cast, or the approval of two parliaments, with an intervening general election and with a simple majority before the elections and a majority of two-thirds at the final vote), but without amending the actual wording of the Constitution. This has been the method used for many of the statutes in connection with incomes policy, among others, the statute imposing the deferment of certain wage increases upon confederations not adhering voluntarily to the agreement on the deferment.

80. In connection with the constitutional reform concerning fundamental rights in 1995, the general constitutional protection of the freedom of association, was supplemented with express provisions guaranteeing everyone the freedom to organize in trade unions as well as in order to protect other interests. In addition, the original provision on the freedom of assembly has been augmented with an express provision on the right to arrange demonstrations without any need to obtain permission, and to participate in them. There was not originally, and no more is there now, any express provision on the right or freedom to strike; but the original 1919 protection was already considered to extend to this right or freedom, although its precise impact in this respect was, and still is, hard to define.

I. Legislation

81. Ordinary Acts of Parliament are the normal method of labour legislation. Finnish labour legislation is abundant, detailed and complicated. With some simplification, there used to exist two main methods for preparing labour legislation. According to the first method, a Government commission with a tripartite composition was set up for the task. The report of the commission often contained a number of dissenting opinions, and in recent decades, employer representatives often remarked that the result of the voting in the commission – as well as the legislation enacted on the basis of the report – was near the opinion of the employee members and far from the employer position; earlier, it would have been possible to present instances of the opposite situation. The other method was that the confederations of employers and employees set up a bipartite commission, possibly with an impartial chairman selected by the confederations. Now, the commission endeavoured to reach a compromise and present a unanimous report, whereupon the confederations asked for a bill based on the report to be presented to the Parliament. Dissenting voices might then be heard from some quarters not represented in the commission, e.g., the Government and municipalities as employers, finding that the proposal neglected the circumstances in hospitals, etc., or the Centre Party, finding that the proposed legislation would merely consolidate the socialist hegemony in the employee representation at the workplaces. The proposal was, however, usually well armoured against such dissents, which seldom could result in anything other than its slight modification.

82. Since the mid-1980s, this picture had, however, changed. The Government Programme, agreed upon by the coalition parties in secret negotiations when setting up a new (majority) Cabinet, has become very decisive in determining the contents of new legislation. This was especially seen during the time of the Blue-Red Cabinet, which in its programme had committed itself to several reforms in labour legislation. The reforms were put into effect almost exactly as they had been written in the programme, without paying much attention to critical opinions presented especially by the employers. The Blue-Green Cabinet in turn met a similar opposition from trade unionists, which by threats of general strikes prevented this Cabinet from fulfilling several of its plans (concerning especially cuts in unemployment benefits). The Blue-Green Cabinet in addition had the main responsibility in effecting the legislative changes made necessary by Finland's joining the EEA and then the EU; this legislation did not meet political opposition, but it involved a lot of strenuous work. The First Rainbow Cabinet endeavoured to secure the cooperation of both sides of the labour market to legislative reforms. Eventually, the cooperation (from both sides), however, became more and more half-hearted, at least in form, and even this Cabinet had to face a threat of a general strike. In addition, the Cabinet, as well as its successor, the Second Rainbow Cabinet, were criticized by the leading party in opposition, the Centre Party of Finland, for diluting and delaying measures that would be necessary to combat mass unemployment and to secure an even pace of development in the different regions of the country.

83. In addition to Acts of Parliament, there are many kinds of subordinate legislation: ordinances (decrees) issued by the President of the Republic, orders given by the Council of State (the National Cabinet) or by a Ministry. Such subordinate legislation is valid only so far as it is given within the powers granted in the Constitution or in legislation of a higher level. There is very little subordinate legislation concerning employment contracts, collective agreements, hours of work and annual holidays. On the other hand, the significance of subordinate legislation is much larger as regards occupational safety and health as well as the organization and functions of Government authorities.

§2. Collective Agreements

I. Ordinary Scope

84. In the Collective Agreements Act of 1976, a collective agreement is defined as an agreement concerning conditions to be observed in employment contracts or in employment relationships. A collective agreement is concluded by one or more employers or employers' associations on the one side, and one or more employees' associations on the other side. A collective agreement is binding not only upon the parties to the agreement but also on such associations, employers and employees as are, directly or through one or more intermediate associations, members of associations which are parties to the agreement. Some duties also fall upon parent associations of such associations which have concluded a collective agreement with the consent of the parent association. The binding effect of a collective agreement, however, is very different for employers and employees, on the one hand, and on associations, on the other.

85. On employers and employees, the binding effect of the collective agreement manifests itself primarily as the regulatory competence of the agreement parties. This competence implies that in employment relationships between employers and employees bound by the agreement, the employment terms embodied in the agreement must be observed by both parties to the relationship. An employer bound by the agreement must also observe its terms in employment relationships with those of his employees who are not themselves bound by the agreement (because of not belonging to any association bound by the agreement) but who perform work covered by the agreement. As such employees are not bound by the agreement, they can only derive rights and no duties or liabilities from it. There are, however, some exceptions to this rule in provisions outside the Collective Agreements Act. Certain provisions allowing exceptions from their contents only by means of a collective agreement entitle any employer bound by the agreement to apply the exceptions also as regards such employees who are not bound by the agreement but are within the sphere where the employer has to observe the terms of the agreement. For example, a collective agreement clause restricting the employee's rights to sickness pay according to the Employment Contracts Act may be applied by an employer bound by the agreement even when the employee in question is not so bound but performs work covered by the agreement. An employer or an employee withdrawing or expelled from an association bound by the agreement will remain bound by it as long as it is in force, and the successor of an employer takes over all rights and duties under a collective agreement to which his predecessor was bound. In any of the respects mentioned, the scope of a collective agreement can, however, be limited in the agreement itself. In the case of two rival employee associations, not willing to sign the same agreement, it is common for each of the associations to conclude an identical agreement, applicable to its members only.

86. The regulatory competence of the collective agreement parties does not extend to their member associations, e.g., in the case of an industry-wide agreement, to the local trade unions. The rights and duties of the associations bound by the agreement are set in the Collective Agreements Act and other legislation, and the parties to the agreement can neither enlarge nor modify or diminish the rights and duties of their member associations. There are some minor exceptions to this rule: within certain limits, the statutory relief for violations of collective agreement duties, the compensatory fine, may be modified in the agreement even as regards violations committed by or against a member association, and arbitration and negotiation clauses in collective agreements are valid also as regards disputes concerning member associations. A member association resigning or expelled from its parent association is relieved of its obligations based on the membership; and according to the prevailing opinion, the member employers or employees of the resigning or expelled association are relieved of their obligations together with their association.

II. General Applicability

87. The Employment Contracts Act and the Seafarers' Employment Contracts Act extend the scope of certain collective agreements beyond the limits set in the Collective Agreements Act. If a national collective agreement can be regarded as general in the field concerned, its terms shall be applied as minimum conditions by all employers in the field (general applicability of collective agreements). The notions 'national', 'deemed as general' and 'the field concerned' have not been defined in the provisions in question. It seems, however, that a collective agreement concluded by national associations on both sides, and possibly also an agreement concluded by a national association of employees and the leading employer or the leading employers in the field concerned is a national agreement irrespective of whether it is an industry-wide or a craft-wide agreement. Accordingly, the 'field concerned' is either the industry in question (e.g., the pulp and paper industry, the construction of buildings, or the wholesale and retail trade) or the craft in question (e.g., the electricians, the foremen and technicians, or the office employees). It also seems settled that a collective agreement is 'deemed as general' if the employers bound by the agreement according to the Collective Agreements Act employ at least about one-half of the employees in the field concerned. Since 2001, there has been a special committee for confirming the general applicability of collective agreements (Act on Confirmation of General Applicability of Collective Agreements, 2001). The Committee has to publish its decisions and all the collective agreements with general applicability are published on the website www.finlex.fi.

88. The general applicability of national general collective agreements in principle implies duties only for the employer and rights only for the employee. Whether the employee is bound by the agreement (by reason of being a member of an association bound by the agreement) is without legal significance. For a collective agreement to create duties for the employee and rights for the employer, it is as a rule necessary that the employer is bound by the agreement according to the Collective Agreements Act. The first exception to this rule was introduced by the comprehensive Hours of Work Act, 1996. This Act provides that employers within the scope of the general applicability of a collective agreement are entitled to apply for the same exemptions from the legal rules on hours of work that the employers within the ordinary scope of the agreement are entitled to apply. Similar exemptions are introduced in the provisions of the Employment Contracts Act on sickness pay as well as with regard to several provisions of the Annual Holidays Act. In distinction from the arrangement under the Hours of Work Act, exemptions under the other statutes mentioned can, however, only be applied in so far as this can be done without any need to resort to a local agreement concluded with a shop steward or other representatives of the employees.

§3. Shop Rules and Employer's Direction and Supervision

89. The Shop Rules Act, repealed by the Cooperation Within Undertakings Act, contained detailed provisions on the required and optional contents of the shop rules as well as on their adoption and confirmation. As of 1 July 1981, shop rules adopted under the Shop Rules Act stand repealed whether or not they have been replaced by shop rules adopted under the new legislation. As in 1991, the Act on Cooperation within Undertakings had been supplemented by provisions on national group cooperation, the tripartite preparation came to the conclusion that Directive 94/45/EC would be implemented by adding the necessary provisions to the same Act. The Act on Cooperation within Undertakings was supplemented in 2005 due to the Directive 2002/14/EC of the European Parliament and of the Council establishing a general framework for informing and consulting employees in the European Community – Joint declaration of the European Parliament, the Council and the Commission on employee representation. In 2007 the overall reform of the Finnish cooperation legislation took place covering also the company group co-operations and new Act on Cooperation within Undertakings was laid down aiming for better readable and understandable legislation. The Finnish Act on Cooperation from 1978 was repealed. At the same time, the provisions concerning cooperation within Finnish and Community-wide Groups of Undertakings were separated from the Act on Cooperation within Undertakings and new Act on Cooperation within Finnish and Community-wide Groups of Undertakings was laid down. It entered into force on 1 July 2007 at the same time as the new Act on Cooperation within Undertakings.

90. According to the Act on Cooperation within Undertakings, the agreement on the working rules (shop rules) and rules for suggestion schemes and any amendments thereto were binding on the employer as well as those employees, within the scope of the agreement, whose personnel group representative had concluded the agreement. The agreement had to be followed as a part of each employee's contract of employment unless otherwise provided in the applicable collective agreement. However, the said agreement did not override an express provision, more favourable for the employee, of a contract of employment. The employer had to provide information about the concluded agreement and its content at the workplace in an appropriate manner. The agreement entered into force within a month from the provision of the information, unless otherwise agreed. As mentioned earlier, the provisions of shop rules are lacking in the present Act on Cooperations within Undertakings (2021).

91. Under the Employment Contracts Act, an employee is in his work obliged to follow instructions given by the employer within his authority. The work is done under the employer's direction and supervision. The employer is free to regulate the same questions which can be negotiated as working rules unilaterally by him.

§4. Custom and Practice

92. The Employment Contracts Act, 1922 provided that as far as contractual terms could not be proved or the contract was invalid, local custom and established usage in that kind of work should apply. A modernized version of this provision was still included in the Government bill for the Employment Contracts Act, 1970, but in Parliament this provision was replaced by the new provisions concerning the general applicability of national collective agreements; the provision concerning invalid employment contracts expressly referred to the terms of the generally applicable collective agreement. In spite of this change, custom and practice could without a doubt still be used where no applicable agreement provisions existed or to interpret agreement provisions; but it was more difficult to use custom and practice outside the enterprise as a base for employment terms more favourable than the minimum terms of the collective agreement in question. In the current Employment Contracts Act there is still no provision on custom and practice. However, custom and practice are, as it has been, one of the legal sources applicable to the employment relationship.

§5. International Sources

93. Finland has been a member of the ILO since 1920. The conventions and recommendations adopted by the International Labour Conference are presented to the Finnish Parliament in a very conscientious manner, albeit sometimes not quite on schedule. Up to 30 June 1998, Finland had ratified seventy-five ILO conventions still binding Finland. The contents of the ratified conventions must, of course, be observed in Finnish legislation, but generally the convention norms are non-self-executing, i.e., they cannot be immediately applied. There are some exceptions to this rule. For example, the Hours of the Work at Sea Act, 1976, allows exceptions from certain of its provisions by means of collective agreements, provided that such exceptions are not against the norms of any international convention binding Finland. Conventions not ratified by Finland as well as recommendations are also an important source for legislation and sometimes also for collective agreements. Thus, the Termination of Employment Recommendation, 1963 (No. 119) was expressly cited in the preamble of the General Agreement on Protection against Dismissals, 1966. The legislation of the EU also includes norms with a bearing upon labour law. The provisions in EU regulations are directly applicable in Finland, while provisions in directives must be implemented in domestic legislation. Failing implementation within the time limit concerned, certain norms in the directive in question can, however, be applied immediately against the State.

94. In addition to the ILO instruments, there are other international treaties which have a bearing upon labour relations. For example, the United Nations Covenants of 1966 on Economic, Social and Cultural Rights and on Civil and Political Rights, as well as the European Social Charter, and the European Convention on Human Rights, to which Finland is a party, contain provisions on employment terms and working conditions as well as on trade union freedom and the right to strike. The provisions of the United Nations Covenant on Civil and Political Rights and of the European Convention on Human Rights have been incorporated in the domestic legal order of Finland and shall thus be applied by Finnish courts and administrative authorities as products of internal Finnish legislation. The Charter of the Fundamental Rights of the EU has the same effect. Moreover, Finland is bound by those provisions in the Covenant on Civil and Political Rights and its Protocol which grant other states as well as private individuals the right to present complaints concerning violations by Finland of the said Covenant. According to the European Convention on Human Rights, as amended, individuals are entitled to present complaints against the Member States to the European Court of Human Rights. Apart from models for legislation, the main direct impact of Scandinavian cooperation on labour relations is the common Scandinavian labour market instituted by a treaty of 1954. According to this treaty and its successor of 1983, nationals of any of the countries need no permit to obtain employment in any of the other countries. The use of national employment services to guide this movement of labour is to be encouraged. For Finland, the effects of the common Scandinavian labour market can mainly be seen in the mass emigration of the working-age population to Sweden in the 1960s; of the 485,000 Finns emigrating in the period from 1946 to 1975, 390,000 moved to Sweden. Now, the provisions of the Scandinavian treaty have largely been replaced by the free movement of persons within the limits of the EU and the EEA and the Union's methods to facilitate this movement.

§6. Relations Between the Different Sources

95. The collision of norms is resolved using what is known as the order of priority and the rule of favourability. The norms governing an employment relationship can be set out in a hierarchy indicating their applicability, this being laid down in legislation. In simplest terms, 'priority' means that the norm highest in the hierarchy is the one to be applied where more than one norm exists governing the same matter at different levels of the hierarchy. The weakest norms are those that are lowest in the hierarchy. The order of priority makes it possible to ascertain whether there can 'legally' be norms of different ranks dealing with the same matter. However, the hierarchy will not necessary provide a solution to a particular dispute. Following is the hierarchy of norms in Finnish labour law:

(a) Mandatory provisions of labour law are by their nature highest in the hierarchy.
(b) The next level comprises norms to be observed in a collective agreement by virtue of the Collective Agreements Act. These are found in collective agreements concluded by a national labour organization (union) on behalf of the employees who are members of that union.
(c) Next are the norms found in a generally binding collective agreement. A condition of employment set out in such an agreement does not, however, ordinarily supersede a condition of employment set out in an employment contract or other source of norms applicable to the employment relationship where the latter condition is more favourable to employees.
(d) This level comprises the semi-mandatory statutory provisions of labour laws, that is, provisions which may be deviated from to the detriment of an employee's benefits through a union-level collective agreement. Authorization to conclude such agreements is set out in the relevant labour law.
(e) The fifth category in the hierarchy comprises the shop rules adopted in a cooperation procedure between the employer and the representatives of the employees.
(f) Level six consists of clauses in individual employment contracts and practices that are tantamount to contractual terms. The Act on Cooperation within Undertakings does not, however, permit a term in cooperation agreement to supersede a term in a collective agreement or employment contract if the latter term is more favourable to employees.
(g) Next are terms in collective agreements which may be derogated from employment contracts.

(h) Eighth in the hierarchy are optional provisions and ninth are norms of customary law.
(i) The last category in the hierarchy consists of orders issued by the employer and on its authority.

96. The rule stating that the contractual term most favourable to an employee is the one that must be applied leads to situations in which the norm chosen is not necessarily the one highest in the hierarchy but the one objectively the most favourable to the employee. Thus such situations are not resolved by consideration for which alternative is best for an individual employee in a particular situation. The favourability rule is applied to all sources of norms where the issue is an employee's benefits, such as wages and wage increments, the duration of his/her annual holiday and compensation for overtime. The most favourable alternative is determined by comparing the range of contractual terms governing the matter at issue. The individual employee's views on what is most favourable must not be allowed to influence the decision; rather, the assessment is carried out objectively contractual term by contractual term. In other words, the different sources of regulation are not compared as wholes. Yet it is not always possible to demonstrate which of two or more norms is the most favourable to an employee, and in such cases resort is had to the hierarchy. Deviations are allowed from the favourability rule if there is an explicit norm to that effect in an Act. For example, the Act on Employment Contracts has a number of provisions, derogation from which to the employee's detriment is possible through union-level collective agreements (semi-mandatory provisions). The Act also contains some provisions from which derogations to the employee's detriment are allowed in an employment contract. If such a contract is made, its terms are observed even where there is a provision in the law that would be more favourable to the employee; otherwise the right to contract would be rendered meaningless.

97. There are also provisions which are meant to resolve some collisions and protect employees. For example, Collective Agreements Act, paragraph 6: Where any part of a contract of employment is at variance with a collective agreement applicable thereto, such part of the contract of employment shall be invalid and superseded by the corresponding provisions of the collective agreement. An invalid will be only the part of the contract of employment which is weaker or more unfavourable for the employee than the equivalent provision in the collective agreement.

98. If an employer, under the Collective Agreements Act, is bound by two incompatible collective agreements purporting to regulate the same employment relationship, the terms of the earlier agreement shall be followed. An employer which is required under the Collective Agreements Act to observe a collective agreement in which the other contracting party is a national employee organization is allowed to apply the provisions of this collective agreement instead of the generally applicable collective agreement.

99. It is commonly provided in a collective agreement that its terms shall be followed even beyond the end of the agreement period until a new agreement is concluded or the negotiations for a new agreement have definitely broken down. In such a case, it is clear that the agreement terms have the full effects of collective agreement clauses during the envisaged period. But in case the negotiations break down, or if the agreement lacks an extension clause the agreement terms no longer have their earlier effect. They are now to be followed in the same manner as employment contract clauses, which implies, among other things, that they can now be modified in subsequent individual contracts. But when some legal provisions allowing exceptions from their contents in collective agreements further provide that such exceptions can be applied even beyond the agreement period, if so agreed in the employment contract, an express individual contract to this effect is needed.

100. The traditional list could be augmented with a point (i): the employer's orders. Although the employer's orders are to be placed at the bottom of the list, the importance of the managerial prerogative is enhanced by the customary rule that in cases of (genuine) doubt concerning the interpretation of employment terms, the employer's interpretation shall be followed until the dispute is finally settled.

Chapter 6. Private International Labour Law

§1. Introduction; Employment Contracts; Employee Protection

101. The EEC Convention on the Law Applicable to Contractual Obligations (Rome, 19 June 1980) was ratified by Finland in January 1999. The contents of the Rome Convention were incorporated in domestic Finnish law with an Act of Parliament, effective 1 April 1999. Employment contracts concluded on 1 April 1999 or later must be governed by the provisions of the convention. Older law (included notably in Chapter 5a of the Employment Contracts Act 1970) applied to older contracts. In the Employment Contract Act 2001 the law applicable to an employment contract with connections with more than one state had to be defined in accordance with the Convention on the Law Applicable to Contractual Obligations, signed in Rome on 19 June 1980 (Treaty 80/934 of 19 June 1980 on the Law Applicable to Contractual Obligations) section 2. Posted employees provisions on the minimum terms and working conditions of employees posted to Finland are laid down in the Posted Workers Act (1146/1999). From 18 June 2016 the provision has been the following: the work carried out in Finland is governed by the law of Finland if the employment contract has no connection to other countries. If the employment contract is connected to two or more countries, the work is governed by the law stated in the Rome I Convention.

102. Some amendments were made to the Act on Posting Workers and they entered into force on 1 December 2020. The amendments are following: more detailed guidelines on pay provisions applicable to posted workers, restrictions to the employer's right to set off receivables against an employee's salary, a new provision on making pay comparisons according to which any payments of an uncertain nature made by the employer would be regarded as compensation for expenses and not as a wage or salary, an extension of applicable collective agreements in transfers within subcontracting or a group of undertakings, application of the same accommodation quality requirements to posted and local workers, additional employment conditions to be applied to long postings of more than twelve months and an obligation for the employer to compensate the posted worker's travel, accommodation and meal expenses arising from travel from the worker's regular place of work in Finland during the posting.

§2. Collective Agreements

103. The Seafarers' Employment Contracts Act applies to contracts (employment contract) applies to contracts (employment contracts) entered into by an employee agreeing personally to perform work for an employer under the employer's direction and supervision in return for pay or some other remuneration on board a Finnish ship or temporarily in some other location appointed by the employer.

The Act applies regardless of the absence of any agreement on remuneration, if the facts indicate that the work was not intended to be performed without remuneration. The Seamen's Annual Holiday Act shall apply to work done in accordance with an agreement by a worker for an employer, subject to the latter's direction and supervision, for pay or other remuneration, on a Finnish ship or, by order of the employer, temporarily elsewhere. The Seamen's Working Hours Act shall apply to work performed by persons serving on board a Finnish vessel plying in foreign transport, for the said vessel or otherwise on the orders of a superior on board the vessel or elsewhere.

Part I. The Individual Employment Relationship

Chapter 1. Definitions and Concepts

§1. Different Categories of Employees

I. General Picture

104. As a general rule, Finnish labour law avoids categorization of employees. The main body of labour law is of general application, making no distinction between, say, wage-earners and salaried employees, or manual and non-manual workers. It has indeed been a definite legislative policy to avoid creating anything that could be regarded as privileges for certain categories of employees and to try to abolish any existing privileges.

105. However, the general applicability of labour law provisions is not a rule without exceptions. Certain employees have been regarded as needing special protection, or certain general rules have been regarded as too inflexible for some kinds of work. A similar effect has been caused by some ILO conventions, which for some categories – such as employees in commerce and offices – require regulations which would be too rigid for employees in general. And as historical differences generally cannot be removed by making the rules favouring certain groups less favourable but only by ameliorating the position of the less favoured groups, the unification process is necessarily slow. Nevertheless, the trend is clear. Even the legal rules concerning seafarers, who until quite recently had legislation of their own for most branches of labour law, have by now been assimilated as far as possible into the general rules of labour law.

106. The small and still diminishing significance in labour legislation of the categorization of employees does not, however, entail a complete uniformity of employment conditions in all other respects. The provisions in legislation generally set minimum conditions only, to be freely exceeded by contract. For some groups, the minimum conditions have been exceeded or widened more than for others. This applies especially to white-collar employees (office workers, foremen, etc.). Even though the salaries of most white-collar employees are no longer substantially higher than the wages of skilled manual workers, white-collar employees often enjoy longer terms of notice, better sickness benefits, etc. Such special rules are nowadays mostly embodied in the collective agreements of the white-collar employees, and as generally, the white-collar employees are separately unionized, their unions naturally try to enhance these favours. But quite as naturally, the unions of other employees try to diminish the differences, and one of the results of these endeavours has been that some groups which were earlier paid on an hourly or piece-rate basis now draw a monthly salary. In this way, the significance of categorization is diminishing even outside legislation.

II. Categories in Legislation

A. Blue- and White-Collar Employees

107. Blue- and white-collar employees were treated separately in some statutes because they were considered to have different interests, especially to the extent that the white-collar employees were seen to have more in common with the employer than blue-collar employees have. Thus, these two categories generally had separate representation in the statutory cooperation at the working places. For this purpose, white-collar employees were in the Production Committees Act (repealed by the Cooperation Within Undertakings Act in 1978) defined as engineers, supervisors, office personnel and other non-manual workers. The Labour Protection Supervision Ordinance, 1973, had a more elaborate definition. According to this definition, a white-collar employee was a person directing and supervising work or engaged in office or planning work, laboratory, marketing or sales work, except in open shops, or in any similar work.

B. Managers and Supervisors

108. According to the Hours of Work Act, 2019, the Act shall not apply to any work which, because of the tasks involved and the position of the employee, may be regarded as being performed by a director of an enterprise, corporation or foundation or of an independent part of such entity, or as constituting an independent task which is immediately comparable to such work of a director Act shall not apply to employees whose working hours cannot be determined in advance and whose use of working time is not subject to supervision and who may thus themselves decide their working hours in relation to the following: (1) work which is to be considered management of an undertaking, corporation or foundation or an independent part thereof by virtue of the relevant duties and of the employee's position otherwise, or independent work directly comparable to such management.

109. To other managerial staff ('middle management', etc.) and supervisors (foremen), the Hours of Work Act is applicable with certain flexibility in some respects. The Act offers no specific definition for managerial staff, but a supervisor is defined as an employee whose principal duties consist of personally directing or supervising work and who takes no part, or takes part only occasionally, in the work performed by the employees placed under his direction or supervision. The employer and the employee may agree on the payment of the remuneration for additional work and overtime and the Sunday work increments as a separate monthly remuneration in respect of employees whose primary duty is to manage and supervise the work of other employees. The agreement on monthly remuneration shall be concluded in writing. Unless otherwise agreed, the agreement may be terminated to expire at the end of the following pay period.

110. Managers and supervisors count as representatives of the employer, *inter alia*, in the sense that the employer has a contractual liability for their acts and omissions concerning employees under their direction or supervision. Even working chargehands, etc., are without doubt regarded as representatives of the employer when they act in their supervisory capacity.

C. Various Branches and Occupations

111. Especially within the field of working time regulation, there have been statutes and provisions regulating hours of work in specified branches and occupations or exempting such branches or occupations from the regulation of working time. At the moment, there are no special working time laws for different branches and occupation except seafarers. There is one Working Hours Act with a wide scope of application.

D. Seafarers

112. The employment conditions of persons employed on board a Finnish ship are laid down in the Seafarers' Employment Contracts Act (2011). Its predecessors, the Seamen's Acts of 1924, 1955 and 1978, distinguished between the master and the seamen – further subdivided into officers (the chief engineer, the mates, the engineers, the chief steward and the radio operator) and ratings – and other persons employed on board, and to a large extent contained different rules for the different categories.

E. Household Employees

113. The Act on the Employment Relationship of Household Employees, 1977, was applicable to any employee who performed household work in the employer's home on the basis of an employment contract. The Act was repealed in 2014.

F. Home Workers

114. As already mentioned, the mere fact that work is to be carried out at the home of the employee or in another place of his own choice does not preclude the contract from being considered an employment contract; and if it is so considered, the employment relationship is governed by labour law also in other respects, unless specifically exempted.

G. *Apprentices*

115. According to the Vocational Education Act, 1998, schooling at a working place was based on a fixed-term employment contract (apprenticeship contract). The Act was repealed and the provisions of the vocational education were moved to the Act on Professional Education in 1998. Almost all the legal rules concerning other employees should also be applied to apprentices unless otherwise provided for in the Professional Education Act. The Legislation for professional education was under return at the moment. The new Act on Vocational Education and Training came into force in 2017. Apprenticeship training mainly comprises workplace education and training through practical job tasks, complemented as necessary with acquisition of competence in other learning environments. Apprenticeship training is based on a fixed-term employment contract between a student aged 15 or older and an employer or, in the case of a student who is in a public-service employment relationship or other comparable employment relationship governed by public law, a written fixed-term agreement between a student and an employer (apprenticeship agreement). A student in apprenticeship training shall have an average of at least twenty-five hours of working hours per week. Training can be based on a training agreement. In training based on a training agreement, a student achieves competence in a workplace through practical job tasks. The student is not in an employment relationship when in training based on a training agreement.

H. *Women and Young Persons*

116. The restrictions on the night work of women as well as on their employment as miners, in painting work using lead white or lead sulphate, etc., have been abolished. There are no other distinctions between the position of men and women in labour legislation. For young persons, there are two kinds of age limits. The contracting capacity of young persons is restricted so as to make their employment in certain cases subject to the consent of their guardians and to protect the health, safety, education and morals of young persons, there are restrictions on the employment, working hours, night work, weights to be carried by them, etc.

§2. The Individual Employment Contract

I. Contract Categories

117. In the systematics of Finnish labour law, the employment contracts of seafarers and apprentices were called 'special employment contracts' as they were regulated more or less at variance with the Employment Contracts Act. Other employment contracts, which were subject to all provisions of the Employment Contracts Act, were called 'general employment contracts'. At the moment, it is not so common to use such distinction.

II. Contract Periods

A. Definite Period

118. According to the Employment Contracts Act, a contract of employment may only in certain circumstances be made for a specified period. A contract for a specified period is permissible if it is reasonable to conclude such a contract, e.g., in order to replace temporarily an employee on a sickness or maternity leave or to perform a definite, non-continuing task. If such a reason is lacking but the contract has nevertheless been concluded for a specified period, or if contracts for specified periods are without a valid reason concluded one after another, the contract is deemed to have been made for an unspecified period. The period may be specified in terms of time, e.g., to last for so many days, weeks, months or years, or to end on a given day. The period may also be specified in an indirect manner, e.g., to the completion of a given job, or until a given employee returns from his sickness leave. A contract concluded for a period longer than five years may be terminated as if it had been concluded for an indefinite period. If the contract of employment has been concluded for a specified period, but the employer allows the employee to work beyond the expiry of the contract period, the contract is deemed to have been renewed for an unspecified period.

119. An apprenticeship contract is always concluded for a specified time, which is the time the apprentice will need according to his personal study programme to fulfil its purpose. Since the beginning of 2017, it has been possible to conclude a fixed-term contract with a person who has been unemployed for the last twelve months.

120. A seafarer's contract of employment is valid indefinitely unless it has, for a justified reason, been made for a specific fixed term. Contracts made for a fixed term on the employer's initiative without a justified reason shall be considered valid indefinitely. It is prohibited to use consecutive fixed-term contracts when the amount or total duration of fixed-term contracts or the totality of such contracts indicates a permanent need for labour.

B. Indefinite Period

121. An employment contract not concluded for a specified period – or deemed to have been concluded or renewed for an unspecified period – is terminated by giving notice. The term of notice may be fixed by contract, but must not exceed six months and must not be longer for the employee than for the employer to observe. If these rules are violated, the term of notice is six months in the former case and the shorter of the stipulated periods in the latter case. If no express term of notice has been stipulated, the period to be observed by the employer is seventeen days, if the employment relationship has continued for one year at most, but one, two, four or six months, if the employment relationship has lasted for more than one, four, eight or twelve years respectively. The notice period to be observed by the employee is fourteen days, if the employment relationship has continued for five years at most, but one month, if the relationship has lasted for more than five years, respectively. An agreement that no term of notice needs to be observed is – unless expressly stipulated otherwise – construed to mean that a notice given during a working day or shift takes effect at the close of the day or shift. It is to be noted that although the legal periods of notice are optional and may thus be deviated from by agreement, collective agreements have in general made them mandatory, excluding deviations by agreements between individual employers and employees. The employer's right to terminate employment relationships by giving notice is restricted by the rules concerning protection against unfounded dismissals.

122. As already said, the contract of an apprentice is always concluded for a specified time.

C. *Trial Period*

123. The employer and the employee may agree on a trial period of a maximum of six months starting from the beginning of the work. If, during the trial period, the employee has been absent due to incapacity for work or family leave, the employer is entitled to extend the trial period by one month for every thirty calendar days included in the periods of incapacity for work or family leave. The employer shall notify the employee of the trial period extension before the end of the trial period.

124. In a fixed-term employment relationship, the trial period together with any extensions to it may comprise no more than half of the duration of the employment contract, and in any event may not exceed six months.

125. If a collective agreement applicable to the employer contains a provision on a trial period, the employer must inform the employee of the application of this provision at the time the contract is concluded.

126. During the trial period, the employment contract may be cancelled by either party. The employment contract may not, however, be cancelled on discriminatory or otherwise inappropriate grounds with regard to the purpose of the trial period.

III. Form and Content of Contracts

A. Form

127. An employment contract may be concluded in any form – orally, in writing, electronically, even impliedly. It may be concluded for either an indefinite or fixed period. As a rule it is in force until further notice (known as a permanent contract). However, an employment contract can be concluded for a fixed period of time if there is a justified reason as defined by the Employment Contracts Act or if the employee himself/herself wishes to commit to the work for a fixed period of time only or if it is a question of an employed person who has been unemployed for the last twelve months. Where a contract is concluded for a fixed term only, the reason may be that it involves the performance of a particular task, working at a particular time of year or other circumstances indicating that there was no intention to undertake the work for an indefinite period. An employment contract is valid indefinitely unless it has, for a justified reason, been made for a specific fixed term. It is prohibited to use consecutive fixed-term contracts when the amount or total duration of fixed-term contracts or the totality of such contracts indicates a permanent need for labour.

128. A fixed-term employment contract binds the parties to it for its duration (*pacta sunt servanda*) and cannot be terminated before the duration of the contract has expired unless this option has been provided for in the contract; such a contract is known as a combined employment contract. In other words, a fixed-term contract may include a termination clause prescribing that notice be given by each party before the agreed term of the contract has elapsed. This option is not laid down in the law but it has been accepted in case law and the literature. The grounds and procedure for giving notice are determined in the same manner as for contracts concluded for an indefinite period.

A fixed-term contract may be concluded for as long a period as desired, but if concluded for over five years it may be terminated after five years in the same way as a contract concluded for an indefinite period.

129. The conclusion of a fixed-term contract always requires agreement to that effect between the parties. If no specific duration for the contract has been agreed on, the contract is to be considered concluded for an indefinite period. A party who appeals to the fact that a contract is a fixed-term one must, if necessary, prove that this is the case. Justified reasons for making a fixed-term contract may include the following: a project of specific duration; seasonal variation in the need for labour (e.g., construction and paving work); work done solely at a particular time of year (e.g., selling ice cream at an ice cream stand); and work involving unpredictable demand or substitute positions (substituting for employees on annual holiday or sick leave). If the employer needs personnel for a task on a permanent basis, the contract concluded may not be a fixed-term one. A fixed-term contract or a series (chain) of fixed-term contracts made at the employer's behest without a justified reason are considered contracts made for an indefinite period. Successive fixed-term contracts are in principle allowed if the justified reason required by the Employment Contracts Act exists for each of them. However, the Act prohibits the use of fixed-term contracts if in number, combined duration or when taken as a whole, they show that the employer's need for the work involved is permanent. Even though a justified reason may exist for each of a series of successive fixed-term contracts, concluding such contracts in succession between the same parties may constitute unlawful contracting when taken as a whole, the result being that the employer can no longer make a fixed-term contract. In the case of successive fixed-term contracts between the same parties, the weightiness required of the grounds for concluding such a contract increases with each. The larger the number of successive fixed-term contracts concluded, the stronger the assumption that the need for personnel is permanent. In judging whether the use of numerous successive fixed-term contracts is permissible, attention must be directed to the same tasks, that is, the range of tasks which the employee or employees in question have performed in the fixed-term employment relationships. In determining whether an employee has done the same work under different contracts, the meaning of 'same work' is not confined to the tasks detailed in the employment contracts, but rather refers to the actual, regular sets of tasks that the employee has performed.

130. A fixed-term contract may be converted into a contract for an indefinite period if the change is agreed upon by the parties or if the employer allows the employee to continue doing the job even though the term of the contract has expired or the ground for the contract being fixed-term no longer obtains (implied extension of the duration of a contractual relationship). A contractual relationship is also deemed to be continued indefinitely where an employer allows an employee to continue working after the period of notice has elapsed.

B. Content

131. The necessary content of an employment contract, already discussed in connection with the definitions of labour law and employment relationship – or employee position – may be summarized in the following manner. For a contract to be an employment contract, it is necessary that in the relationship based upon the contract one of the contract parties shall – or, exceptionally, may – perform work for the other party, that the latter party is entitled to direct and supervise the work, and that the work is not intended to be done without remuneration; but it is not necessary that these characteristics can be seen or heard in the words of the contract. In addition to these characteristics, an employment contract has no required content. Any employment terms on which the contract is silent are derived from other sources.

IV. Capacity to Contract

A. Married Persons

132. The capacity of any person – man or woman – to make contracts with outsiders is not in any way restricted on account of being married, and nor is the validity of an employment contract concluded by one spouse dependent on the approval or consent of the other spouse. On the other hand, there are restrictions in the Marriage Act, 1929 on the capacity of the spouses to make contracts with each other. An employment contract may be concluded concerning the work of one spouse for the trade, business, farm, etc., of the other spouse, but not concerning household work in the home of the spouses. Even in the former case, the contract is to be regarded as an employment contract only when remuneration for the work was expressly stipulated or evidently intended or in the case where it is, in the circumstances, equitable to require remuneration for the work.

B. Minors

133. Persons under the age of 18 are under age.

134. A person having care and control of a child under 15 is competent to make an employment contract on behalf of the child, but on the consent of that person, the child may also conclude the contract himself. After the child has attained the age of 15, he is competent to conclude the contract himself. If the employment contract of an employee under 18 is not made in writing, the employer shall, at the request of the employee or the person having care and control and before the contract is concluded, state the contract terms in writing, except in the case of a contract on household work in the home of the employer for not more than one day.

135. The employment contract of a person under 18 may be rescinded by the person having care and control of him in the interest of the education, development or health of the minor. In other respects, the capacity to conclude a contract also includes the capacity to terminate it. Independently of the contracting capacity, a minor is entitled to receive his earnings himself and to dispose of them, except where otherwise ordered by the local Guardianships Authority in the interests of the minor.

C. Persons Declared Legally Incompetent

136. A person who has been declared legally incompetent is himself capable of entering into a contract as an employee and to terminate his employment, unless forbidden by a court order in his own interest or precluded on the grounds of his incompetence.

Chapter 2. Rights and Duties of the Parties in the Course of the Employment Relationship

§1. Duties of the Employee

I. General Provisions

137. According to the Employment Contracts Act, an employee must perform the tasks assigned to him conscientiously. In performing his tasks, he must follow the instructions of the employer with regard to the manner in which the work is to be performed, the quality and extent of the work and the time and place for its performance, provided that the employer acts within his competence. (It is not, however, always clear whether the instructions of the employer are given within his competence or whether the existing conditions of work have tacitly become parts of the employment contract and hence cannot be altered unilaterally by the employer.) The employee should also refrain from anything that is contrary to what may reasonably be expected from an employee in his position or liable to cause prejudice to his employer. There are similar provisions on the duties of the employee in the Seafarers' Employment Contracts Act.

II. Fidelity

A. *Business and Trade Secrets*

138. For the duration of the employment, the employee shall neither exploit for his own use nor divulge to a third party any of his employer's business or trade secrets that have been entrusted to him or otherwise come to his knowledge. The possibilities of extending this duty beyond the end of the employment relationship are strictly limited.

During the term of employment, the employee may neither utilize unlawfully nor divulge to third parties the employer's trade secrets. If the employee has obtained such information unlawfully, the prohibition will also continue after termination of the employment relationship. Provisions on the protection of trade secrets are also laid down in the Trade Secrets Act (595/2018). Liability for any loss incurred by the employer applies not only to the employee who divulged the trade secret but also to the recipient of this information, if the latter knew or should have known that the employee had acted unlawfully.

B. *Competing Activities and Contracts*

139. Except with his employer's consent, no employee shall carry out such work for another person or otherwise exercise such activity as would cause manifest prejudice to the employer as a competing activity which is contrary to fair employment practice. The employer is, however, deemed to have given his consent, if he knew about the competing activity when the employment contract was made and did not expressly stipulate that the competing activity shall be discontinued. An employment contract concluded by an employee in violation of his duties under a previous contract of employment is not invalid but the employee is liable for damages for the neglect of his duties under either of the contracts (or both of them, as the case may be). If the second employer knew of the violation, he is liable for damages to the first employer jointly and severally with the employee.

§2. Duties of the Employer

I. General

140. The employer's duties contain provisions on the general applicability (extension) of collective agreements and equal treatment in employment. Since 2015 non-discrimination has been regulated in a separate law. There are also detailed provisions on the employer's duty to pay wages, on his duties in the interest of the safety and health of the employees, etc. In some other respects, the provisions expressly concerning the duties of the employer are very meagre. Certain standards of behaviour for the employer and his representatives can, however, be inferred from the provisions entitling an employee – as a general rule – to rescind his contract of employment if the employer or his representative grossly insults him.

II. Specific Duties

A. To Provide Work

141. Another inference from the rescission provisions of the Employment Contracts Act – seen together with the preparatory materials – is that the employer shall give the employee a sufficient amount of work irrespective of whether the employee is paid on time or piece-work rates. However, there is still no provision in the Employment Contracts Act on giving a sufficient amount of work. If an employer is entitled to terminate a contract of employment by means of notice, he may alternatively transfer the employee – except a seafarer – to part-time work, observing the same period of notice as in the case of termination. If an employer who has part-time employees seeking full-time work seeks employees for similar part-time or full-time work, such work shall in the first place be offered to such part-time employees as far as this is possible with regard to the nature of the work. Training for the new work shall be arranged by the employer as far as is reasonable. Such former employees who are entitled to be offered reinstatement have, however, priority over the part-time employees.

142. In case of variable working hours clause, employee's working hours, as a specified period, vary between a minimum and maximum amount under the employment contract, or a working hours arrangement in which the employee undertakes to perform work for the employer when separately asked to do so.

143. Agreement on variable working hours may not be made at the employer's initiative if the employer's labour need to which the agreement relates is fixed.

144. Any agreement that the minimum working hours included in a variable working hours clause will be fewer than required by the employer's labour need may not be made at the employer's initiative.

If the actual working hours over the preceding six months demonstrate that the agreed minimum working hours do not correspond to the employer's actual need for labour, the employer must, at the employee's request, negotiate an amendment to the working hours clause to correspond to the actual need. The negotiations must be undertaken within a reasonable time and the employee has the right to use an assistant in the negotiations. If no agreement is reached on new minimum working hours, the employer must present in writing relevant grounds justifying how the valid working hours clause still corresponds to the employer's labour need.

B. *Tools and Working Materials*

145. Tools and working materials shall be supplied by the employer, except as far as it has been agreed otherwise or a contrary practice prevails in the branch concerned. There are provisions in some collective agreements on the duty of some employees – e.g., carpenters – to have and use certain tools of their own (and on the compensation to be paid by the employer for the employee's use of his own tools).

§3. Occupational Safety and Health

I. General

146. There are in the Employment Contracts Act and the Seafarers' Employment Contracts Act some general provisions concerning occupational safety and health. The most important statute in the field is, however, Occupational Safety and Health Act containing general as well as special provisions. The seafarers earlier had their own Protection of Ship Labour Act, 1967, but as of 1988, they are included under the Occupational Safety and Health Act. Various statutes contain additional provisions on safety and health within specific branches or regarding specific hazards. Moreover, various statutes contain provisions with the aim of protecting the safety and health of young people in employment; but these provisions are treated in a later context.

147. The provisions of the Occupational Safety and Health Act as well as of the Mines Act and other such statutes are to a great extent of a general nature. They are further implemented by means of subordinate legislation, often in a very detailed form, for various industries and activities. We have thus, e.g., orders for the prevention of noise in work, orders concerning the use of tractors, and orders for the following: mining work, manufacturers using the viscose method, dock work, construction work, ski lifts, etc. The safety and health conditions at the workplaces are further to be developed in cooperation between the employer and the employees and the observance of the duties laid down in legislation – subordinate legislation included – is officially supervised.

148. The Occupational Safety and Health Act is one of the general statutes in labour law. In principle, it applies to work carried out under the terms of an employment contract and to work carried out in an employment relationship in the public sector or in comparable service relation subject to public law. In addition, there are several provisions which enlarge the scope of application. The Act is applied, for example, to work done by apprentices and students in connection with education and by persons involved in employment measures, to work associated with rehabilitation and rehabilitative work experience, work done by persons serving a court sentence and to work or work activities done by persons undergoing treatment or kept in a place for treatment or a comparable institution. The Act is also applied to work done by conscripts and women in voluntary military service with some restrictions and to work done by persons in non-military national service and to work done by persons belonging to a contractual fire brigade while voluntarily participating in rescue services.

II. Duties and Rights of the Employee

149. In addition to the duty of the employees to cooperate with the employer to ensure and promote occupational safety and health, every employee must, in observing the instructions and advice received, take care of his own safety and health at work as well as of the safety and health of fellow employees as far as they are influenced by his work. Besides this general duty, there are few specific duties for employees concerning safety and health. If an employee has been provided with personal protective equipment, he must use it, take good care of it, and immediately inform the employer or his representative and the labour protection representative of any faults or defects in the protective equipment. He must also immediately inform them of any faults or defects in the machinery, equipment or tools in his use or care, if the faults or defects might involve a safety or health risk and he cannot himself remove them. Employees are also to wear working clothes which do not entail a risk of an accident, and if an employer is legally required to arrange medical examinations for his employees, no employee may, except on reasonable grounds, refuse to undergo such an examination.

150. If the work involves serious danger to the life or health of an employee or other employees, he is entitled to refrain from performing the work as far as is necessary with regard to the safety and health of the work. The employer or his representative shall be informed as soon as possible. The employee has no duty to compensate for damage caused by an action within his competence to refrain from work.

III. Duties of the Employer

151. The main responsibility for safety and health lies with the employer. In order to protect the employees against accidents at work and health defects arising out of work, the employer must take all precautions which are reasonable with regard to the nature of the work and the conditions in which it is performed as well as the age, sex, skill and other qualifications of the employee. The working environment must be constantly observed, and proper measures must be taken in order to search out and prevent accidents, health hazards and dangerous situations. For action to promote safety and health at work and the employees' working capacity, the employer must have a programme, which covers development requirements for the employment conditions and the influence of factors connected with the working environment. Safety and health goals derived from the action programme shall be observed in developing and planning the workplace, and they shall be discussed with the employees or their representatives. As already mentioned, the employer must also in other respects cooperate with his employees in safety and health matters.

152. The main body of the Occupational Safety and Health Act consists of provisions concerning the specific duties of the employer with regard to safety and health. The contents of the different provisions laying down the duties of the employer might best be summarized by citing the titles of the provisions: Planning of Work and Working Environment; Planning the Dimensions of Work and Utensils to Suit the Employee; Hygiene; Night Work; Structures at, and Dimensions of Working Premises; Ventilation; Lighting; Temperature and Humidity; Excessive Dampness, Draughts, Temperature, Glare and Radiations; Dust, Fumes, Gases and Vapours; Substances Dangerous to Health; Noise, Vibration and Pressure; Orderliness and Cleanliness; Personal Protective Equipment; Periodic Employment in More Hygienic Conditions and Shortening of Working Hours, and Systematic Breaks; Fire Prevention; Risks of Large Accidents; Electric Wiring and Equipment; Hoisting, Transports and Traffic; Risks of Falls and Drowning; Repairs, Installations and Maintenance; Machinery and Equipment; Explosive, Inflammable and Corrosive Substances; Care of Dangerous Materials; Instructions and Notices; First Aid; and Home Work. Most of these provisions are not very precise, however, and do not give the employer exact instructions. Instead, they must be supplemented with the varying conditions of every workplace: 'The ventilation on working premises shall be efficient and suitable'; 'machinery shall be suitably constructed, located and installed so as to prevent accidents to those using the machinery in their work as well as to other persons at the workplace'; etc. Such open provisions are to a certain extent supplemented in the regulations for various industries and activities mentioned earlier. But in the absence of such regulations, or in cases where the regulations are open, it lies ultimately with the employer to ascertain himself what the provisions require of him. The Occupational Health Care Act lays down the duties of employers in combating health hazards connected with employment.

IV. Duties of Third Persons

153. In order to protect employees against safety and health hazards, the Occupational Safety and Health Act does not lay down duties solely on those protected persons and their employers but on certain third persons. All makers, importers, vendors and lessors of machinery, tools and other technical equipment are thus under a duty to ensure that the equipment sold, let or exhibited by them is safe for use. This entails that the equipment must be fitted with the protective devices needed for its normal use. Nor must the equipment, in use, involve the employees concerned with undue safety or health hazards. And instructions for installing, using and maintaining the equipment must be delivered together with the equipment. These requirements also refer to second-hand equipment. Thus a factory owner may not sell any used machines in an unsafe condition unless he makes sure that the equipment is really scrapped or that it is made safe before it is put into use. An independent contractor undertaking to install any machinery shall ensure that the appropriate safety devices for the equipment are properly in place. Similar provisions as to makers, etc., of machinery, etc., apply to makers, importers, vendors and transferors of materials which are dangerous to health, and of chemicals without regard to whether they are dangerous to health. Providers of plans of working premises, machinery, working methods, etc., shall ensure that provisions on employee protection are observed in the plans. In cases of subcontracting of labour, both parties to the contract shall be regarded as employers of the subcontracted employees if those employees work under the direction and supervision of the party for whom the work is performed. There are special provisions to protect the work at a shared workplace.

154. Packages of one ton or more sent by ship shall have their gross weight in kilograms marked plainly and durably before they are loaded. If premises have been let to be used as a workplace, the lessor must allow the lessee to carry out such repairs or alterations in the building as are required of him under the Act. A landowner or tenant who sells gravel or other similar material to be dug out by the customers shall, in the absence of a contrary agreement with the employer of the workmen, ensure that the quarry does not become dangerous.

§4. Employee Privacy

I. Collection, Maintenance and Use of Information

155. The Act on the Protection of Privacy in Working Life lays down provisions on the processing of employees' personal data, the performance of tests and examinations on employees and the related requirements, technical surveillance in the workplace, and retrieving and opening employees' electronic mail messages. The Data Protection Act specifies and supplements the EU's General Data Protection Regulation and its national application. The Act provides, among other things, for the appointment, organization and powers of the supervisory authority on data protection matters. In addition to general data protection legislation, Finland has specific legislation on the processing of personal data. *See* more on the website of The Office of the Data Protection Ombudsman (www.tietosuoja.fi).

156. The Act on the Protection of Privacy in Working Life applies not only to those in an employment relationship but also to civil servants and *mutatis mutandis* to job applicants. Also covered by protection of privacy is information on any criminal record an employee might have and on his/her reliability. This protection is afforded by provisions elsewhere in Finnish legislation.

157. Essentially, every individual has the right to decide where his/her personal data are sent and how. It is natural that when a job has been advertised and when an employment relationship exists, the employer needs personal data on an applicant and employee. The point of departure in the Act on the Protection of Privacy in Working Life is that an employer is only entitled to process personal data on an employee that are necessary for the purposes of the latter's employment relationship. These data must pertain to the parties' to the relationship exercising their rights and discharging their obligations or to benefits which an employer provides to an employee; or the need to use the data must stem from the particular nature of the employee's duties. Examples of data which are necessary are data on an employee's education or qualifications, as well as data relating to whether his/her health, skills, experience and so on meet the requirements of the duties to be undertaken. By contrast, data such as the person's family status, type of housing or amounts owed on bank loans are not considered necessary. Even with the consent of the employee/applicant, no exception is allowed to the requirement that the data be necessary for the sense of the Act. Personal data on an employee are to be collected primarily from the employee himself/herself. Use of other sources to obtain such data requires the employee's consent. This consent is not required, however, if the data are obtained from an authority for a purpose prescribed in the law. The employer must nevertheless inform the employee of these data before they are used in making any decisions.

158. Collection, maintenance and use of information concerning individuals are regulated in the Data Protection Act, 2018. It specifies and supplements Regulation (EU) 2016/679 of the European Parliament and of the Council on the protection of natural persons with regard to the processing of personal data and on the free movement of such data, and repealing Directive 95/46/EC (General Data Protection Regulation), and its national application. The provisions on telecommunication are in the Information Society Code (2014).

159. 'Sensitive information' may, without the consent of the persons in question, be collected and filed only to the extent that doing so fulfils a legal duty. Sensitive information includes all information concerning the health, illnesses and disabilities of individuals as well as care measures applied to them. Sensitive information also includes data on race or ethnic origin; societal; political and religious opinions; membership in a trade union; and criminality, punishments and sexual orientation. There are, however, several legal duties which require that especially health information is filed, e.g., in order to comply with the provisions of the Employment Contracts Act on paid sick leave, maternity leave, job protection, etc. For the fulfilment of the employer's duties it is, however, in general enough to record the mere existence of the illness or pregnancy, or of the absence due to it, and the dates concerned. The name of the illness, or other medical details, are seldom of any concern to the employer, and they cannot thus be recorded. The prognosis of a severe illness or accident is, however, needed as it tells whether the loss of working capacity entitles the employer to terminate the employment; but even in such a case, the name of the illness or accident and other medical details are irrelevant. Associations and other entities representing societal, political and religious opinions may handle data on their members' and connected persons' opinions. Data on membership in a trade union may be handled by the union itself as well as by any federation (or confederation) to which it belongs. Data on union membership may also be handled by the employer in so far as is needed to fulfil the employer's rights and duties within labour law.

160. If an employer has an employee's or applicant's health examined, this examination and any related testing must make use of professional healthcare personnel and healthcare services. The rationale of this requirement is to ensure that any check-ups, tests and examinations are performed only by professionals entitled to do so and that the information and results obtained are reliable. Information on an employee's state of health, illness, disability or treatment he/she has undergone is considered sensitive. As a rule, an employer may not process such data. The employer may, however, do so if the data have been obtained from the employee or, where the employee has given his/her written consent, another source, and if the processing of the data is necessary to determine the employee's salary during sick leave or to provide comparable benefits relating to employee health. Such data may also be needed to determine if an employee has a justifiable reason to be absent from work or to ascertain his/her capacity to work. Data on an employee's state of health may only be processed by a person whose job description includes preparing or making decisions on employment relationships or executing such decisions. An employer must specify who these persons are or define the duties which involve the processing of health-related data. Personnel processing such data have a secrecy obligation with regard to the data even after their employment relationship has ended.

161. A doctor's certificate or statement concerning the employee's working capacity given to the employer by the employee may, however, be supplied to the occupational health service provider for the purpose of carrying out the occupational health care duties laid down in the Occupational Health Care Act, unless the employee has forbidden this.

162. The employer must store any data in its possession concerning the employee's health separately from any other personal data that it has collected. Data concerning health shall be erased immediately after the grounds for processing have ceased to exist. The grounds and necessity of processing shall be evaluated at least every five years.

§5. Remedies and Penalties for Violations

I. Breaches in the Contractual Relationship

163. The main remedies for the wronged party for violations of duties in the employer–employee relationship are his right to terminate the employment contract and his right to damages. A punishment (fine or even imprisonment) is foreseen in certain cases. Termination by way of rescission or otherwise is treated in detail below, and so are the normalized indemnities for cases of wrongful termination. Compensatory fines for violations of collective agreements are likewise treated below. So are pecuniary compensations for non-fulfilment of the negotiation duty under the Cooperation Within Undertakings Act (in matters concerning job protection, etc.) and for violations of provisions on sex discrimination. Where a normalized indemnity is not provided for, an employer who wilfully or through negligence fails to meet his obligations is liable to compensate the damage of the employee in full. An employee is liable to damages to the extent it is considered reasonable under the circumstances. Where he is only slightly at fault, no compensation is payable; but if the damage was caused wittingly, full compensation shall be paid unless there are special reasons to allow a reduction.

164. A fine is laid down for employers violating certain provisions in the Employment Contracts Act. Employers violating provisions of statutes on safety and health, privacy, annual vacations, hours of work, etc., are also as a rule liable to fines. An employee violating certain provisions on bribery or trade secrets is also liable to a fine or to imprisonment for not more than two years and a motor vehicle driver violating the EU regulation on road transport is liable to a fine. Provisions on penalties were earlier included in the various statutes on employment contracts, safety and health, hours of work, etc. In connection with a codification of criminal law, all provisions providing for an (alternative) prison term as well as some other penalty provisions considered more important were rewritten and transferred to the Criminal Code in 1995 (as regards trade secrets and bribery, already in 1990). Provisions imposing fines for minor transgressions remained in labour law statutes, and provisions on penalties for violations of the EC regulation on road transport and of the European Agreement Concerning the Work of Crews of Vehicles Engaged in International Road Transport (AETR) are included in the Road Traffic Act, 1981, as amended in 1998.

II. Breaches Against Third Parties

165. If an employee in the course of his work causes damage to a fellow employee or an outsider, the damage must be compensated by the employer, as a rule in full. The employer is subrogated to the claim, but only to the same extent as if the damage had been caused to the employer. With the exception of damage caused wittingly or of the insolvency of the employer, the third party cannot sue directly the employee. Even in these exceptional cases, the liability of the employee is restricted as the case of damage suffered by the employer.

Chapter 3. Working Time, Annual Vacations, Holidays

§1. Working Time

166. The Finnish law of working time regulation has traditionally been embodied in many rather complicated statutes. There used to be, to begin with, a general statute, the Hours of Work Act. Several branches, however, had their working time regulated in statutes of their own. Such special statutes were the Hours of Work in Commerce and Offices Act, 1978 the Work in Bakeries Act, the Janitors' Hours of Work Act, 1970, the Hours of Work in Agriculture Act, 1989, the Act on the Employment Relationship of Household Employees, the Hours of Work at Sea Act, and the Act on Hours of Work in Coastal and Inland Navigation, 1982. Within the scope of the EEC Regulation on the unification of social legislation relating to road transport (EEC 3820/85), its provisions were to be applied with priority to the provisions of the Hours of Work Act. The following branches and activities remained outside the legal regulation of working time: homework, forestry work paid at piecework rates, timber floating, fishing, office work in public administration, and, within certain limits, fieldwork of commercial travellers and representatives. Taking into account the branches and activities regulated by the special statutes or remaining outside legal regulation, the general Hours of Work Act, 1946, was applicable in the following main areas: manufacturing, handicrafts, rail, road and air transport, telecommunications, catering, construction work, hospitals, prisons and institutions for social welfare, customs and post offices as well as police and fire departments. Bakeries and road transport were subject to the general Hours of Work Act in so far as the Work in Bakeries Act or the EEC Regulation did not contain diverging provisions. The applicability of the legal regulation of working time to supervisors and managerial staff has already been discussed. A comprehensive codification of working time regulation was, however, enacted in 1996. The new Working Hours Act has replaced not only the Hours of Work Act, 1946, but also most other statutes on the regulation of working time. In addition, the legal regulation of working time now covers some fields which still were outside the regulation, especially office work in public administration. Seafarers, however, still have their own rules, and the EEC Regulation on road transport as well as one section of the Work in Bakeries Act, 1961, have remained effective. The new act entered into force on 23 November 1996 with the exception of the limits of overtime, which have been applicable since 1 January 1997. The European Agreement concerning the work of crews of vehicles engaged in international road transport (AETR, 1970) has been incorporated in Finnish legislation as of 15 August 1999.

The tripartite work on updating Working Hours Act was completed in 2019 and the new law came into force at the beginning of 2020.

I. Normal Working Time

A. The Working Hours Act

167. According to the Working Hours Act, the general rule for normal working hours is that they should exceed neither eight a day nor forty a week. It is, however, possible to exceed the weekly limit – but not the daily limit – if the employer lays down a schedule in advance providing for working hours not exceeding forty a week on average. A simple model for such a regulation would be a two-week timetable with six days of eight hours each one week and four similar days the other week; but the timetable might also be much longer, up to fifty-two weeks, and more complicated. An employer and an employee may agree to extend the daily regular working time by no more than two hours subject to the provisions of the collective agreement applicable to the work concerning agreement on regular working time. In this case, the weekly regular working time shall average no more than forty hours over a period of no more than four months. Weekly regular working time may not exceed forty-eight hours. The agreement may be concluded for a fixed term or indefinite term. An agreement concluded for an indefinite term or for a fixed term of at least two weeks shall be made in writing. An agreement on regular working time concluded for an indefinite term may be terminated to expire at the end of the adjustment period. A fixed-term agreement for a period of more than one year may be terminated after four months of conclusion in the same manner as an agreement concluded for an indefinite term. An employer and an employee may agree on flexible working hours so that the employee may, within set limits, determine the timing of his or her daily working hours. When agreeing on flexible working hours, at least the following shall be agreed: (1) consecutive fixed working hours, (2) the daily limits for and placement of flexible working hours, (3) the placement of rest periods and (4) the maximum accumulation of hours in excess or in deficit of the regular working time. When working flexible hours, the daily regular working time shall be reduced or extended by a flexible period which shall not exceed four hours. Weekly regular working time may average no more than forty hours over a reference period of four months and the employee may work more or less than this amount of hours within the set flexible working hours limits. At the end of the reference period, the accumulated excess hours may not exceed sixty hours and the accumulated deficit of hours may not exceed twenty hours. The employer and the employee may agree that the accumulated excess hours shall be reduced through paid leave given to the employee. At the employee's request, the employer shall strive to give such leave in the form of full workdays. An agreement concerning flexible working hours concluded for an indefinite period may be terminated to expire at the end of the reference period. An agreement concluded for a fixed term of more than one year may be terminated after four months from its conclusion in the same manner as an agreement concluded for an indefinite term.

168. There are new provisions of the flexiwork and working time account in the new law. An employer and an employee may agree on flexiwork whereby the employee may independently decide on the placement and place of performance of at least half of the working time. When agreeing on flexiwork, at least the following shall be agreed: (1) the days to which the employee may allocate the working hours; (2) the placement of the weekly rest period; (3) the fixed working hours, if any, however, not their placement between 23:00 and 06:00; and (4) the working time applicable after expiration of the agreement on flexiwork. In flexiwork, the weekly regular working time may not average more than forty hours over a period of four months.

In the Working Hours Act, a working time account means a system for reconciling working time and time off by which working time, earned time off or monetary benefits converted into time off may be saved and combined. The employer and the shop steward or, when one has not been elected, the elected representative or other employee representative or the employees or a group of employees collectively may agree in writing on the introduction of a working time account. An agreement on a working time account concluded by a representative shall be binding on those employees whom the representative is deemed to represent.

169. In certain branches and activities, it is allowed to use period-based working time. Regular working time may be organized so that it does not exceed 120 hours over a period of three weeks or eighty hours over a period of two weeks. The branches and activities where such arrangements are possible include, for example, security and guard duties, surveillance and traffic control duties, rescue duties and prison administration.

170. hospitality and cultural sectors and in camp operations, press services, editorial radio and television work, and comparable generation and transmission of online content, film production and postal services as well as in telecommunications services requiring night work, early childhood education and care services requiring night work, and in social welfare, health care and veterinary services operating for most of the day, passenger and freight transportation and in the loading and unloading of ships and railway cars, mechanical forest and forest improvement work and in short-distance timber transport, performed off-road and dairy operations.

171. Nationwide federations of employers as well as individual employers, on one side, and nationwide federations of employees, on the other, have great freedom in fixing the normal working hours by collective agreement without regard to the daily, weekly or periodic limits mentioned in the preceding paragraphs. The only legal limitation applicable is that the normal hours shall not exceed an average of forty a week in a period to be determined in the agreement but not to exceed fifty-two weeks. An employer bound by such an agreement shall apply it to his employees without regard to whether they are bound by it or not. In case an employer is bound to apply a collective agreement because of its general applicability, the employer and the employees, represented in general by their shop steward, may agree on the application of the collective agreement terms also to the extent that they deviate from the legal provisions on working time.

172. Working time includes the time spent working and the time an employee is obliged to be present at a place of work at the employer's disposal. Time spent travelling shall not be regarded as working time unless such time is to be simultaneously considered the performance of work. An employer and an employee may agree on stand by and the compensation paid for it. When on stand by, the employee shall be available to the employer so that the employee can be called for work. Time spent on stand by shall not be regarded as working time unless the employee is required to remain at the workplace or in its immediate vicinity. Stand by may not unduly hamper the employee's leisure time. The employee shall be aware of the amount of compensation for stand by or the grounds for the determination of the compensation and of the terms of the stand by when concluding an agreement on stand by. The restrictions imposed by stand by on the employee's leisure time shall be taken into consideration in the amount of the compensation. When stand by duty is essential due to the nature of the work and for extremely compelling reasons, a public servant and officeholder cannot refuse it.

173. For every workplace, the employer shall draw up a schedule of hours of work, indicating the times at which work begins and ends as well as the breaks for meals or rest. The schedule shall be brought to the notice of the employees in good time and at the latest one week before the beginning of the period covered. After the close of the minimum time of notice, the schedule may be amended only with the consent of the employees or on grave reasons connected with the organization of the work. Where the nature of the work makes it very difficult to draw up a schedule, the Regional State Administrative Agencies may grant a partial or total exemption. Exemptions are also allowed in nationwide collective agreements. Exceptions to the rules on notice time and amendments may be made in nationwide collective agreements.

B. Other Statutes

174. In order to comply with the requirements of the ILO Convention on Hours of Work (Commerce and Offices), 1930 (No. 30), the Hours of Work in Commerce and Offices Act, 1978, included some restrictions unknown to the general Hours of Work Acts of 1946 and 1996. The repeal of the Hours of Work in Commerce and Offices Act in connection with the enactment of the comprehensive Working Hours Act, 1996, has made it necessary for Finland to denounce the ILO Convention in due course.

175. The provisions on seamen's hours of work are based on a normal working time of eight hours a day and forty hours a week.

II. Work Beyond Normal Hours

A. *The Working Hours Act*

176. The Working Hours Act distinguishes between two kinds of work beyond normal hours: overtime work and emergency work. There are no general prerequisites for overtime work except that it presupposes the personal consent of the employee concerned for every separate occasion. The consent can, however, be given for a certain shorter period of time if this is needed for the organization of the work. An agreement on stand by implies a consent to any overtime needed during the stand by time.

B. *Maximum Working Time*

177. The working time of an employee, including overtime, may not exceed an average of 48 hours per week over a period of four months. Emergency work can be done if the forces of nature, an accident, or another unforeseen circumstance has caused a cessation in the normal running of the enterprise or threatens to cause such a cessation or peril to life, health or property. Emergency work can be done to the extent that it is required because of those occurrences just mentioned without any limit either daily, weekly or yearly or any other precise limits than that emergency work must not continue on account of the same occurrence beyond two weeks; nor is the consent of the employees concerned necessary. All occasions of emergency work shall, however, immediately be reported to the labour protection authorities, which may, as far as is needed, take steps to limit or terminate the prolongation of hours. Emergency work should be taken into account in the maximum working time.

178. Overtime and emergency work in excess of the normal daily hours of work shall be paid with time and a half for the first two hours and with double time for any extra hours. Overtime and emergency work not in excess of the normal daily hours of work shall be paid with time and a half. This means, e.g., that in applying a normal five-day working week, the first ten hours of Saturday work are to be paid with time and a half and any exceeding hours with double time. In work where the eight-hour day is not applicable, the first twelve hours of overtime and emergency work in a two-week period, or the first eighteen hours in a three-week period, as the case may be, shall be paid with time and a half and any exceeding hours with double time. There are special provisions for the cases where the period to be applied is interrupted by the expiry of the employment relationship or by annual holidays, sickness or another valid reason. It is possible to agree with a managerial employee or a supervisor about a monthly lump sum to be paid in lieu of overtime pay reckoned for every hour. It is also possible for nationwide employers' and employees' associations to deviate from the legal provisions concerning the pay for overtime and emergency work. All other agreements to diminish the employees' pay for overtime and emergency work or to include it in the pay for normal hours of work are null and void. By agreement, pay for overtime and emergency work may, however, be replaced with corresponding paid free time. Any work beyond the working time agreed to in the employment contract or in a collective agreement, but not in excess of the statutory normal working hours, must be separately compensated with normal wages.

C. *Other Statutes*

179. Seafarers have a duty to work overtime when ordered to. Regular daily overtime shall, however, be avoided, nor may overtime work in general exceed sixteen hours a week. Compensation shall be given in certain cases in money and in other cases in free time, with a possibility to agree on free time in the former and on money in the latter cases.

III. Rest Periods and Sunday Work

A. *The Working Hours Act*

180. If the daily hours of work are in excess of six hours, the employees – except those whose presence at the workplace is essential to the continuance of operations – are entitled to a rest period of at least one hour, during which they shall be free to leave the workplace. Employers and employees may, however, agree upon a shorter rest period of at least half an hour. In shift work and in work where the normal hours are only limited to an average of forty hours a week during a period of a certain number of weeks, with no daily or weekly maxima, the employees are entitled to a rest period of at least half an hour or to an opportunity to eat during the course of their work. When the daily working time exceeds ten hours, after eight hours of work, the employee shall additionally have the right to take a break of no more than thirty minutes. Rest periods and breaks shall not be reckoned in the hours of work when the employee is freely permitted to leave the workplace. Exceptions to these provisions may be agreed to in nationwide collective agreements.

181. The daily working time of a motor vehicle driver may not exceed eleven hours within the consecutive twenty-four-hour period following a daily rest period. When there is no other way practicably to organize the work of a motor vehicle driver, the daily working time may be extended to no more than thirteen hours, provided that the working time does not exceed twenty-two hours within the forty-eight-hour period following the daily rest period that follows the extended working hours. The daily working hours of a motor vehicle driver shall not exceed eleven hours during the twenty-four hours following a daily rest period.

182. The employees shall be granted an uninterrupted weekly rest of at least thirty-five hours. An average within a period of two weeks is, however, allowed, provided that a rest of at least twenty-four hours is granted each week. In continuous shift work, the weekly rest shall be at least twenty-four hours every week and on average at least thirty-five hours during a period of twelve weeks. The same arrangement is also permitted on account of technological circumstances or the organization of the work, but only with the personal consent of the employee. If possible, the weekly rest shall be given on Sundays. Deviations from the provisions on weekly rest are permitted in emergency work and in certain agricultural work and other limited cases. No employee who has not personally undertaken to work on Sundays is obliged to do so except in the case of emergency work and such work which by reason of its nature is regularly carried out on every day of the week.

183. Work performed on Sundays or church festivals as well as on Independence Day or May Day shall be paid with double time. Employees may be required to work on Sundays and public holidays (Sunday work) only when this has been agreed in the employment contract, or with the employee's consent. However, no consent is required if the nature of the work is such that it is regularly performed on these days. In the case of overtime or emergency work on such a day, both grounds for a pay increase shall be taken into account, making double time and a half or treble time, as the case may be. The payment for Sunday work does not authorize an exception from the provisions concerning the weekly rest. Where work is performed, in the instances mentioned in the preceding paragraph, during weekly rest periods, such work shall be compensated with time off or, with the consent of the employee, with double wages. Sunday is reckoned from midnight to midnight, save in the case of an agreement to reckon it as another period of twenty-four hours from the normal hour to report for work. Exceptions to the rules on weekly rest and Sunday work may be made in nationwide (i.e., industry-wide or craft-wide) collective agreements.

B. Other Statutes

184. A seafarer has to be given a sufficient rest period of at least six continuous hours every day. Seaman whose duties are divided into watches shall each day be given a rest period of at least ten hours, which may be divided into two units, one of them comprising at least six hours. However, the daily rest period may two times each week be shortened to six hours, provided that the seamen are accorded a weekly rest period of at least seventy hours. In addition to this rule, there are no express provisions for weekly rest for seafarers in foreign trade. However, work on Saturdays, Sundays and holidays is in many cases – and when in port almost invariably – to be regarded as overtime work and shall be compensated separately.

IV. Night Work

185. Provisions concerning night work of young persons will be treated separately. According to the Hours of Work Act, Work performed between 23:00 p.m. and 06:00 a.m. shall be regarded as night work and it is restricted only if it is on a regular basis. Night work on a regular basis shall be permitted:

(1) in work that may be organized as period-based work;

(2) in shift work;
(3) in maintenance and repair work that is essential to maintaining the regular operations of the employer;
(4) in work that cannot be performed at the same time as work regularly performed at the workplace;
(5) in the maintenance and cleaning of public roads, streets, other transport corridors and airports as well as means of transport;
(6) in pharmacies;
(7) at peat sites during the peat extraction season, and at sawmill drying houses;
(8) with the employee's consent, at bakeries; however, no consent shall be required for work performed between 05:00 a.m. and 06:00 a.m.; and
(9) with the employee's consent, in urgent sowing and harvesting, in work directly related to parturition or treatment of domestic animals, and in other agricultural work that owing to its nature cannot be postponed.

Employers who regularly employ night workers shall bring this information to the attention of the occupational safety and health authority if it so requests.

In period-based work and in continuous shift work, an employee may, according to the work schedule, work no more than five consecutive shifts where at least three of the working hours fall between 23:00 and 06:00, after which the employee shall be given uninterrupted leave of at least twenty-four hours. Two additional shifts as referred to above may be worked consecutively when the employee consents separately to both additional shifts.

186. In especially hazardous work or work that is highly stressful either physically or mentally, the working time may not exceed eight hours over a period of twenty-four hours in which the employee performs night work. More specific provisions may be laid down by Government Decree or more specific regulations agreed by collective agreement as to when work is to be considered to be especially hazardous or highly stressful either physically or mentally.

187. The employer must organize transport to work for a night worker if (1) transport to work is necessary and common in the area and (2) if there is no satisfactory public transport available with regard to routes or timetables at the time when the work shift begins or ends and the worker has no car or other vehicle at his or her disposal. There is no right to transport to work if the worker cannot use a car because of a driving ban imposed for a criminal offence or violation. For transport to work, the employer can charge the employee a fee equivalent to the fee paid for the use of public transport. The employer shall negotiate with the staff before making the decision on organising transport to work.

§2. Annual Vacations

188. The Annual Holidays Act applies to work carried out as part of an employment relationship or civil service relationship unless provided otherwise in the law. The Act is also applied, albeit in limited scope, to those working at home. The Act does not apply to work that, on account of the nature of the employer's operations, is interrupted each year and in which the employees are, under a collective agreement (agreed with the employers' and employees' national associations) entitled to paid leave that is at least equivalent to the annual holiday provided for in the Annual Holidays Act. According to the Act, an annual holiday is earned for the time spent working. Certain periods of absence are considered equivalent to time at work for purposes of holiday credit, and annual holiday accrues during those times (time equivalent to hours at work). The Act has a provision setting out two means of earning an annual holiday: fourteen days and thirty-five hours. In addition, the Act provides for an employee's right to leave corresponding to the annual holiday. The rules on earning holiday credit cannot be applied at the same time, in parallel or in an overlapping fashion. Only one or the other may be applied. The length of an employee's annual holidays is determined primarily by the length of uninterrupted employment with the same employer. However, holiday credit is earned following the transfer of an enterprise or going to work for an employer that is controlled by the employee's previous one. Annual holiday does not accrue for a mere time at work; rather, time at work must meet the requirements set out in the Act. The duration of the annual holiday for a particular annual holiday season (2 May–30 September) is calculated with reference to the employee's time at work during the previous holiday credit year (1 April–31 March). If, by the end of the previous annual holiday credit year, an employee's employment relationship has lasted at least one year, he/she is entitled to two and a half weekdays of holiday for each full holiday credit month. Otherwise, he/she is entitled to two weekdays for each full holiday credit. When the number of days of holiday is calculated, any fraction of a day is rounded up to constitute one full day of holiday. Only weekdays are counted as days of holiday. In calculating how long an employment relationship has continued uninterrupted, periods are not counted during which employment is suspended because the employee is doing compulsory military service, voluntary military service for women or non-military service.

189. Annual holiday is earned for all of the calendar months falling within the holiday credit year during which an employee has at least fourteen days at work. How long the working day has no significance, nor does it matter whether the hours worked have been the employee's regular working hours, additional work, or overtime. (Additional work refers to work done on the employer's initiative which does not exceed regular working hours; overtime refers to work carried out on the employer's initiative in addition to the regular working hours.) If an employer and employee have agreed in the employment contract that the work will be done on so few days that the fourteen-day requirement is not met, a full holiday credit month is defined as a month during which the number of hours worked by the employee is at least thirty-five. Annual holidays can also be earned for days on which an employee is prevented from working. Such periods include periods of absence for which an employer is required by law to pay employee wages. A second such case, with some restrictions, is the time at which an employee is absent from work in order to meet statutory requirements for the maximum average number of hours that may be worked in a week. In addition to these provisions, the Act provides an exhaustive list of criteria of types of absence for which holiday credit accrues. These include maternity, special maternity, paternity or parental leave; illness or accident (up to seventy-five days per annual holiday credit year or, if the employee's incapacity continues after the end of the holiday credit year, at most seventy-five working days for the particular illness or accident); and being laid off (at most thirty working days at one time). Periods not considered the equivalent of time at work include child-care leave, job alternation leave, unpaid leave, military service, non-military service, participation in an industrial action and unauthorized absences. Starting 1 April 2016, a maximum of 156 days of maternity and parental leave and, correspondingly, 156 days of paternity and parental leave are counted as time at work for purposes of annual leave. In practice, this means that 51 days of parental leave following a mother's maternity leave and, correspondingly, 102 weekdays of a father's period of parental leave are counted as time at work.

190. The Annual Holidays Act contains a provision covering employees who do not earn holiday credit according to fourteen-day or thirty-five-hour rule described above. In such cases, an annual holiday is earned not on the basis of time at work but solely on the duration of the employment relationship. The provision entitles an employee to two weekdays of leave for each calendar month in which the employment relationship has been in force. It also guarantees four weeks' leave where the employment relationship has lasted at least one year.

191. In principle, it is the employer who has the authority to decide on the specific time when the annual holiday may be spent within the statutory holiday season. In some instances, the employer and employee may agree on the time. As a rule, annual holiday earned is always spent as a holiday and cannot be exchanged for money. Holiday is earned, and given, in the form of weekdays. A holiday week consists of six weekdays even when employees work a five-day week. The proportion of summer holiday in the annual holiday, twenty-four days, is given during the holiday season, this being 2 May to 30 September. The days of annual holiday that an employee has earned in excess of twenty-four days are to be spent at a time stipulated by the employer between the end of the holiday season and the beginning of the next one, that is, between 1 October and 30 April. This portion of the annual holiday is what is known as the winter holiday. The summer and winter holidays must be given in continuous periods. Where a holiday exceeds twelve weekdays, the excess days may be taken in segments if this is essential for ensuring that the work may proceed uninterrupted.

192. An employer must explain in advance to employees or their representatives the general principles observed at the workplace in the granting of annual holidays. Before fixing the time when the holiday may be taken, the employer must grant the employees an opportunity to express their views on the matter. Where possible, the employer has to take the views of the employees into account and act impartially in setting the dates for holidays. When fixing the dates for holidays, an employer must notify employees of the dates at least one month before the beginning of the holiday. If this is not feasible, notification must be given at least two weeks in advance.

§3. Paid Public Holidays

193. While at work, an employee earns annual holiday as well as holiday pay for the holiday that accrues. The point of departure in section 9 of the Annual Holidays Act is that an employee receives the same pay during his/her holiday as he/she would receive if working. The actual calculation of an employee's annual holiday pay is performed in a number of different ways depending on how he/she is paid (weekly or monthly salary, average daily salary or percentage-based salary). Any fringe benefits forming part of an employee's remuneration are granted in full during the annual holiday. If a benefit cannot be used during the annual holiday, the employee must be compensated through a monetary payment. The annual holiday pay is to be paid before the beginning of the holiday. If the holiday is granted in segments, the proportion of the annual holiday pay corresponding to the length of the segment must be paid before the segment begins. Notwithstanding, where a period of holiday is no more than six days, the holiday pay may be paid on the day when wages are ordinarily paid. The employer must provide the employee with a statement detailing how the holiday pay has been calculated, with the statement showing the size of the holiday pay or other payment and the bases on which it has been calculated.

194. Sunday pay must also be paid for work on other public holidays, but there are no rules of law on compensation for such days if no work is performed. The problem has, however, been diminished not only by the introduction of the five-day week but also by transferring some Church festivals to Saturdays. Midsummer Day and All Saints' Day are now every year on a Saturday, and Annunciation is always on a Sunday while the Second Day of Pentecost has disappeared altogether. The following Church holidays are still (or again) either on varying days of the week or on fixed days of the week other than Saturdays or Sundays; New Year's Day (1 January), Epiphany (6 January), Good Friday, Easter Monday, Ascension Day (a Thursday), Christmas Day (25 December), and St Stephen's Day (Boxing Day, 26 December). By law, May Day (1 May) has the same position. When the five-day week was introduced, it was planned that if any of the usual working days (Monday to Friday) happened to be a public holiday, Saturday should instead be a working day, thus entitling the employer to forty hours of work and the employee to wages for forty hours, in spite of the holiday. By collective agreements, the number of such Saturdays was, however, gradually diminished by entitling the employee to wages for a holiday without any duty to work on the Saturday in question. This development was completed in 1978. As of 1992, Epiphany and Ascension Day were, however, returned to their former positions. The fate of the Saturdays of the Epiphany and Ascension weeks has not yet been totally solved. In manufacturing and other industries not immediately in the service of the public, Easter Saturday, Midsummer Eve (a Friday) and Christmas Eve (24 December) are according to collective agreements paid holidays.

Chapter 4. Remuneration

195. In an employment relationship, remuneration is the main obligation of the employer, constituting the counterpart of work performed. In principle, the amount of the remuneration can be freely agreed to between the parties. There is no general minimum wage system proper. However, the relevant collective agreement must be followed, and for most employees, the general applicability (extension) of certain collective agreements has the essential effects of a genuine minimum wage system.

196. The criterion of remuneration that an employment relationship must fulfil can be met by any remuneration which has economic value. Thus, it can be money, goods, fringe benefits or a combination of these three. If the employer and employee have agreed on monetary remuneration, this must be paid to the employee in the 'currency of the land', that is, euro, unless the parties agree otherwise. Wages are to be paid to a bank account specified by the employee and must be available to the employee on payday. Wages may be paid in cash only for a compelling reason. The costs of the payment procedure are borne by the employer. An employee is to receive a written calculation of his/her wages every time they are paid indicating the size of the pay and its components. Where wages are paid in cash, the employer has to have a receipt signed by the employee or other written account verifying the payment. An employer with an accounting obligation must attach the receipt or other written account to its records. If the scale of the remuneration has not been agreed on in the employment contract or collective agreement, it must be conventional and reasonable.

§1. Payment of Wages

197. Wages stipulated in money shall be paid in respect of each pay period. Wages based on a day or a shorter period as well as piece-work wages shall be paid at least twice a month (i.e., usually with pay periods of two weeks or half a month). In other cases, the pay period shall not exceed one month. A period up to one month may also be applied to piece-work wages paid as supplements to time wages for periods longer than one day, and a pay period longer than one month may be agreed to in part-time jobs and as regards profit shares and commissions paid in addition to other remuneration. The remuneration shall be paid on the last workday of the pay period (Saturdays excluded), unless otherwise agreed. (As regards hourly and piece-work wages, it is customary to have an agreement on a calculation period, allowing the remuneration to be paid a certain number of days after the close of the pay period.)

198. Payment of a seafarer's wages may be demanded when the ship is in port but not more often than once in seven days in any one country.

199. Cash remuneration shall be paid immediately after working hours at or near the workplace, unless otherwise agreed. When the remuneration is to be paid into the employee's bank account or by way of a bank or postal transfer service, the expenses entailed shall be borne by the employer, and the remittance or transfer order shall, unless otherwise agreed, be sent in such good time that the remuneration may be presumed to be at the disposal of the employee on the due date. Bills of exchange must never be used for the payment of wages, nor may cheques or other payment orders drawn on a bank or the post office be used except with the express consent of the employee.

200. Any remuneration payable to an employee shall not be set off against counterclaims to the extent that the remuneration is legally free from distrain. This means that of the remuneration due, in general, two-thirds – after tax – shall be paid to the employee, while the remaining third may be used for the set off. The right to set off does not depend on the nature or amount of the counterclaim, and any agreement to enlarge the employer's right to set off is null and void.

§2. Failure to Pay Wages

201. If any wages or other debts arising from the employment and due at the termination of the employment are not properly paid, the employee is entitled to full wages for the period of delay up to a maximum of six days, but in certain cases only after he has protested against the delay. Where the employment relationship is not terminated, a failure to pay wages, etc., only entitles the employee to interest on the unpaid amount.

202. Under the Act on the Guaranteed Payment of Wages, 1998, the payment of wages is assured by the Government in the event of the employer's bankruptcy or insolvency. Under guarantee, the employee is entitled, up to a maximum amount of EUR 19,000, to a payment for wages and other debts arising out of the employment which has not been due for more than three months when the employee's application is filed. The employee's claim under guarantee is in the first instance met out of public funds by the appropriate Centre for Economic Developments, Transport and the Environment (Uusimaa ELY centre). The Government is then subrogated to the employee's claim against the employer. As, however, a large part of such claims cannot be recovered from the bankrupt or insolvent employers in question, the remainder is levied from all employers in connection with their obligatory fees to the unemployment insurance.

Chapter 5. Suspension of the Execution of the Employment Contract

203. The employment relationship is in principle governed by what is known as 'remuneration for work done', that is, remuneration is paid solely for work that has been performed. Some exceptions to the principle can be found. The Act on Employment Contracts entitles employees to pay during sick leave and, among other situations, if work cannot be done because the materials necessary for it are lacking.

204. If work cannot be done for reasons relating to the employer, an employee is entitled to full remuneration for as long as the obstacle persists. However, the employer need not pay the wage supplements based on actual performance of work. A requirement for remuneration to be paid is that the employee be available to the employer for work but the work cannot be done for reasons attributable to the employer. For example, an employer may have forgotten to order the materials necessary for painters to do their work or neglected to equip an office with telephone connections, rendering telemarketing impossible. Other reasons attributable to the employer include shortcomings in how work has been organized and obstacles which the employer could have removed through repairs without appreciable difficulty.

205. If the performance of work becomes impossible for a reason independent of the employer and employee (force majeure), the employee is entitled to remuneration for as long as the obstacle persists up to a maximum of fourteen days. Reasons falling into this category include fires at the workplace, extraordinary natural events (floods or storms) or similar occurrences.

206. An employee may also be prevented from doing his/her work due to industrial action by other employees. Those prevented from working for this reason are entitled to pay for at most seven days. The industrial action may not impact the affected employees' contractual terms or working conditions. If such a connection, known as a related interest, exists, that is, the industrial action being taken may impact the contractual terms of the employees who are prevented from doing their work, the employees have no right whatsoever to remuneration for the period during which the impediment continues.

207. The Act on Employment Contracts does not provide a definition of 'full pay'. This remains to be determined in each individual case, primarily on the basis of the employment contract or relevant collective agreement. An employer may deduct from an employee's pay the various supplements based on working conditions, such as the compensation for shift work, Sunday work and holiday, if the employee's right to these supplements is based on actual work done.

§1. ILLNESS

208. If an employee is prevented from working due to illness or accident, he/she is entitled to wages for nine weekdays (the days when he/she would be working during this period) following the onset of illness or occurrence of the accident. After this period, the employee's right to sick pay under the Health Insurance Act applies, with this being paid by the Social Insurance Institution, not the employer. Collective agreements often provide for longer periods of sick pay than those set out in the Employment Contracts Act. On the other hand, collective agreements may also deviate from the standard in the Act, providing weaker coverage: for example, they may make the first day of sick leave unpaid, with the right to remuneration not applying until thereafter. The right to sick pay presupposes that the employee is incapable of working due to illness or accident. An employee is not entitled to sick pay if he/she has caused the incapacity intentionally or through gross negligence. Inability to work and absence from the workplace following cosmetic surgery or a fertility treatment procedure, for example, is not construed as an absence due to illness provided that the procedures do not constitute treatment of illness. In such situations, a physician's certificate attesting to an inability to work will entitle an employee to be absent from work, but normally a clearly stated diagnosis or medical diagnosis code must be provided before the employee will receive pay for the period of absence.

209. The employee's rights described in the preceding paragraph may be restricted by collective agreement only. Such an agreement may, however, also be applied to such employees who are not themselves bound by it but who are, under the Collective Agreements Act, entitled to the benefits provided for in the agreement. Such restrictions may also be applied by employers within the scope of the general applicability of the collective agreement under the Employment Contracts Act, but only in so far as a local agreement is not needed to apply the restriction. Any such clause can also be applied after the expiry of the collective agreement in question and until the next agreement takes effect, but only if expressly stipulated by the parties to the employment relationship. It is common to stipulate in collective agreements that in the case of a disability not lasting for more than, e.g., one week, no wages are due for the first day of absence. However, employees with a service of at least, e.g., six months may also be entitled to wages for the first day of sickness and continue to receive wages up to, e.g., three weeks, the daily benefits under the compulsory sickness insurance for the corresponding time either being deducted from the wages or paid directly to the employer.

210. According to the Seafarers' Employment Contracts Act, employees who are prevented from performing their work by an illness or accident are entitled to pay during illness, shipmasters up to a maximum of ninety days, other employees up to a maximum of sixty days in foreign traffic and up to a maximum of thirty days in domestic traffic. Employees are entitled to pay during illness during the lay-off, provided that the disability to work can clearly be attributed to circumstances caused by work. Employees are not entitled to pay during illness if they have caused the disability wilfully or by gross negligence.

§2. Lay-off

211. An employment relationship may be suspended by agreement for a definite period or until further notice. During the period for which the relationship is suspended no work is performed and no wages are paid, while the relationship is maintained in all other respects. With the same effect, the employee may be unilaterally laid off by his employer under the same conditions as should be applied for terminating the employment relationship. If in the case of temporary reduction of the workload no alternative work or training can be found (or the employee does not accept the work or training available), the employee may be laid off for not more than thirty days, even though the conditions for terminating the relationship entirely are not fulfilled. In laying off an employee, a period of notice of fourteen days shall be observed (lay-off notice). When the employer perceives the necessity of a lay-off because of a reduction of the workload, an advance explanation of the grounds of the lay-off shall be presented without delay as soon as the employer becomes aware of the need for the lay-off to the employees' representative or the employees jointly and, in case at least ten employees are concerned, to the competent manpower authority. At workplaces, within the scope of the Cooperation Within Undertakings Act the intended lay-off shall in addition be handled in consultations as provided for in that Act.

212. The employer's right to lay off employees may, in addition, be enlarged by collective agreement or an agreement under the Cooperation Within Undertakings Act whether the right to lay-off can also be enlarged by individual employment contract is unclear. The possibility that the right to lay off employees may be enlarged by agreement means in effect that while the employer's right to terminate an employment relationship is restricted by mandatory provisions, the restrictions are to a large extent only optional in regard to lay-offs. Therefore, collective agreement clauses concerning lay-offs and dismissals have a more independent position as regards lay-offs than as regards dismissals. Some collective agreements allow a shorter period of notice than fourteen days in cases of an unforeseen reduction of workload. An employee laid off is not debarred from accepting other work for the lay-off time. In the case of a lay-off until further notice, such notice shall be given at least seven days before the resumption of work, unless otherwise agreed.

§3. Study Leave

213. Under the Study Leave Act, study leave is granted for general, vocational, professional, and trade union education and training. An employee is entitled to a study leave after having been in the employer's full-time service for one year (with or without interruptions), and the maximum amount of study leave the employer is obliged to grant him is two years in the course of five years in the employer's service. Service of at least three months entitles the employee to a study leave of five days. Under certain conditions, the employer may postpone a study leave asked for, and an employee may postpone a study leave already granted but not yet begun. Moreover, an employee on study leave may in certain cases interrupt the leave and report back to work. Exceptions to most provisions of the Study Leave Act may be concluded in a collective agreement. Such exceptions are applicable also to employees who are not themselves bound by the agreement, and on certain conditions also by employers who are only within the scope of the general applicability of the agreement. A certificate from the school or institution shall, on demand, be presented to the employer. An employee neglecting his studies to the extent that he cannot obtain a certificate forfeits, for the next two years, his right to a study leave. The employer has no duty to pay the employee any remuneration for the time of the study leave. Study leave is no ground for the employer to terminate an employment relationship.

§4. Military Service

214. According to the Act on the Continuation of Contractual and Public-service Employment and People Fulfilling Their National Defence Obligation, 2009, the employment relationship of a person summoned to military service shall not be terminated by the employer during the service. With some exceptions, concerning employers' deaths and bankruptcies as well as transfers of business, employees returning from military service shall be reinstated. When the service ends or is interrupted, the employee has the right to return primarily to the job in which the employee was previously engaged. If this is not possible, the employee should be offered equivalent work in accordance with the employment contract or service relationship, and if this is not possible either, other work by agreement. The Act is also applicable to persons performing civilian service in lieu of military service and to women's voluntary military service. Employers violating provisions of the act are liable to a fine. There is no legal duty for the employer to maintain the income of the serviceman during the suspension of the employment relationship. In the case of training meetings for reservists (lasting usually from one to three weeks) many collective agreements, however, provide for an augmentation of the Government pay by the employer.

§5. Accommodation During the Suspension

215. Where an employee is provided with accommodation either as a part of his employment contract or under a rental agreement in connection with his employment relationship, he is entitled to continue to use the accommodation during the suspension of the relationship. Any agreement to the contrary is null and void. For a weighty reason – e.g., if the dwelling of the suspended employee is needed for a substitute – the employer may assign the employee another suitable dwelling, any removal costs to be borne by the employer. The provisions concerning accommodation during the suspension are not applicable to suspension because of military service.

Chapter 6. End of the Employment Relationship

§1. By Mutual Consent

216. It is always possible to end an employment relationship by mutual agreement. This means, *inter alia*, that if one of the parties wants to terminate the relationship, the other party may relieve him of the duty to observe the term of notice.

§2. During a Trial Period

217. In the case of a valid agreement for a trial period, or during the trial period determined in an apprentice's contract, either of the parties may terminate the employment relationship with immediate effect. No period of notice need thus be observed during the trial period. An employer terminating an employment contract during the trial period need not show the unsuitability of the employee for the job. A termination on discriminatory or other unfair grounds is, however, unlawful and entitles the employee in general to normalized damages. If the employer terminates the contract during the trial period, the same procedure shall be followed as in other cases of individual termination.

§3. At the End of the Contract Period

218. An employment contract lawfully concluded for a specified period comes automatically to an end at the close of the agreed period. It was said earlier that the contract period may also be specified in an indirect manner, e.g., to the completion of a given job, or until a given employee returns from his sickness leave. If in such a case the termination of the contract period depends on a circumstance known to the employer but not to the employee, the employer shall in good time notify the employee about the forthcoming termination.

219. Neither of the parties to an employment contract lawfully concluded for a definite period has the right to have the contract extended against the will of the other party. There is accordingly no job security beyond the agreed period. The parties may renew the contract either for a new specified period or for an indefinite period. Successive renewals for specified periods may, however, show that there is no lawful reason for a limited contract period. In such a case, the contract is deemed to have been extended for an unspecified period. An extension may also come about without an express agreement. If the employer allows the employee to continue his work after the expiry of the contract period, the contract is also deemed to have been extended for an unspecified period.

220. The Employment Contracts Act also contains a provision on the age at which an employee must resign. An employee's employment relationship ends without termination and notice of termination at the end of the calendar month during which the employee reaches the age of retirement, unless the employer and the employee agree to continue the employment relationship. The retirement age is 68 for those born in 1957 or earlier, 69 for those born in 1958–1961, and 70 for those born in or since 1962. The employer and the employee may agree on a fixed-term continuation of an employment relationship without having to state the justified reason required by the Act.

§4. By Means of Notice

221. An employment contract for an unspecified period is normally terminated by a notice given by one of the contract parties to the other. The statutory terms of notice to be observed in different cases have been discussed earlier. The notice shall be served, orally or in writing, to the opposite party in person or, in the case of an employer, to his representative. If such a service is impossible, the notice can be served by mail or by email or letter. A notice sent in this way is deemed to have been served on the seventh day after it was sent, but not during a vacation or during a comparable absence of at least two weeks. An employer who dismisses an employee without observing the period of notice is liable to pay full wages for the neglected time. An employee who leaves his employment without observing the period of notice is liable to pay a normalized indemnity amounting to his wages for the neglected period. Notice by either side to terminate a seafarer's employment shall be served in the same way as mentioned above.

I. Job Security

222. An employer shall not give notice to an employee except in cases mentioned in the Employment Contracts Act (or the Seafarers' Employment Contracts Act, as the case may be). The provisions concerning job security are different depending on whether the contract is terminated because of a reason connected with the individual employee (called individual termination) or because of lack of work (collective termination). The protection against unfounded dismissals becomes effective immediately upon the conclusion of any employment contract for an unspecified period; as to the effect of a stipulation concerning a trial period. Notice given in violation of job security provisions is not devoid of effect. The employment relationship will end as indicated by the employer in his notice, but he becomes obliged to pay an indemnity to the employee for an unjustified dismissal. The legal provisions concerning job security are mandatory. Any stipulation purporting to enlarge the employer's right to terminate contracts of employment is accordingly null and void. In addition to the job security provisions protecting employees in general, there are special provisions to protect shop stewards and other representatives of the employees against unjustified dismissals.

A. *Lawful Grounds for Termination*

223. The Employment Contracts Act prescribes mandatory (non-derogable) grounds on which an employer can terminate an employee's contract. An employer may terminate an employee's contract for a reason relating to the employee's person, known as an individual ground, or due to changes in the conditions under which the employer operates, known as a collective ground. The general condition for termination is always that the reason be proper and weighty, as prescribed in Chapter 7, section 1 of the Act. In addition to this, an individual or collective reason set out in the Act must be established. By contrast, an employee may terminate an employment contract freely; that is, the Act prescribes no grounds that must be presented for doing so. The employee must, however, remember to give notice to the employer (notice of termination) and to observe the period of notice thereafter. Cancellation of a contract concluded for an indefinite or for a fixed period requires the existence of a reason for cancellation set out in the Employment Contracts Act (a particularly weighty reason). An employment relationship that is terminated on unlawful grounds cannot be forcibly reinstated, that is, by court judgment. The protection accorded to employees in such instances largely takes the form of financial compensation which the court orders the employer to pay.

The Employment Contracts Act sets out a list of unlawful grounds for termination relating to the employee's person:

(1) illness, disability or accident affecting the employee, unless working capacity is substantially reduced thereby for such a long term as to render it unreasonable to require that the employer continue the contractual relationship;
(2) participation of the employee in industrial action arranged by an employee organization or in accordance with the Collective Agreements Act;
(3) the employee's political, religious or other opinions or participation in social activity or associations;
(4) resort to means of legal protection available to employees.

224. The catalogue is not exhaustive. Any other ground presented by the employer makes the dismissal justified only if the ground can be regarded as especially weighty. The catalogue shows nevertheless that an especially weighty reason may be connected either with the capacity or with the conduct of the employee.

225. A collective termination is permissible if work has been significantly reduced for financial or production-related reasons or for reasons arising from the reorganization of the employer's operations and not only temporarily and if the employee cannot, with regard to his skills and capacities, reasonably be placed in or trained for new tasks. Lack of work is not considered to be only temporary if it has lasted, or is expected to last, more than ninety days. These basic provisions are completed with a list of reasons which in no case can be regarded as lawful grounds for collective terminations. In essence, this list refers to presumed cases of concealed individual terminations.

B. Termination Procedure

226. Also the procedure to be followed by an employer in terminating an employment contract is different in cases of individual and cases of collective termination. Before the notice for an individual termination is served, the employee shall be accorded an opportunity to be heard about the reasons for the intended termination. To the hearing, the employee is entitled to call an assistant. The notice must be served within a reasonable time after the employer comes to know of the reason for terminating the employment. On request, the reasons for the termination and the day on which the contract shall end must without delay be given to the employee in writing. A suit concerning the termination of a contract of employment must be brought within two years of the date on which the employment ended. The legal provisions on procedure in matters of individual termination are mandatory except that they can be parted from in collective agreements (job security agreements) concluded between industry- or craft-wide federations of employers and employees. Such agreement clauses may also be applied by employers bound by the agreement under the Collective Agreements Act on their employees who are not themselves bound by the agreement. The clauses may also be applied by employers within the scope of the general applicability of the job security agreement under the Employment Contracts Act, but only in so far as a local agreement is not needed for the application.

227. Before notice is given for collective termination, the matter should be discussed according to the cooperation procedure, if the Cooperation Within Undertakings Act is applicable. A collective agreement may also impose a duty to negotiate. In other cases, the employer must in good time explain to the employee to be dismissed the grounds for termination of employment and the alternatives. If the termination concerns more than one employee, the explanation may be given to a representative of the employees or, if no such representative has been elected, to the employees jointly.

228. The employer shall notify the employment and economic development office without delay if employment contracts of at least ten employees shall be terminated for financial or production-related reasons. The notification shall indicate the number of employees whose employment contracts shall be terminated, the vocation or working duties and the time of termination of employment. The employer is obliged to inform the employee of his right to an employment plan referred to in the Public Employment and Business Service Act.

229. An employer intending to terminate a seafarer's employment for a reason discovered on board shall, before notice is served to the employee, submit the matter for discussion by the Ship's Committee, consisting of the master as chairman, of an officer appointed by the master for each particular case, and of two representatives of the personnel. A notice given by a seafarer may also in certain cases be submitted to the committee. The committee is, however, only entitled to recommend a course of action to the parties concerned, not to decide whether the employment shall be continued or not. In case an intended termination – whether individual or collective – need not be discussed by the Ship's Committee, the employee shall be accorded an opportunity to be heard, with a right to call an assistant to the hearing.

230. If the employer needs new employees within four months of termination of the employment relationship for the same or similar work that the given employee notice had been doing, the employer shall offer work to this former employee if the employee continues to seek work via an Employment and Economic Development Office. However, if the employment relationship has lasted without interruption for at least twelve years prior to its termination, the re-employment period shall be six months. If the answer is in the affirmative, work shall in the first place be offered to these persons. Any failure of the employer in this respect entitles the employee to an indemnity but not to reinstatement.

C. Consequences of Unlawful Terminations

231. If an employment contract is terminated without reason, that is, if the contract has been terminated or cancelled where none of the reasons cited in the Employment Contracts Act obtained, the employee is entitled to compensation from the employer. Even where termination of the contract has occurred unlawfully, the employment relationship cannot be reinstated unless the employer and employee agree to do so. In other words, an employee may receive financial compensation for unlawful termination or cancellation. An employee is also entitled to compensation if he/she has had to cancel the employment contract for a reason relating to a breach of contract by the employer. The employee must demand compensation and only a court of law can order the employer to pay compensation unless the employer and employee have reached an agreement on the matter. The compensation ordered for unlawful termination is a lump-sum payment, the size of which may range between three and twenty-four months' salary. A shop steward or elected employee representative may receive compensation amounting to at most thirty months' salary. In certain cases, the compensation paid may be below the minimum of three months' salary. Factors increasing or decreasing the amount paid include the prospects which the terminated employee has of receiving work corresponding to his/her profession or education. The compensation paid to the employee has to be reduced by the amount of any unemployment benefits or labour market subsidy paid to him/her at the time. The procedures by which the compensation may be reduced are laid down in detail in the Act.

232. In the case of an unlawful collective termination, the employer shall compensate the actual damage to the employee. Neglect of the consultation duty under the Cooperation Within Undertakings Act is discussed below.

II. Special Grounds and Terms of Notice

233. In certain circumstances, one of the parties to an employment relationship, or both of them, are entitled to terminate the relationship by using a shorter term of notice than would otherwise have been applicable. Moreover, notice may in these cases also be given to terminate a contract for a specified period, thereby ending the employment relationship before the close of the stipulated period.

A. *Death, Bankruptcy or Business Reorganization Procedure*

234. If the employer dies or is declared bankrupt, the administrators of the estate as well as the employee may terminate the employment relationship with fourteen days' notice. The statutory periods of notice apply, and the relationship may be terminated immediately. Accordingly, neither the death nor the bankruptcy of the employer ends the employment relationship automatically. However, termination is not prevented by provisions on job security. Until the termination of the relationship, the remuneration of the employee shall be paid from the estate. This means, in the case of bankruptcy, that the remuneration from the time at which the bankruptcy is considered to have begun until the end of the employment relationship is paid in priority to all debts of the bankrupt, without regard to whether or not the administrators of the estate can make use of the employee's services. There is no time limit within which the special right of notice ought to be exercised, as long as the employment is based on the contract concluded with the deceased or bankrupt employer. If the contract is renewed with the administrators, the special right of notice can be used no longer.

235. If the employer is subject to a court-directed business reorganization procedure, the employment contract of the employee may be terminated with fourteen days notice, but only on specific grounds connected with the needs of the reorganization.

236. The death of an employee terminates the employment relationship at once. Remuneration for all work done as well as compensation in lieu of annual holidays earned but not used by the employee shall be paid to his estate. The bankruptcy of an employee is no grounds for a special right of notice for either party to the relationship. The employee may of course be in such a position that his bankruptcy is a sufficient reason for the employer either to terminate the relationship by way of notice or even to rescind the employment contract.

B. *Change of Ownership*

237. When an undertaking is transferred or leased, the contracts of employment are automatically transferred to the new owner or lessee. The assignee may not terminate an employee's employment contract merely because of the assignment of the enterprise. The employee may terminate an employment contract concluded with the transferor. In the case of notice given by the employee, the termination becomes effective at the time of the transfer; but if the employee did not know about the forthcoming transfer one month before, he may choose a later day within one month from the time he was informed about the transfer. Assignment of the employer's business refers to assignment of an enterprise, business, corporate body, foundation or an operative part thereof to another employer, if the business or part thereof is to be assigned, disregarding whether it is a central or ancillary activity, remains the same or similar after the assignment. When an enterprise is assigned as referred to above, rights and obligations and employment benefits related to them under employment relationships valid at the time of the assignment devolve to the new owner or proprietor. The assignor and the assignee are jointly and severally liable for the employee's pay or other claims deriving from the employment relationship that has fallen due before the assignment. Unless otherwise agreed, however, the assignor is liable to pay the assignee employee claims that have fallen due before the assignment.

Where an enterprise is assigned by a bankrupt estate, the assignee is not liable for the employee's pay or other claims deriving from the employment relationship that has fallen due before the assignment, except if controlling power in the bankrupt enterprise and in the assignee enterprise is or has been exercised by the same persons on the basis of ownership, agreement or other arrangement.

C. Suspension of Employment

238. An employee who is laid off is entitled to give notice to terminate his employment relationship at any time during the lay-off. Any agreement to the contrary is null and void. However, if he already knows when the lay-off will come to an end, he has no right to give notice to end the relationship during the last seven days of the lay-off.

239. A lay-off in itself is no reason for the employer to terminate an employment relationship. If an employer, however, for any other reason gives notice to terminate an employment relationship during a lay-off and the lay-off was not preceded by a term of notice at least as long as required for a termination of the employment, the employee shall be compensated with the loss of remuneration for the term of notice, unless otherwise agreed. If a lay-off has continued for at least two hundred calendar days and the employee for any reason then terminates his employment, he has the same right to compensation as if the notice had been given by the employer, except if the employer offers him work within one week from the day of notice. During a lay-off, employees are entitled to terminate their employment contract without a notice period regardless of its duration. If the date when the lay-off ends is known by the employee, this right shall not apply for seven days preceding the end of the lay-off period.

§5. By Rescinding the Contract

I. Right to Rescind the Contract

240. The employer is only upon an extremely weighty cause entitled to cancel an employment contract with an immediate effect regardless of the applicable period of notice or the duration of the employment contract. Such a cause may be deemed to exist in case the employee commits a breach against or neglects duties based on the employment contract or the law and having an essential impact on the employment relationship in such a serious manner as to render it unreasonable to expect that the employer should continue the contractual relationship even for the period of notice.

241. Correspondingly, the employee shall be entitled to terminate the employment contract with immediate effect if the employer commits a breach against or neglects its duties based on the employment contract or the law and having an essential impact on the employment relationship in such a serious manner as to render it unreasonable to expect that the employee should continue the contractual relationship even for the period of notice.

242. A rescission takes effect immediately, except that a seafarer's employment generally continues to a convenient port. An extremely weighty reason is defined as any omission or behaviour of one of the parties, or any change of conditions belonging to the risks of this party, because of which it cannot reasonably be demanded that the other party continue the employment relationship. There is no longer a list of events which the employer may regard as extremely weighty reasons. An employment contract can in general be rescinded, e.g., if one of the parties has misled the other party in any essential respect at the conclusion of the contract or if one of the parties through his carelessness jeopardizes safety at the workplace or assaults the other party or grossly insults him. The employee's permanent disability to perform work as well as his persistent failure to fulfil his obligation to work may allow a rescission. The employee, again, is generally entitled to rescind his contract if, e.g., his remuneration is not paid according to the contract or if he is not given a sufficient amount of work (disregarding whether or not his earnings are reduced in line with the work). On account of a strike or lock-out, the employment contract may not be rescinded, except if such a measure has been taken in violation of the provisions concerning mediation in labour disputes, or if the measure is at variance with the Collective Agreements Act or the collective agreement in question. In these excepted cases, a strike or lock-out thus may be, but is not necessarily, an important reason, sufficient for a rescission of a contract of employment. The contract of an apprentice may be rescinded like any ordinary employment contract. Upon leave of the organizer of apprenticeship education the fixed-term contract of an apprentice may in addition be unilaterally rescinded on grounds on which one of the parties to an ordinary employment contract would be entitled to terminate the relationship by means of notice.

II. Modalities of the Rescission

243. The procedures to be followed in rescinding a contract of employment are the same as in the case of an (individual) termination by notice. Additional requirements for the employer may be laid down by agreement. An employee (except a seafarer) intending to rescind his contract of employment must first provide his employer with an opportunity to be heard. No supplementary requirements can be imposed on the employee by agreement. Similarly, the employer's, but not the employee's, right to rescind the contract may be restricted by agreement.

244. If an employee has been absent from work for seven days without presenting a lawful excuse within that time, the employer may consider the contract of employment to be rescinded without any need to notify the employee. However, if it later appears that the employee had a lawful excuse not only for being absent but also for not notifying the employer, the rescission is annulled. The employee has a similar right of rescission if the employer is absent in a like manner without having any representative on the spot. With some exceptions, the right to rescind an employment contract can only be exercised within seven days after the cause for rescission has arisen or, if it is of a continuing nature, has come to an end.

245. A rescission without a sufficient – important – reason will nevertheless end the employment relationship as indicated by the party rescinding the contract. The wronged party is entitled to actual damages as for any other breach of contract. If the employer rescinded the contract although there were insufficient grounds even for terminating the relationship by ordinary notice, the provisions on normalized indemnity in cases of wrongful individual termination seem to be applicable in addition. (It is to be noted that, e.g., a strike not justifying a rescission does not justify a dismissal by notice either.) A rescission based on the fault of the other side entitles the wronged party to compensation for the damages caused by the untimely end of the relationship according to the principles generally applicable in employment relationships.

§6. Modalities at the End of an Employment Relationship

I. Certificate

246. On the termination of an employment relationship, a certificate shall be issued by the employer to the employee, at his request, showing the period of employment and the kind of work performed. If so requested, the certificate shall also state the reason for the termination, and if so requested, it shall include a testimonial to the employee's ability, diligence and conduct; but neither the reason for the termination nor a testimonial may be included in the certificate without such a request. An employer contravening these provisions or trying to convey any concealed information by means of the certificate is liable to a fine. For seamen, the modalities for signing off shall be observed.

247. A certificate may be requested also by a former employee or by the next of kin of a deceased employee. If, however, ten years have elapsed since the end of the employment relationship, the employer is not bound to deliver the certificate if he cannot do so without undue inconvenience. Under the same conditions, a new certificate shall be issued to replace a lost or destroyed certificate. These rules mean, in effect, that records of their employees which are complete enough for the issuance of certificates, must be preserved by employers for ten years after their relationships have ended.

II. Accommodation

248. The right to use accommodation forming part of the remuneration ends in principle when the employment contract ends. To this principle there are, however, some important exceptions entitling the employee or his family to use the accommodation for an extended period, not exceeding in any case seven months after the termination of the employment. The employer has, however, a right to a reasonable rent for the use and the same right to assign another dwelling for the use of an employee or his family as in the case of suspension. If the employer had rented the dwelling from a third party, the employee – or his next of kin, as the case may be – is under certain conditions entitled to be subrogated in the relationship between the former employer and his landlord. If the employee's accommodation is subject to a separate rental agreement, such an agreement does not end automatically, but it must be terminated by a separate notice, as provided in the chapter on Employment Dwellings of the Lease of Dwellings Act, 1995.

Chapter 7. Protection of Certain Categories of Employees; Discrimination

249. In this chapter, protection of certain categories of employees for their own sake is described. Protection of shop stewards and other representatives of their fellow employees, primarily intended to enable them to fulfil their duties without fear, is discussed in Part II below.

§1. Women and Parents

I. Women in General

250. For women, night work used to be somewhat more strictly limited than for men. These restrictions have, however, been repealed as of 1 January 1989. The restrictions concerning the employment of women of any age in painting work using paints containing white lead or lead sulphate have also been repealed. So have, as of 1 October 1998, the restrictions on the employment of women in mines or similar underground work, since Finland is no longer bound by the Underground Work (Women) Convention, 1935 (No. 45) of the ILO.

II. Maternity and Paternity

A. Parental Leave

251. According to the Employment Contracts Act and the Seafarers' Employment Contracts Act, an employee is entitled to a maternity, paternity or parental leave for the period to which the maternity, paternity or parental benefit is deemed to relate. At present, such benefit is payable to the mother for a period of 105 weekdays (Saturdays included), generally beginning thirty weekdays before the calculated date of confinement (maternity benefit), to the father for six to twelve weekdays in connection with the confinement and for six weekdays at another time (paternity benefit), and after the end of the maternity benefit period, to the mother or to the father, according to their agreement, for 158 weekdays, augmented with sixty weekdays per each additional child in the case of twins, triplets etc. (parental benefit). The employer has no legal duty to pay any remuneration for the time of the leave. Some collective agreements, however, grant employees the difference between their usual wages and the maternity benefit for a certain period of time, e.g., six weeks, and under the Seamen's Act, an employee with an uninterrupted service of at least six months is entitled to wages for the time of maternity leave according to the provisions concerning sickness leave. As far as an illness connected with pregnancy or childbirth prevents a woman from performing work at times other than during her maternity or parental leave, she is entitled to sickness benefits as for any other illness. A pregnant employee is entitled to medical examinations during working time without loss of earnings, if the examinations cannot be otherwise arranged. In case a chemical substance (including, from 1 July 2000, tobacco smoke), radiation or contagious disease, connected with the work of a pregnant worker or with the circumstances of her workplace, is considered to cause danger to the development of the foetus or to the pregnancy, she shall be endeavoured to be transferred, until the beginning of her maternity leave, to other tasks which are suitable to her in regard to her skills and experience, in case it has not been possible to remove the dangerous factor from the work or the circumstances of the workplace. In case a transfer is not possible, she is entitled to a *special maternity leave* and a special maternity benefit for the period in question. Any agreement restricting the employee's right to maternity leave is null and void. With her consent, however, the employee may perform such work during the leave period which does not entail any danger to herself or her child, but both parties are entitled to stop such work at any time and no work may be performed during the last two weeks before the calculated date of confinement and the first two weeks after the childbirth. Any work so performed does not restrict the employee's right to maternity benefit under the Sickness Insurance Act. Paternity benefit and parental benefit to the father are only paid if he stays at home for the days in question. Parental benefit to a mother who has returned to work is only granted as a fixed sum per day (and not on the basis of previous earnings, as in other cases).

252. After the end of the parental leave, either of the parents (but not both of them simultaneously) is entitled to a *child-care leave* until the child reaches the age of three years. A home care benefit is payable for the period in question in case the child is not in municipal day care. If a child under ten suddenly falls ill, one of the parents is entitled to an unpaid *temporary child-care leave* of at most four workdays. If both parents of a child work outside the home, one of them is under certain conditions entitled to a shortened time off work (six hours a day and thirty days a week, if not otherwise agreed to) until the end of the calendar year when the child enters the comprehensive school (as a rule the year the child attains the age of seven; *partial-child-care leave*). A person adopting a child under seven years of age is entitled to parental benefit for about eight to nine months. The parental allowance system was reformed in August 2022. The reform seeks to recognize equally all kinds of situations, including those involving diverse families and various forms of entrepreneurship and self-employment. The goals are to allocate family leave entitlements and care responsibilities equally between the parents, to strengthen non-discrimination and equality in working life, reduce the gender wage gap. The new family leave model will provide families with much more opportunity, flexibility and freedom of choice than the current system in terms of their family leave decisions.

Parents will have a total parental allowance entitlement of 320 working days. If a child has two parents, the days are divided equally between the parents, i.e., they will both be entitled to 160 working days. The pregnant parent is entitled to an additional forty days of pregnancy allowance before the payment of the parental allowance is set to begin. Parents can agree to give up as many as sixty-three days of their entitlement to the other parent or some other person who provides care for the child. *See* more: https://www.kela.fi/web/en/family-leave-reform-2022.

B. Protection Against Dismissals

253. No employment contract may be terminated because of the pregnancy of the employee or because the employee is exercising his or her right to certain family leave. Termination shall be deemed to have taken place on the basis of the employee's pregnancy or family leave unless the employer can prove there was another legal reason. However, the employer is entitled to terminate the employment contract of an employee on family leave on financial and production-related grounds if the employer's operation ceases completely. This prohibition is also applied to a rescission of the employment contract, no matter for what reason. Any agreement to diminish the protection of the employee in these respects is null and void. It seems, however, that the employment may be terminated because of the employer's bankruptcy, death or court-directed business reorganization. A notice given in violation of the protection nevertheless terminates the employment, but makes the employer liable to pay a normalized indemnity. An employee returning from maternity, paternity, parental, special maternity, child care, temporary child care, or partial-child-care leave is entitled to be reinstated to the former job or to a comparable job.

§2. Young Persons

254. The main rules on the protection of young persons in employment are to be found in a special statute, the Young Workers' Act, 1993, as amended. This Act is applicable to employees and other working persons under the age of 18. In addition, there are scattered provisions on the protection of young persons in employment in various other statutes as well as in the EEC Regulation on the unification of social legislation relating to road transport and in the AETR Agreement.

I. Employment

255. The capacity of young persons and their guardians and custodians to conclude and terminate contracts of employment has been discussed earlier. The general minimum age for employment is fifteen years. In addition, the young person shall no longer be liable to compulsory school attendance. However, a person having attained the age of 14 or attaining that age during the calendar year in question may be employed during a school vacation for very light work, as listed by the Ministry of Employment and the Economy, for not more than one-half of the vacation in question, and during school term for short work prestations. Permission may be granted for the temporary employment of still younger children as performers or assistants at artistic and cultural performances or similar occasions.

256. In addition to the requirements under the general provisions on occupational safety and health, the employer shall ensure that the job is not detrimental to the physical or mental development of the young employee or requires more effort than is appropriate to his age and strength. The employer shall also ensure that a young employee who does not have the necessary skill or experience for his job is given training, guidance and personal supervision to prevent him from being a danger to himself and others. More detailed provisions in regard to jobs considered unsuitable for persons under 16 or 18, as the case may be, have been given in an ordinance and by the Ministry of Employment and the Economy. With some exceptions, every young employee shall be given a medical examination at the employer's expense either before entering employment or within one month thereafter.

257. Persons aged 16 or older when commencing work may be employed in work meant in the Seafarers' Employment Contracts Act.

II. Working Time

258. The normal hours of work of a young person over 15 (but not over 18) are the same as the normal hours of work of an adult employee in the same kind of work. A young person over 15 may perform no more overtime work than eighty (or, with a dispensation, 120) hours during a calendar year. His normal and overtime hours may not together exceed nine a day or forty-eight a week. He may perform emergency work only if no person over 18 is available. He shall have a rest of at least twelve consecutive hours between each working day. If his daily rest has been curtailed because of an emergency, he shall be given a compensating rest as soon as possible, at the latest within three weeks. The hours of work of an employee under 15 may not exceed seven a day or thirty-six a week. No overtime or emergency work beyond these limits is allowed. He shall be granted a daily rest of at least fourteen consecutive hours. The maximum working time during school terms for a person, whether over or under 15 years, who is still liable to compulsory school attendance is two hours on school days and seven hours on other days, with a weekly maximum of twelve hours at work and a daily aggregate maximum of eight hours at work and at school. A weekly rest of at least thirty-eight consecutive hours shall be granted to all employees under the age of 18.

259. The hours of work shall fall between 6 a.m. and 10 p.m. for young employees over 15 and as a rule between 8 a.m. and 8 p.m. for employees under 15. Employees over 15 may perform work in two shifts until midnight, if approved and supervised by a public authority for purposes of vocational training. Emergency work may be performed by young employees over 15 beyond the hours otherwise applicable. In household work, working time may be extended until 11 p.m. on special grounds and with the consent of the employee. The working time regulation described here is not applicable in ship work. A young seafarer whose duties are not divided into watches shall every day be given a continuous rest of at least eight hours.

§3. DISCRIMINATION

I. In General

260. The ILO Conventions on Equal Remuneration, 1951 (No. 100), and Discrimination (Employment and Occupation), 1958 (No. 111) have been ratified by Finland. These conventions belong, however, to the so-called promotional conventions, which do not oblige the ratifying countries to enforce their contents by legislation, but only to promote the realization of their aims by the means available. The Equal Remuneration Convention could thus be ratified in 1963, when the discrimination of women had been completely abolished from the Government's own wage and salary system. However, it was also important, although not absolutely essential for the ratification that the direct dependence of wages upon sex was abolished from collective agreements at about the same time. In the Government bill proposing the ratification of the Discrimination (Employment and Occupation) Convention in 1969, it was pointed out that Finnish legislation no longer contained any discrimination prohibited in the convention but that the ratification would oblige the Finnish Government to promote the abolition of such discrimination in practice. As existing discrimination of this kind, the bill mentioned the difficulties of women seeking access to leading positions and to well-paid skilled work in factories but also the difficulties faced by the gypsies seeking work.

261. In principle, an employer is to treat all of its personnel equally. Differential treatment is possible if an employer can present an acceptable and objective reason for the practice. Such a reason may derive from the employee's duties, position and working conditions. Preferential treatment is also generally permitted. For example, an employer may provide employees with an extra rest period where they require special protection; older employees fall into this category. An employer must be consistent in all of its actions and treat employees uniformly; for example, who is given a warning in the workplace cannot differ depending on the worker. An employer is to treat all employees equitably, with no discrimination, throughout the duration of the employment relationship as well as during the recruitment phase that precedes this. Part-time employees and employees working under fixed-term contracts may not be subjected to less favourable working conditions based solely on the duration of their contracts or working hours than employees working under indefinite contracts or on a full-time basis. Exceptions to this principle are allowed if the employer has a justified, objective reason. The reason may not be arbitrary and the benefits involved must be allocated on a consistent and uniform bases. One approach that has been allowed is that employees must reach certain thresholds, expressed as numbers of years of service, before being granted a benefit, providing that the thresholds are the same regardless of the duration of the employment relationship or number of working hours. For example, an occupational health plan could offer health care services to all employees who have worked for, say, six months. Benefits based on conditions of employment can be granted in keeping with the principle of *pro rata temporis*; that is, the scope of benefits is proportionate to the number of working hours.

Provisions on 'general' discrimination are laid down in the Non-Discrimination Act and on sex-discrimination in the Act on the Equality Between Women and Men. Without a justified reason, an employer may not place an employee in a different position than others on the basis of age, origin, nationality, language, religion, belief, opinion, political activity, trade union activity, family relationships, state of health, disability, sexual orientation or other personal characteristic.

II. Sex Discrimination

262. Discrimination based on gender is governed by the Act on Equality between Women and Men (hereinafter 'the Equality Act'). Gender discrimination may take the form of discrimination based on gender, gender identity or gender expression and occur for reasons relating to pregnancy or childbirth.

The Equality Act introduces a duty for authorities, educational institutions and employers to promote the equality of women and men. Employers thus shall endeavour to have both women and men as applicants for jobs, to further the equal placement of women and men in various tasks, to prepare equal career opportunities for them, and to develop working conditions so as to make them suitable to both women and men. The main body of the Equality Act, however, aims at the suppression of actual discrimination.

263. The anti-discrimination provisions of the Equality Act begin with a general clause stating that sex discrimination is forbidden. Discrimination is defined to consist of the putting of women and men in different positions on account of their sex, or of the putting of persons in different positions on account of any reason depending on pregnancy or childbirth or on account of parenthood, the liability to support one's family or any other reason connected with sex. If the factual result of any course of procedure is that persons are factually put in different positions on account of any of the reasons just mentioned, such a course of procedure also counts as discrimination. There are some exceptions to the definition of discrimination. It is thus permissible specifically to protect women because of pregnancy and childbirth, and to introduce a planned favouring of one sex ('positive discrimination') in order to carry into effect the aims of the Equality Act. As regards employers within the scope of the Cooperation Within Undertakings Act their personnel or training plans or action programmes for safety and health shall include measures for a more rapid realization of equality between women and men in the workplace.

264. The Equality Act also contains specific duties and liabilities for employers. If an employer in hiring or promoting, or in selecting employees for education, disregards a person who is more merited than the selected person of the other sex, he is guilty of discrimination except if he can show that he had an important and acceptable reason, based on the nature of the job or task, or another acceptable justification not connected with the sex of the persons in question. If an employer in hiring or promoting, or in selecting for education, discriminates against a person on account of pregnancy, childbirth or another reason connected with sex, or on account of such reason restricts the duration or continuation of an employment relationship, or if an employer on account of sex applies to one or several employees less favourable wage or other terms of employment than to one or several other employees of his performing similar work or work of equal value, or if he directs or distributes work or arranges labour conditions in a manner clearly disfavouring an employee in comparison with an employee of the other sex, or if he impairs the working circumstances or employment terms of an employee after the latter has had recourse to the rights or duties provided for in the Equality Act, or if he terminates an employment relationship or suspends or transfers an employee because of the sex of that employee, he is also guilty of discrimination, except if he can show an acceptable justification not connected with the sex of the persons in question. And if an employer fails to fulfil his duty to ensure as far as possible that no employee is subjected to sexual harassment or derangement, he is likewise guilty of discrimination. In all these cases, the employer is liable to pay the wronged party a compensation. If in a matter of hiring, promotion, or selection for education, two or more persons have been discriminated against, the compensation shall be divided between them. An employer shall not advertise a job to be applied for only by women or only by men, except if he has an important and acceptable reason connected with the nature of the job or task or if the advertisement is based on a plan of positive discrimination, as mentioned above. An employer who is guilty of sex discrimination shall in addition to the pecuniary compensation (if any) compensate the actual damages of the victim.

265. If anyone is of the opinion that he has been discriminated against in hiring, promoting or selecting for education, as mentioned in the preceding paragraph, the employer shall upon demand and without delay give him a written explanation over the selection. Such an explanation shall include the selection grounds applied and describe the education and experience of the successful person as well as any other merits or circumstances which have clearly influenced the selection. An explanation shall in similar manner be given to an employee who considers that he has been discriminated against in any other manner described in the preceding paragraph. Suits to recover pecuniary compensation or actual damages for discrimination in employment and prosecutions for sex discrimination are tried by regular courts. The observance of the Equality Act is supervised by an Equality Ombudsman and a national non-discrimination and equality tribunal. The tribunal consists of a chairman and a vice-chairman, who must be learned in law, and of three other members. The delegation shall include both men and women, and among the members there shall be persons with knowledge of equality and labour matters. The Equality Delegation can forbid anyone who has violated the general prohibition of sex discrimination or any of the specific anti-discrimination provisions of the Equality Act to continue or repeat the violation. Such an order may be combined with a threat of a pecuniary penalty; but the person concerned may also be granted a reasonable time to alter the conditions or procedures in question. Decisions of the tribunal may be appealed to the Supreme Administrative Court.

Chapter 8. Covenant of Non-competition; Statute of Limitations; Inventions by Employees

§1. Covenant of Non-competition

266. The competition between an employee and an employer during the existence of the employment relationship has been treated earlier. After the termination of the employment relationship, the employee is in principle free to compete with his former employer either by founding a competing business of his own or by entering into the service of a competitor of the former employer. Only on a particularly weighty reason, connected with the employment relationship, is it possible to conclude an agreement restricting the freedom of an employee to compete with his employer after the termination of the employment relationship.

267. For a particularly weighty reason related to the operations of the employer in the employment relationship, an agreement made at the beginning of or during the employment relationship (agreement of non-competition) may limit the employee's right to conclude an employment contract on work to begin after the employment relationship has ceased with an employer which engages in operations competing with the first-mentioned employer, and also the employee's right to engage in such operations on his or her own account.

268. In assessing whether very serious grounds exist for instituting an agreement of non-competition, consideration shall also be given to the nature of the employer's operations and any need for protection related to keeping a trade secret or to special training given to the employee by the employer, and the employee's status and duties together with other similar matters.

269. If a restriction period of not more than six months has been agreed upon, the employer shall pay the employee a compensation equivalent to 40% of the employee's salary for the restriction period. If a restriction period has been agreed on more than six months, the employee shall be paid a compensation equivalent to 60% of the employee's salary for the restriction period. The restriction period can be agreed on a maximum of one year from the termination of the employment contract. The compensation shall be paid during the restriction period during the pay periods observed during the employment relationship, unless otherwise agreed after the termination of the employment contract. Instead of compensation for loss, the agreement may include a provision on contractual penalty, which shall not exceed the amount of pay received by the employee for the six months preceding the end of the employee's employment relationship.

270. An employer is entitled to terminate the agreement of non-competition observing the period of notice the length of which shall be at least one-third of the length of the restriction period, but at least two months. However, the termination right no longer applies after the employee has terminated the employment contract.

271. An agreement of non-competition does not bind the employee if the employment relationship has been terminated for a reason deriving from the employer.

§2. Statute of Limitations

272. Employees' pay claims become statute barred five years after the due date, unless the period of limitation has been interrupted before that time. The same period of limitation also applies to other claims referred to in the Employment Contracts Act. However, the period of limitation concerning bodily injury caused to an employee is ten years. After the termination of employment, a claim as referred to above (claims) will expire unless the suit is filed within two years of the date on which the employment ended. If the provisions of the collective agreement on which the employee's claims are based are manifestly ambiguous, however, the claim will become statute barred as laid down above.

273. Several statutes in labour law foresee, however, shorter periods of limitation. Overtime pay and vacation pay must thus generally be claimed within two years, reckoned in both cases from the end of the calendar year during which the payment became due. Pecuniary compensation under the Equality Act must be claimed within one year from the actual infringement, and normalized indemnity or actual damages for an unlawful termination of an employment contract within two years from the serving of the notice. These shorter periods of limitation can only be interrupted by bringing an action in court. A prosecution for an infringement of provisions in labour legislation shall in general be instituted within two years from the facts. The general limitation period of ten years is applied to claims concerning actual damages, except damage claims for wrongful terminations.

§3. Inventions by Employees

274. The right of inventors to exploit their inventions is regulated in the Patents Act, 1967. There is, however, a separate Employment Inventions Act, 1967, to regulate the reciprocal rights and duties of an inventor and his employer. According to this Act, an employee who has made an invention which can be patented has the same legal position as an independent inventor if there is no other provision in the Act or in an agreement between the inventor and his employer. The exceptions to the main principle in the Act are important enough. However, the Act also restricts the powers of the parties to deviate from the main principle by way of a contract.

275. Inventions made by the employee are divided into four categories on the basis of their proximity to the employment relationship:

(1) If an invention is a result of the activities of the employee to fulfil his obligation to perform work, or if his experience gained in the employer's establishment has played an essential part in it, it is included in the first category if

the utilization of the invention lies within the employer's line of business. If the utilization of the invention lies outside the employer's line of business, the invention is only referred to the first category if it was the result of a specified task given to the employee. For an invention of the first category, the employer is entitled to obtain rights which are as far reaching as he wishes.

(2) An invention which came about in a manner not so intensively connected with the employment as in the first category, but with a connection, is referred to the second category, but only if the utilization of the invention lies within the employer's line of business. The employer is entitled to obtain a right to use an invention of the second category. If he is interested in larger rights to the invention (e.g., exclusive rights to use it, or transferable rights to it), he is entitled to acquire such rights by agreement with the inventor with priority over other speculants.

(3) The third category comprises any invention the origin of which is in no way connected with the employment of the inventor but the utilization of which lies within the line of his employer's business. The employer has no immediate rights to such an invention, but he is entitled to acquire any right to the invention, by agreement with the inventor, in preference to other speculants.

(4) All other inventions, i.e., inventions which neither originated with a connection with the inventor's employment nor lie within his employer's line of business, are referred to the fourth category. As regards these inventions, the inventor's employer is in the same position as any outside person. An invention is considered to have been made during the inventor's employment, if patent for the invention is applied for within six months after the end of the employment and the inventor does not make it probable that the invention originated after the end of the employment. However, any agreement between an employer and an employee restricting the latter's rights as regards inventions which he may make more than one year after the end of his employment is null and void.

276. The employee is entitled to reasonable compensation for any right to his invention which his employer may obtain either through the operation of the law or by virtue of a contract. Any agreement restricting the employee's right to compensation is null and void unless it is concluded after the invention was made.

Chapter 9. Settlement of Disputes over Rights

277. Disputes over rights in labour questions are decided by several official organs. To a certain extent, such disputes may also be referred to procedures agreed to by the parties – either by the parties to the dispute, or by parties to a collective agreement binding the parties to the dispute. Disputes over interests are in principle to be settled by the parties themselves. There are official organs and procedures intended to help the parties to reach a settlement, but the functions of these organs and procedures are limited to such assistance; they cannot be used to impose any settlement on the parties. It is, however, possible for the parties themselves to entrust the settlement of disputes over interests to an outside person or body.

§1. Regular Courts

I. The Court System

278. Finland has a three-tier system of regular courts. Civil as well as criminal matters are tried by the same courts. As of 1993, the courts of first instance were unified. The jurisdiction of a Court of First Instance comprises one or more municipalities. The court is composed of full-time learned judges with a permanent appointment and of part-time lay jurors elected by the municipal council for a period of four years. The composition of the court is one or two learned judges and three to four jurors for more severe criminal cases and some other (mainly family law) cases, one learned judge for minor criminal cases, and three learned judges for most civil cases, labour law cases (except prosecutions) included. The jurors have an individual vote each in the court, and they sit on equal footing with the learned judges both on law and on facts.

279. From the courts of first instance, appeal lies with the courts of appeal. There are five courts of appeal, composed of full-time learned judges with a permanent appointment and sitting as a rule in panels of at least three members. From the courts of appeal, appeal lies with the Supreme Court, but only with leave of the said court. The Supreme Court is composed of justices with a permanent appointment, and it sits as a rule in panels of five justices. For especially important decisions, e.g., if a panel would be about to overrule a principle embodied in earlier Supreme Court decisions, the Supreme Court sits in a plenary composition, comprising all justices of the court. Although the doctrine of *stare decisis* is not recognized in Finland, earlier decisions of the Supreme Court are seldom departed from by the court itself and still more seldom by lower courts.

II. Competence and Procedure

280. All labour law disputes not belonging to the competence of other organs are heard and tried by the regular courts. This means that the following matters lie within the jurisdiction of regular courts:

(i) disputes concerning the interpretation of individual employment contracts;
(ii) disputes concerning other claims based on individual employment contracts or on legislation pertaining to such contracts;
(iii) disputes concerning individual claims based on collective agreements as far as such disputes are not to be tried by the Labour Court;
(iv) disputes concerning claims for overtime compensation, holiday pay, etc., based on legislation on hours of work, annual holidays, etc.; and
(v) prosecutions for violation of labour legislation (on employment contracts, equality, hours of work, annual holidays, safety and health, etc.) and claims for damages because of such violations.

281. Court procedure in Finland has been, and to a considerable extent still is, informal, inexpensive and easy for the parties. Not only are civil and criminal matters tried by the same courts, but prosecutions and private claims based on the same facts are regularly tried together, which makes it very easy for an employee to present a claim for, say, overtime pay in connection with the public prosecutor's claim for punishment for the violation of the Hours of Work Act. The procedure was thoroughly modernized in civil cases in 1993 and in criminal cases in 1997. The modernization has made the court procedure more efficient and speedy, but also somewhat more formal and expensive. Also in the appellate courts, procedure has recently been thoroughly modernized. Appeals may be based on questions of law as well as on issues about facts.

§2. The Labour Court and Grievance Procedure

I. Composition of the Labour Court

282. The Labour Court is a single specialized court for matters connected with collective agreements. The Labour Court is composed of a president and two other neutral members, four employers' members, four employees' members and four additional members for cases concerning public officials. There are two substitutes for each member, except for the president. A temporary vice-chairman may be appointed to the Labour Court for a fixed period, not exceeding three years, if this is warranted by the caseload or other special reasons. The presidency and the vice-chairmanship of the Labour Court are full-time posts. Other members of the court have their full-time duties elsewhere. The president and the vice-chairman shall be learned in law and conversant with the duties of a judge. The two other neutral members shall be learned in law and conversant with labour conditions. The employers' and employees' members must also be conversant with labour matters. High officials of the main organizations of employers and employees serve in these posts. The Labour Court regularly sits in panels of two neutral members, two employers' members and two employees' members.

283. All members of the Labour Court and their substitutes are appointed by the President of the Republic for a term of three years. They may be (and usually are) reappointed. If a person in Government service is appointed president or vice-chairman of the Labour Court, he is entitled to retain his former post and to return to it after his service at the Labour Court is over. The employers' and employees' members shall be appointed from among candidates recommended by the most representative confederations of employers and employees, respectively. The president of the Labour Court draws a salary which is approximately equal to the salary of the justices of the Supreme Court.

II. Competence of the Labour Court

284. Disputes within the competence of the Labour Court are of two principal kinds: interpretation of collective agreements, and breaches against duties based on the contents or existence of collective agreements. Within its competence so defined, the Labour Court tries individual as well as collective disputes over rights. If the settlement of an individual claim depends on the interpretation of a collective agreement, the Labour Court can, however, if it finds it expedient, confine its judgment to the interpretation issue and direct the parties of the individual dispute to institute proceedings at the competent regular court, which then has to settle the individual claim in accordance with the decision of the Labour Court in the interpretation issue. If the determination of another case at a regular court requires special knowledge pertaining to collective agreements, the regular court may ask the Labour Court for an advisory opinion on the matter; but the advisory opinion is not binding on the regular court. Such advisory opinions are mainly asked in suits based on the general applicability of certain collective agreements as the general applicability is based neither directly on any collective agreements nor on legislation pertaining to collective agreements but merely on provisions in the Employment Contracts Act, claims based on the general applicability are regarded as referring to employment contracts and not to collective agreements and hence to belong to the jurisdiction of regular courts and not of the Labour Court. If an individual claim is based on an undisputed clause in a collective agreement but there is a dispute unconnected with the agreement (e.g., on the number of hours worked), such a claim will be settled by a regular court.

III. Procedure at the Labour Court

285. Suits at the Labour Court are regularly brought by and against the parties to the collective agreement in question. This means, e.g., that if the outcome of an employee's wage claim against his employer is dependent on the interpretation of the industry-wide collective agreement governing the employment relationship, the interpretation issue shall be settled in a suit brought at the Labour Court neither by the individual employee nor against the individual employer but by the employees' federation party to the agreement against the employers' federation party to the agreement. And if a local trade union is charged with a breach of the peace obligation based on an industry-wide collective agreement, any suit to recover a compensatory fine – the regular remedy for breaches of duties based on collective agreements – from the local union is brought at the Labour Court neither by the factory owner who suffered the damage nor against the local union but by the employers' federation party to the agreement against the employees' federation party to the agreement. The member association or individual employer or employee against whom the claim is presented shall, however, also be called to be heard at the trial. Anyone so heard is entitled, e.g., to present evidence, but he does not have the legal position of a party to the lawsuit.

286. There are two exceptions to the rule that only parties to collective agreements may appear as parties to lawsuits at the Labour Court. If, on the defendant side, an employer or employee is charged with a violation of employment terms embodied in a collective agreement – as distinguished from a violation of the peace duty or the surveillance duty – a claim for a remedy for such a violation shall be presented in a suit against the individual employer or employee in question, and not against the association party to the agreement. And on the plaintiff side, a member association, employer or employee may itself institute proceedings upon the consent of the association party to the agreement, or upon the express refusal of that association to institute the proceedings. Such a possibility is, however, open to members only. Even though an employer bound by a collective agreement shall, in general, apply its terms also to unorganized employees, such an employee has no independent standing to sue at the Labour Court. If the trade union party to the agreement does not shoulder his claim, he cannot have it settled by judicial means, unless the agreement is generally applicable and he can accordingly have the dispute settled by a regular court.

287. If the collective agreement in question provides for a grievance procedure, but the grievance is submitted to the Labour Court before the procedure is exhausted, the case shall be dismissed except when the complainant is not to blame for the non-exhausture of the procedure. The procedure at the Labour Court begins with an exchange of briefs, followed usually by a pre-trial conference – sometimes two or more such conferences – between the chairman and clerk of the court and the representatives of the parties. The purpose of the prehearing procedure is to ascertain which demands, facts and other circumstances are in dispute and which are undisputed. During the prehearing procedure, the parties shall present all their written evidence and nominate the witnesses to be heard at the main hearing. If no witnesses need to be heard, the case may be decided without a main hearing. At the main hearing before the full court, the parties present their cases, referring to their briefs and the transcript of the prehearing conferences, the witnesses are examined and cross-examined, and the parties give their final statements. A postponement of the main hearing is granted only exceptionally. In urgent cases, the judgment of the court may be formulated and proclaimed in connection with the main hearing, but usually a separate conference of the members of the court is held to formulate the judgment. All members of the court have an equal vote, and any dissenting opinions are published. However, about three-quarters of the judgments of the Labour Court are unanimous.

288. Decisions of the Labour Court are often declaratory judgments not needing any enforcement. Decisions involving compensatory fines or other money payments are legally enforceable. There is no regular appeal from the judgments of the Labour Court. An extraordinary appeal or an application for a new trial may be presented to the Supreme Court on account of procedural errors, other grave errors in law, or substantial new evidence. The decisions of the Labour Court are used as precedents both by the court itself and by the organizations.

289. If a request for an advisory opinion of the Labour Court concerns a distinctive collective agreement or several such agreements – as they usually do – the parties to the agreement or agreements are accorded an opportunity to present their opinions on the question. If the collective agreement parties disagree on the matter, a normal procedure with one or more prehearing conferences and a main hearing is arranged at the Labour Court for the collective agreement parties; the parties to the individual dispute at the regular court are not invited to take part in the proceedings at the Labour Court.

IV. Grievance Procedure

290. Most collective agreements provide for a grievance procedure for the settlement of disputes concerning the application of the agreement in question. The typical industry-wide collective agreements in manufacturing provide that if a disagreement between an employee and his immediate supervisor cannot be settled between them, grievance negotiations shall be conducted first between the supervisor and the shop steward of the department and then between the management and the chief shop steward of the plant. If these negotiations fail, a memorandum shall be drafted stating the issue and the standpoints of both parties, and either party may ask for negotiations between the industry-wide federations (collective agreement parties) by sending the memorandum to the federation concerned. At the federation level, agreement may be reached, or the matter may be remitted to new negotiations at the local level (often with instructions given by the federations), or the negotiations may fail. Only in the last case may the dispute be brought before the Labour Court. Outside manufacturing, the grievance procedure is often not so minutiously regulated, with the result that disputes reaching the Labour Court may be less well prepared.

§3. Arbitration

291. Disputes which would otherwise belong to the jurisdiction of the Labour Court may be referred to arbitration. A plea that a collective agreement be declared rescinded belongs, however, to the exclusive jurisdiction of the Labour Court and cannot be referred to arbitration. In practice, arbitration is not often used instead of a lawsuit at the Labour Court. The main exception to this rule is constituted by the typographical industry, where the collective agreements provide for arbitration in virtually all disputes over rights. In some other fields, e.g., the pulp and paper industry, arbitration has been introduced, but only to a limited extent. Arbitration may also be substituted for civil proceedings at regular courts, but as far as is known, arbitration has a practical significance within labour law only as regards managerial and comparable employees. Arbitration cannot be substituted for criminal proceedings. If a valid agreement provides for arbitration in a given dispute but the dispute is nevertheless submitted to the Labour Court or a regular court, the case will be dismissed upon the demand of the defendant. However, if the defendant does not plead this defence at the beginning of his appearance, he forfeits his right to do so, and the case is to be decided on its merits by the court.

292. Arbitration presupposes an arbitration agreement. Trial at the Labour Court can only be replaced by arbitration by virtue of an arbitration clause in a collective agreement. To replace a trial at a regular court by arbitration, a separate arbitration agreement in writing is sufficient. An arbitration clause or a separate arbitration agreement may be very short, just stating the potential disputes subjected to arbitration, or the actual case where there is a separate arbitration agreement. In all other respects, the provisions of the Arbitration Act, 1992, shall be applied. The contracting parties are, however, free to replace most of these provisions with agreement clauses.

293. If not otherwise agreed to by the parties, there shall be three arbitrators, one to be appointed by each of the parties and the chairman to be selected by the appointed members. If a party fails to appoint an arbitrator, or the appointees fail to select a chairman, a regular court shall, upon application of either of the parties, fill the vacancy with a qualified person. The award of the arbitrators is final and, if not of purely declaratory nature, legally enforceable. The award may, however, be contested on the ground of a decision ultra vires or because of procedural or formal errors. Contestation on the merits of the case is not allowed, except as regards the arbitrators' decision concerning their own fees.

§4. The Labour Council

294. The composition of the Labour Council and its administrative functions have already been discussed. As a judicial organ, the Labour Council had until 1996 the competence to decide questions concerning the scope of the most important statutes concerning employee protection (such as the Hours of Work Act, 1946, the Annual Holidays Act, and the Occupational Safety and Health Act) as well as of a number of separate provisions of these statutes. Decisions of the Labour Council were binding upon employers, employees, organizations, authorities and courts of law. The competence of the Labour Council to give binding decisions was, however, abolished in 1996.

295. The Labour Council retained the task of giving advisory opinions on the interpretation and application of the most important statutes concerning employee protection. Advisory opinions may be requested by labour protection authorities, confederations on employers and employees, and courts of law. Even though the advisory opinions of the Labour Council are not binding, they have in practice been deviated from only exceptionally, and both the binding decisions and the advisory opinions of the Labour Council have been widely used as precedents. It remains to be seen whether advisory opinions of the Labour Council will after the 1996 reform be requested to the same extent as earlier and whether the new advisory opinions will retain the same authority as precedents as the earlier decisions and opinions.

§5. Administrative Tribunals

296. In addition to ordinary courts and specialized organs already described, Finland has a system of administrative tribunals. Except for matters concerning public officials outside the scope of this Encyclopaedia, labour law was until quite recently outside the jurisdiction of all lower administrative tribunals. In connection with the reshaping of the Labour Protection Administration in 1993, appealed from the decisions of the Labour Protection Offices of the Labour Protection Districts (were, however, directed to the Provincial (administrative) Courts, which will be, as from 1 November 1999, replaced by (regional) Administrative Courts. There will be in continental Finland six regional Administrative Courts and in the autonomous Province of Åland another Administrative Court with some differences from the other Administrative Courts in regard to organizational position and jurisdiction. The Administrative Court sits as a rule in panels of three full-time learned judges with a permanent appointment. The highest organ of decision in disputes concerning administrative law is the Supreme Administrative Court, which is in composition and stature quite comparable to the Supreme Court. To the Supreme Administrative Court, appeal lies not only from the regional Administrative Courts and other lower administrative tribunals but also from the Ministries and the Council of State (National Cabinet) itself.

Part II. Collective Labour Relations

Chapter 1. Trade Union Freedom

§1. General Rules

I. International Commitments

297. The history of trade union freedom in Finland has already been described. Finland has ratified the ILO Conventions Nos. 87 (1948) on Freedom of Association, 98 (1949) on the Right to Organize and Collective Bargaining, and 135 (1972) on Workers' Representatives. Finland is thus under the control of the ILO organs as to the fulfilment of her obligations under these conventions. Finland has also ratified the United Nations Covenants of 1966 on Economic, Social and Cultural Rights and on Civil and Political Rights. Both covenants contain provisions on trade union freedom, and Finland is bound by the provisions of the latter covenant and its protocol which grant other states and private individuals the right to present complaints concerning Finnish violations of the covenant to the Human Rights Committee established under the covenant. Similarly, Finland has ratified the European Convention on Human Rights of 1950 and the European Social Charter of 1961. Both of these instruments also contain provisions concerning trade union freedom; Finland is subject to the compulsory jurisdiction of the European Court of Human Rights; and the fulfilment of Finland's obligations under the European Social Charter is also controlled as provided for in the Charter.

II. Freedom of Association

298. Associations in general – trade unions and employers' associations included – are governed by the provisions of the Associations Act, 1989, as amended in 1989, 1992 and 1994. An association intended to have corporate personality shall have statutes fulfilling certain formal requirements, and it shall be registered by the National Patent and Register Board upon application. If the formal requirements are fulfilled, the registration cannot be denied; and from the decision of the National Board, appeal lies to the Supreme Administrative Court. The members of a registered association are not personally responsible for the obligations of the association. An unregistered association has no legal personality, and any persons who have incurred an obligation on behalf of such an association – but not other members of the unregistered association – are personally liable for the fulfilment of the obligation. However, Finnish trade unions and employers' associations are generally registered under the Associations Act and hence have a corporate personality. As will be seen, they must in fact be registered in order to be capable, e.g., of concluding collective agreements.

§2. The Protection of Trade Union Freedom at the Workplace

I. Freedom to Join and Be Active

299. The Employment Contracts Act makes it unlawful and punishable for an employer to prevent an employee from belonging to or joining a lawful association. It is also still unlawful – but no longer punishable, if the provisions of the Criminal Code concerning violence, etc., are not violated – for an employee to interfere with his employer in the same manner; but to interfere in this manner with a fellow employee is since 1995 not only unlawful but again also punishable. Also preserved is the provision declaring any agreement not to belong to an association null and void. Being active in an association is given the same protection as belonging to or joining it. It is accordingly unlawful and punishable for an employer to prevent an employee from working for a lawful association and unlawful for an employee to interfere with his employer or a fellow employee in the same manner, and any agreement not to be active in an association is null and void. Since the repeal of the Act to Protect Labour Peace in 1945, there were until 1995 no comparable legal provisions – except for the Criminal Code provisions on violence, etc. – to protect the employers' and employees' right not to belong to an association. In connection with the reform of the constitutional provisions on fundamental rights in 1995, the constitutional protection of the freedom of association was augmented with an express clause protecting the right of everyone to stay outside an – or any – association. In connection with the transfer, also in 1995, of penalty provisions from various labour law statutes to the Criminal Code, penalty of a fine was introduced for anyone forcing an employee to belong to or join a trade union or political association.

300. According to most collective agreements, employers and employees are entitled to decide freely about joining trade associations (i.e., trade unions and employers' associations). This provision protects not only the right to join an association and to belong to it but also the right not to belong to an association. Moreover, in addition to the prohibition of any interference by an employer or employers' organization in the freedom of association of the employees, and vice versa, any internal interference of either side in the freedom of association is also made a breach of the contractual duties towards the other side. In practice, such a breach has real significance only when its effects are felt by the other side, e.g., when the organized employees decline to work with an unorganized person and the operation of the employer's undertakings are thereby endangered.

301. The protection of trade union freedom is further implemented by certain provisions introduced by the Non-discrimination Act and the Employment Contracts Act. Trade union activity is one of the grounds for discrimination prohibited by these provisions. It is accordingly unlawful and punishable for an employer not only to dismiss an employee or to decline to hire a person because of his trade union activity but also to discriminate against an employee on that ground in any other way, e.g., in promotions, allocation of work, or remuneration.

II. Duty to Provide Meeting Space

302. The Employment Contracts Act further provides that in any workplace, the employer shall allow the employees and their trade unions to use an appropriate space free of charge for meetings and organizational tasks in connection with employment matters. Such meetings, etc., shall, however, be conducted during meal and other breaks or outside working hours and without interfering with the operation of the undertaking, and if the employer has no appropriate space available, he is under no obligation to procure premises for the purpose. An employer violating these provisions is liable to a fine. Many collective agreements include further provisions on the fulfilment of the employer's duties as well as on the procedure to be followed by the employees and their organizations, e.g., requisitioning meeting space and conducting meetings.

III. Check-off of Union Dues

303. There are no legal provisions entitling trade unions to any direct economic assistance from the employer side. However, in connection with the incomes decision of 1968 the employers' confederations in principle agreed to deduct union dues from wages and salaries, and provisions to this effect were in fact included in most collective agreements. According to these provisions, deduction can only be effected upon a written authorization of the employee concerned; but once such an authorization has been given – and as long as it is not withdrawn by the employee – the employer is duty bound to deduct the union dues from the wages and salaries of the employees concerned and to remit the deducted amounts to the accounts of the trade unions in question.

IV. Facilities and Protection of Employees' Representatives

304. Trade unions and their members are usually represented at the workplace by shop stewards. Most collective agreements contain provisions defining the extent to which the chief shop steward of the establishment shall be free from other work without loss of pay in order to conduct his official duties. The agreements further contain provisions protecting the shop steward's remuneration, often protecting the development of his remuneration as compared with other employees. In addition, there are agreement clauses on office space and other facilities for the chief shop steward.

305. The shop stewards mentioned in the preceding paragraph also enjoy preferential protection against dismissals and lay-offs. According to the Employment Contracts Act, the employment of a shop steward may only be terminated or suspended with the consent of the majority of the employees represented by him or if the work performed by him ceases totally (i.e., no one in the establishment will be engaged in that kind of work) and no suitable alternative work can be found. However, as regards rescission of the employment contract for grave misconduct or another weighty reason, the shop stewards do not have more preferential positions than other employees. In the case of wrongful dismissal of a shop steward, the employer is liable for a normalized indemnity, as in the case of other employees, but the shop steward is no more entitled to reinstatement than any other employee. The job security of shop stewards is still enhanced by collective agreements. For example, most collective agreements provide that except in the case of a total closing-down of an establishment, the chief shop steward of the establishment can only be dismissed if it is jointly established by the employer and the employee side that no suitable work can be found for him, and other stewards are almost as well protected as the chief shop steward. A dismissal violating these contractual rules but not the legal job security of the shop steward entitles him to an indemnity but does not lead to punishment of the employer.

306. The protection accorded to shop stewards is extended to other representatives of the employees. Thus, the labour protection representative of the employees shall be released, without any loss of earnings, from their normal work for their duties in that capacity. They also enjoy the same job security as shop stewards. The labour protection agents elected in accordance with collective agreements enjoy a more limited right to time off. They are protected against dismissals because of their acts and omissions in this capacity, but they have no privileges as compared with other employees in regard to dismissals for other reasons. The personnel representatives under the Cooperation Within Undertakings Act are entitled to time off without loss of earnings not only for the cooperation proceedings under the act but also for their internal preparation in close connection with the cooperation proceedings. The act does not accord the personnel representatives under the act any special job protection; but as the personnel representatives are in most cases either shop stewards or labour protection representatives, they enjoy the job security of these officials. A representative of the personnel under the Act on the Representation of the Personnel in the Administration of Enterprises as well as his substitute are also entitled to time off, without loss of earnings, for participation in the meetings where they represent the personnel and also for their internal preparations in close connection with the meetings. They are in addition entitled to job protection like shop stewards, except that no fine can be imposed for the wrongful dismissal of the substitute of a representative.

Chapter 2. The Trade Unions and the Employers' Associations

§1. The Trade Unions

I. The Central Organization of Finnish Trade Unions

307. The earlier history of the Finnish trade union movement has been described briefly in connection with the history of the trade union's freedom. In the 1930s and during World War II, the SAK, founded in 1930, in fact had a fairly influential position in comparison with its membership figures. Immediately after the war had ended, the membership figures began to rise steeply. However, political strife led to a split in the organization. It was the opinion of many Social Democrats that Communists and left-wing Socialists were using the trade union movement for their political purposes. As the situation could not be altered within the SAK, some of the Social Democrat-dominated constituent federations of the SAK broke out from the organization, rival federations were founded for some others which remained within the organization, and in 1960, most of the outbreakers and the rival federations founded a new confederation, which adopted the name of the first SAJ, founded in 1907. But apparently, many Social Democrats within the trade union movement preferred the strength of their own old federations to the immediate aims of their political confreres, and so some of the rival federations remained rather insignificant, and in some fields, no rival federations at all were founded. As a consequence, the SAJ remained weaker than its founders probably had expected. Nevertheless, the rival unionism both weakened the trade union movement as a whole and was an inflationary factor, when rival unions tried to surpass each other in their wage demands. Very soon after the founding of the SAJ, endeavours were begun to bring the cleavage of the trade union movement to an end, but only in 1969, when the political situation within the left had changed, was a real unification achieved. To unite the trade union movement, the SAK was reformed with new statutes, allowing larger independence to the constituent federations, the outbreakers or rival federations joined the new SAK or were merged with the member federations, and the SAJ was dissolved. In connection with the reorganization, it was agreed to simplify the membership structure of the SAK. As a consequence, the number of the federations, which had been about sixty in 1969 – outbreakers and rival federations included, disregarding whether they had joined the SAJ or had remained independent – was diminished to twenty-right by 1975 and to twenty-two by 1994. By 1997, the number had again risen to twenty-seven, due mainly to the transformation of directly owned Government enterprises into private-law companies. The figures in Table 5 show the development of the number of individual trade union members in the organizational field of the SAK.

Table 5 Individual Trade Union Members in the SAK and SAJ

Year	*Affiliation*	*Number of Members*
1908	SAJ	24,000
1917	SAJ	157,000
1928	SAJ	90,000
1938	SAK	70,000
1943	SAK	86,000
1945	SAK	300,000
1948	SAK	306,000
1953	SAK	240,000
1958	SAK	239,000
1960	SAK	228,000
	SAJ	53,000
	Independents	90,000
	Total	371,000
1965	SAK	248,000
	SAJ	105,000
	Independents	72,000
	Total	425,000
1970	SAK	650,000
1975	SAK	920,000
1980	SAK	1,032,000
1985	SAK	1,055,000
1990	SAK	1,071,000
1994	SAK	1,115,000
1997	SAK	1,100,000

The number of members in SAK was 992,716 at the beginning of 2016 53.8% of members were men and 46.2% women. And in the beginning of 2022 the number of members was 835,652 (45% women and 55% men). SAK has eighteen member associations.

The federations are in general formed on an industrial basis. They endeavour to organize all the employees of the industry in question disregarding the skills and tasks of the individual employees. Thus, the Paper (Workers') Federation tries to organize all the employees of the paper and pulp mills in Finland. There are, however, some craft federations endeavouring to organize all employees with certain skills or tasks disregarding the trade of their particular employers. The most notable example of a craft federation is the Finnish Electric Workers' Federation, which caters not only to the employees of electrical contractors, the electrotechnical industry and electric power plants but also to the electricians of shipyards and of the maintenance departments of factories of all kinds. The Metal Workers' Federation, too, has members within the maintenance departments of the, say, paper and pulp mills and sawmills. Neither of these federations, however, conducts an independent bargaining policy in these industries any more: the Metal Workers Federation signs a protocol with the (Employers') Federation of the Wood Industry, essentially duplicating the provisions concerning maintenance work in the collective agreement with the Paper Federation or the Wood and Special Branches Federation, as the case may be; and while the agreements of the Finnish Electric Workers' Federation are in the form independent collective agreements, their contents are almost identical with the collective agreements of the main industries. However, even though the painters and plumbers belong to the Building Workers' Federation, this federation endeavours to maintain the independence of these (and some other similar) fields in the manner that not only are independent collective agreements drawn up and concluded for painters as well as for plumbers, but these agreements are applicable not only to painters and plumbers in the service of painting and plumbing contractors but also to painters and plumbers employed by construction firms, applying the collective agreement for the construction industry – also concluded with the Building Workers' Federation – to their other employees. Moreover, the Finnish Electric Workers' Federation as well as, in regard to painters and plumbers, the Building Workers' Federations endeavours to maintain the independence of these fields also in the local representation of employees by claiming – with varying success – that there shall be independent shop stewards, labour protection representatives and labour protection committees for electricians of manufacturing firms as well as for painters and plumbers of construction firms.

308. The various federations of the SAK are regularly composed of local unions. The federations of the local unions – as well as the SAK itself – are registered associations under the Associations Act. The Building Workers' Federation also has regional associations, which, too, are registered associations and have the local unions in the region as members. Most federations, however, only have a district organization composed of organs or officials of the federation. The district organization of the SAK likewise consists of organs and officials of the confederation. But in addition there are local trade union organizations in different localities. These organizations are registered associations composed of the local trade unions of various industries and crafts in the locality. The main tasks of the local trade union organization are educational and informative, but they may also organize local support for industrial actions of their member unions. They do not, however, engage in negotiations with the employer side. There are about 170 such local trade union organizations.

309. The business of a local union is conducted by its members at large, convened in a general meeting, or by its board and officers, elected by the annual general meeting or – in the case of other officers than the chairman, such as the vice-chairman, secretary or treasurer – by the board. A local trade union may comprise employees of a single employer or workplace only, but it may also draw members from several or all workplaces of the industry or craft in the locality. In the latter case, the union members at a single workplace (where more than but a few members are employed) regularly form an unregistered subsidiary of the local trade union, the *työhuonekunta*, here translated as 'the shop circle'. The shop circle of a large workplace often has an organization similar to that of the local union, with the chief shop steward often functioning as chairman and the departmental shop stewards as board members.

310. A general meeting of a member federation of the SAK is regularly convened at intervals of two to five years. It is composed of representatives elected by the members of the constituent local unions. Proportional elections have gradually been introduced in most federations. The election campaigns are usually conducted between Social Democrats and Left Wing Alliance, with some occasional candidates and even representatives from the Centre of Finland. The council, the board and the most important officers of the federation are elected by the general meeting to sit until the next general meeting. In recent years, many federations have abolished the general meeting. If this is the case, the council of the federation is elected by the members with proportional elections, and the board and the most important officers are elected by the council for a fixed period. The council is convened a few times a year to decide, e.g., upon the adoption of a new collective agreement and to fill any vacancies occurring in the board or among the officers elected at the general meeting. The day-to-day business is conducted by the board and the officers. The adoption of a collective agreement may be submitted by the council to balloting by the membership at large, and it may also be delegated to the board, subject to conditions set by the council. The organization of the SAK is similar to the organization of its constituent federations, except that the representatives of the general meeting, convened every fifth year, are elected by the organs of the federations. Union dues amount on average to 1% of the wages. Of the dues collected, 18% on average are allotted to the local union, 75% to the federation and 7% to the SAK.

II. The White-Collar Confederations

311. The SAK is in principle a general confederation, open to all employees. However, the SAK considers itself a part of the labour movement, together with the political parties of the left, the Workers' Sports Federation, etc. White-collar employees traditionally identify themselves neither with the trade union movement of the blue-collar employees nor with the labour movement. The SAK has essentially remained a confederation of blue-collar employees, and the white-collar employees have – after their unionization eventually began – formed organizations of their own. Even though the proportionate part of the supporters of the political parties of the left has increased among white-collar employees and elections to the general meetings of the federations are in many cases conducted along political lines (with United Bourgeois and Social Democrats usually as the main adversaries), the proclaimed policy of the white-collar unions is neutrality among the political parties – any partisan engagement of the unions would alienate a considerable portion of the union membership. However, some supporters of the left among Government officers of the white-collar and especially professional grades remained, especially during the 1970s, outside the traditional unions of white-collar and professional employees and instead joined the SAK-affiliated unions founded by Government employees of blue-collar grades.

312. The oldest associations of white-collar employees can trace their roots to times more than hundred years ago. The associations of those times were, however, founded with a view to further the coherence and profession of their members, not to further defend their economic interests. In fact, the economic position of white-collar employees – especially in Government service – was in general favourable until World War I. But the inflation during and after the war and the democratization of the budget power from the Imperial Majesty to the Parliament changed the state of things drastically. The white-collar employee associations already in existence or newly founded assumed the defence of the economic interests of their members. For the better fulfilment of this purpose, the leading associations of Government officials, municipal officials and industrial white-collar employees founded the predecessor of the later TVK in 1922, although several associations of white-collar employees remained outside the confederation at least until its reorganization in 1944. The two other confederations of white-collar employees, the STTK and the Confederation of Unions for Academic Professionals in Finland (Akava) also have member federations with a history of more than hundred years, but the confederations were only founded after World War II, the STTK in 1946 and the Akava in 1954. Before the establishment of these two confederations, many of their individual members had belonged to associations affiliated to the TVK but had begun to feel to be in a minority position in that confederation. Similar reasons were a contributing factor in the subsequent growth of the two confederations, although a large part of the growth consisted of people who were unorganized earlier. The situation changed abruptly during the depression in 1992, when TVK went bankrupt (because of unsuccessful financial undertakings). Its member federations remained independent for a while. Eventually, they joined other confederations, predominantly the STTK, which was renamed as the 'Finnish Confederation of Salaried Employees STTK'. The development of the white-collar confederations can be seen in the membership figures in Table 6.

Table 6 Membership Figures of White-Collar Federations

Year	*TVK*	*STTK*	*Akava*
1923	10,000	–	–
1928	13,000	–	–
1938	17,000	–	–
1943	15,000	–	–
1944	61,000	–	–
1948	64,000	9,000	–

Year	*TVK*	*STTK*	*Akava*
1958	110,000	13,000	22,000
1965	152,000	16,000	29,000
1970	212,000	27,000	42,000
1975	287,000	85,000	78,000
1980	325,000	115,000	162,000
1985	375,000	130,000	214,000
1990	388,000	155,000	278,000
1994	–	623,000	325,000
1997	–	637,000	347,000

Source: Akava had 596,947 members in 2016 and 615,000 members in 2022.

313. Both confederations of white-collar employees consist of member federations and associations. In addition, there are some federations which have remained outside the confederations. Since the reorganization of the SAK around 1970, these independent federations are all of a white-collar character. The following table gives the 1994 membership numbers of the most important of the member units of the two confederations as well as of some of the independent federations. (Some independent federations, such as the Air Line Pilots' Federations and the Air Controllers' Federation, are outside the official statistics.)

314. The white-collar federations, especially the federations affiliated to Akava, are essentially of a craft union character. However, the negotiation activities are centred on the confederation level to a far larger extent than in the case of the SAK. This is also especially true in regard to Akava's small federations. The trade union character of Akava has, however, sometimes been questioned by others, since some of the Akava federations (such as the federations of dentists, lawyers and physicians) include members who are self-employed and may even employ other members of the same federation.

III. Union Density

315. No official statistics have been compiled on union density, but studies conducted by Dr Timo Kauppinen and his associates at the Ministry of Labour include calculations and estimations on the development of the union density of all white-collar employees, all blue-collar employees and all employees, and the following figures on this question are mainly based on these studies. The percentage of unionized white-collar employees includes, however, members of such organizations, which only gradually assumed the role of trade unions. The percentage of 'real' trade unionists among white-collar employees would, therefore, be almost negligible until World War I and essentially lower than in the table up until World War II. Another comment is that the method to count the number of potential trade unionists was changed in 1976. The percentages given for 1980, 1985 and 1988 are therefore not comparable with the figures for earlier years. For 1980, the old method would give 88% for white-collar employees, 75% for blue-collar employees and 82% for all employees; but for 1985 and 1988, calculation according to the old method is no longer possible. The traditional method, used in the table, would give a union density of 87% for 1989 and a density of 97% for 1994. The traditional method, however, exaggerates the density to some extent because the numerator (actual union members) includes a growing number of individuals not included in the denominator (potential union members), e.g., students. A revised calculation gives a union density of 72% for 1989 and a density of 81% for 1995. No separate figures have for these years been calculated for white-and blue-collar employees (*see* Table 7).

Table 7 Union Density

	Union Density of:		
Year	*White-Collar Employees*	*Blue-Collar Employees*	*All Employees*
1908	24	5	6
1916	24	7	9
1917	44	25	27
1918	24	7	9
1928	38	13	17
1938	29	9	13
1943	29	10	14
1945	45	34	37
1948	50	35	39
1953	51	25	32
1958	52	22	30
1960	48	28	34
1965	43	41	42
1970	59	55	57
1975	76	72	74
1980	94	67	81
1985	91	70	81
1988	96	74	86

Union density exceeds 95% in paper and pulp manufacturing, shipping, typographic industry, and newspapers. Even in the service occupations, the union density, which remained low until fairly recently, is now at least around two-thirds. As regards white-collar occupations, union density is approaching 100% in many branches of public service (such as teachers, nurses, doctors, municipal employees) and is very high among the supervisors and technicians in manufacturing, while the growth has been slower in many other kinds of white-collar employment in private service.

IV. International Relations

316. In addition to contributing to the work of the ILO, the trade unions are engaged in extensive international cooperation. The SAK was originally a member of the World Federation of Trade Unions (WFTU), but withdrew from that organization in 1951 and joined the International Confederation of Free Trade Unions (ICFTU) in 1957. Some member federations of the SAK, however, retained their membership in the WFTU for a longer time, and the SAK itself used to send observers to the meetings of the WFTU. The SAK also performed mediating functions in ameliorating the relations between the two world federations. Also the trade unions of the former socialist countries have, however, left the WFTU, which now has members in some developing countries only and does not have relations with the SAK or any of its member federations. The TVK was also a member of the ICFTU since 1970. The Akava joined this federation in 1992 and the STTK in 1993. Both the SAK and the TVK were founding members of the European Confederation of Trade Unions (1973) and the Scandinavian Confederation of Trade Unions (1972). These regional organizations were joined by the Akava in 1991 and by the STTK in 1993. All these existing confederations are also represented in the Trade Union Advisory Committee of the Organisation for Economic Co-operation and Development, and so was the TVK. The SAK, the TVK and the STTK also had regular relations with the trade union movement of the Soviet Union now replaced with cooperation with Russian and Baltic, especially Estonian trade unions; and for decades, all confederations have maintained a lively cooperation with their Scandinavian counterparts on confederation as well as federation levels. In 1995, after Finland had joined the EU, the three existing confederations founded a common office in Brussels, called KEY-FINLAND. At present, the name is Finunions.

§2. The Employers 'Associations'

317. Employers became organized on the heels of the employees. The typographic industry was a forerunner here also: the Employers' Federation of the Graphic Art Industries was founded in 1900. The metal trades followed shortly after, and in 1906 a decision was made to set up an association to be a uniting link for the various employers' federations. The new association began its activities the following year, concurrently with the Finnish Trade Union Confederation. Since 1917, it was called the STK and gradually its membership grew to comprise practically all employers' federations and associations in manufacturing, construction, transportation and maintenance. In 1993, the STK was, however, merged with the Confederation of Finnish Industries (TKL), an association founded to promote the interests of manufacturing and other industries in other respects than in employment relationships and with a membership structure almost identical to the STK. The result of the merger is called the Confederation of Finnish Industry and Employers (TT). Due to the low union density in service industries, it was not until 1945 that it was in the interests of the employers in these fields to organize. In that year, the independent Employers' Confederation of Service Industries (LTK, now PT) was set up to organize employers in the wholesale and retail trade, banking, insurance, hotels and restaurants, and other similar fields. For a long time, the employers were members directly to the LTK, without any intermediate federations; but in 1974, the new statutes of the confederation introduced its division into member federations to which the employers in the respective fields belong.

318. The TT and PT merged to become EK in 2005. The Confederation of Finnish Industries (at the moment Elinkeinoelämän keskusliitto EK) is the leading business organization in Finland. It represents and defends the interests of the Finnish business community EK represents the entire private sector and companies of all sizes. It has twenty-seven member associations and 16,000 member companies across all business sectors. Member companies employ 980,000 workers.

319. Suomen Yrittäjät ry is an interest and service organization for small and medium-sized enterprises from all fields around entire Finland and their owners. It represents 115,000 enterprises.

320. As in the case of trade unions, the development and significance of the employers' associations are described with two sets of statistical figures. The first set gives figures on the membership of the employers' confederations at different points in time, while the second set renders the present strength of the confederations and the federations. But as the principle 'one man – one vote' is inapplicable here, two figures are needed throughout: the number of member employers and the number of their employees.

321. The employers' associations, too, have extensive international activities. The EK is a member of BUSINESSEUROPE, the European-level association for employers, commerce and industry and International Organization of Employers (IOE).

Chapter 3. Institutionalized Relations Between Employers and Employees

§1. Relations at the Enterprise Level

322. There are five different basic institutions for employer-employee relations at the enterprise level. Four of these basic systems are statutory, while the fifth one is mainly based on agreements and practice. In the statutory systems, trade unions have no immediate formal position, although their practical significance is often considerable. The non-statutory system, again, is built up to consist of relations between the employer and the trade union, but sometimes the connection of the system to the formal structure of the union may in practice be rather loose. The non-statutory system serves, however, as the main base of one of the statutory systems, while the other statutory systems have been set up for specific purposes, namely labour protection (mainly safety and health), personnel representation in the administration of enterprises, and participation in the profits of enterprises. The cooperation system for labour protection also serves as a subsidiary base for the statutory system first mentioned, while that system in turn has a role in the operation of the two remaining statutory systems. Therefore, the following description begins with the non-statutory system (the shop steward system), followed first by the statutory system for labour protection, then by the statutory system for cooperation within undertakings (employee participation), and finally by the (newer) systems for representation in the administration of enterprises and participation in the enterprise profits.

I. The Shop Steward System

A. Development and Foundations of the System

323. Representatives of the employees were first mentioned in the Shop Rules Act, 1922. According to this Act, it was possible to include provisions in the shop rules on how notice should be given to the employer about the election of the employees' delegates under the law or a collective agreement. The employers were, for a long time, however, disinclined to recognize any other representatives of the employees than the general representative under the Industrial Inspection Act, 1927. Meanwhile, the shop steward system was developed by the trade unions as an internal union organization at the workplace. The shop stewards were finally recognized by the first General Agreement, concluded in 1944. The sparse provisions of the General Agreements of 1944 and 1946 on this subject were first supplemented by various collective agreements and finally replaced by the more elaborate Shop Steward Agreement, 1969, in turn superseded by a new agreement in 1990 and finally by provisions in the comprehensive General Agreement of 1997. There are similar arrangements in agreements concerning the shop stewards of some branches (e.g., the Metal Trades), which have remained outside, or are no more within, the scope of the general Shop Steward Agreement or the new comprehensive General

Agreement, as well as of white-collar employees. The job security of shop stewards and the compensation for their time off are concurrently regulated by the Employment Contracts Act; and the General Agreement contains provisions on time off, generally without loss of earnings, for shop stewards participating in trade union training.

B. Contents of the System

324. The shop steward system embodied in the General Agreement, 1997 (the Agreement was updated in 2001), consists of a chief steward for the establishment, a shop steward for every department, and a substitute for the chief shop steward. The agreements concerning white-collar employees augment the shop steward network of a normal manufacturing establishment with two or three more shop stewards: one for the technicians and supervisors and another for the clerical and other comparable personnel, plus possibly a representative of the professional grades. According to the General Agreement, the shop stewards shall be elected by the local trade union concerned. The union is entitled to organize the elections at the workplace, which entails that the shop stewards are commonly elected by the union members at the establishment or department, as the case may be, and certified to the employer by the union. The personal employment relationship of a shop steward is not altered on account of his election. Accordingly, he shall personally follow the general employment conditions of the workplace as well as the working hours, supervisors' orders, etc.

325. The shop steward is the representative of the local trade union at the workplace. In this capacity, the shop steward has dual tasks. First, he shall represent the interests of the trade union and its members towards the employer and see to it that the employer honours his obligations – especially those based on collective agreements – towards the union and its members. If differences concerning the remuneration or employment conditions of an employee cannot be settled between him and his first-line supervisor, negotiations concerning the difference shall first be conducted between the shop steward of the department and the supervisor and second, if these negotiations fail, between the chief shop steward and a management representative at an appropriate level. This pattern for grievance negotiations is regularly followed even in cases not concerned with disputes over rights. In more important questions – concerning, e.g., wage rises for several employees – the shop stewards are in practice often seconded by *ad hoc* representatives of the employees in question. If the negotiations fail even at the chief shop steward level, either of the parties may demand that the negotiations be continued between the contracting parties of the collective agreement in question.

326. The other side of the shop steward's tasks as a representative of the local trade union at the workplace is directed towards the union members there. A part of these tasks consists of purely internal union matters of no concern to the employer (as far as they do not interfere with the operation of the enterprise). But the shop stewards shall also see to it that the union members honour the obligations of the union towards the employer, especially as regards labour peace. Any omissions of the shop steward in this respect are imputed to the union.

II. Cooperation Organs for Labour Protection

A. *Development and Foundations of the System*

327. The first beginnings of institutionalized cooperation within the field of labour protection were embodied in the Industrial Inspection Act, 1927, empowering the employees at any workplace under the inspection system to elect a general representative from among themselves to represent them in inspections as well as in other cases where the employees are legally entitled to receive a document concerning working conditions at the establishment either for information or for consultation. These provisions were supplemented by provisions in legislation concerning hours of work and annual holidays, entitling the general representative to inspect the employer's records on overtime and Sunday work, holiday pay, etc. The principle of cooperation in matters of safety and health is also stressed in the Occupational Safety and Health Act and in the Employment Contracts Act. However, it was not until the enactment of the Labour Protection Supervision Act, replacing the Industrial Inspection Act, 1927, and 1987 called the Act on Labour Protection Supervision and Appeals in Labour Protection Matters and 2006 Act on Occupational Safety and Health Enforcement and Cooperation on Occupational Safety and Health at Workplaces, that a more sophisticated institutional framework for this cooperation was introduced by statute. A comparable system already been created by the Agreement on Safety Work at Workplaces, concluded in 1969 between the STK, the SAK and the STTK. This agreement and its successors of 1974, 1976 and 1990 are no more in force. At present, the statutory framework is supplemented and, under authority granted in the Act on Occupational Safety and Health Enforcement and Cooperation on Occupational Safety and Health at Workplaces, etc., to some extent modified by the comprehensive General Agreement of 1997. Companion agreements exist for construction work, office work, etc. There is also some scope for local agreements, covering one workplace and concluded between the employer and the local trade unions concerned. Local as well as confederation- or federation-wide agreements validly concluded have to be acquiesced in also by such employees who do not belong to any of the associations concluding the agreement. The cooperation organs have also been given some tasks in the Occupational Health Care Act. Finally, a Protocol to the General Agreement of 1997 includes some very general provisions on workplace catering, replacing identical provisions in the Protocol to the 1990 Agreement on Labour Protection Cooperation at Workplaces, which in turn had superseded the more elaborate Workplace Catering Agreement, 1976.

B. Contents of the System

328. The Act on Occupational Safety and Health Enforcement and Cooperation on Occupational Safety and Health at Workplaces, etc., makes it a duty for the employer and the employee to cooperate in labour protection matters. For each workplace, the employer shall appoint a labour protection supervisor, if the employer does not himself act in that capacity, to be responsible for the cooperation. At any workplace where at least ten employees are regularly employed, the employees shall – and at other workplaces may – elect a labour protection representative (and two substitutes for him) from their own number for a period of two calendar years to represent them in this cooperation as well as in relations with the labour protection authorities. The white-collar employers are entitled to elect a labour protection representative of their own and substitutes for him, but if they do not make use of this option (regularly they do), they are entitled to vote in the election of the first mentioned labour protection representative and are represented by him. At a workplace with a shop steward system, the competence of the labour protection representatives is restricted to matters concerning the safety and healthiness of the work (except where the same person has been elected both shop steward and labour protection representative). It has not yet been definitely settled whether this expression only covers what is commonly meant by industrial safety and health, thus deferring matters concerning hours of work and annual holidays at such workplaces to the exclusive competence of the shop stewards, or whether such matters are also included under the said legal expression. Special provisions exist for labour protection supervisors and labour protection representatives at workplaces where employees of many employers are working.

329. At a workplace where at least twenty employees are regularly employed, there shall according to the main rule also – and elsewhere may – be a labour protection committee for the furtherance of the safety and healthiness of work. The labour protection committee shall consist of representatives appointed by the employer and elected by the employees. If no agreement is reached as to the number of the representatives of the various parties (i.e., the employer, the white-collar employees and the blue-collar employees), this question shall be settled by the AVI. By agreement, the statutory labour protection committee may be replaced by another arrangement, provided that the possibilities of the employees to handle matters concerning labour protection at the workplace are not diminished. The General Agreement of 1997 provides for a further elaboration of the safety organization by a network of labour protection agents, to be elected by the employees from among themselves. The job security and time off of the labour protection representative, the members of the labour protection committee, and the labour protection agents have been discussed earlier.

330. The tasks of the labour protection supervisor, the labour protection representative, the labour protection committee and the labour protection agents are of a cooperative and advisory character. They assist in official inspections carried out at the workplace by the labour protection authorities, make themselves acquainted with the safety and health conditions of the workplace and their development, make representations to the employer for improvements concerning dangerous working conditions and work methods, make plans for safety and health education at the workplace, take care of safety and health information at the workplace, give their opinion on the employer's plans concerning workplace health care, etc. The labour protection representative shall also, when necessary, inform the labour protection authorities of safety and health defects at the workplace, and he is entitled to examine any documents and registers the employer is required to maintain in accordance with the labour protection legislation, but, with one important exception, the law gives none of the mentioned labour protection organs any powers of decision. The power and the responsibility rest with the employer.

331. The exception mentioned above consists of the right of the labour protection representative to interrupt the work of employees represented by him, in case the work involves immediate and serious danger for the life or health of an employee and only as far as is necessary for the safety and healthiness of the work. The labour protection representative shall inform the employer about the interruption, if possible in advance and in any case without delay. The employer may, after having ascertained that no such danger exists, order that the work shall be reassumed. Such measures of the employer shall be reported without delay to the labour protection authorities, which shall take immediate action to decide the dispute if no agreement on safe continuation of the work is reached at the workplace.

III. Workplace Participation

A. Production Committees and Other Earlier Systems

332. In the new political situation after World War II, plans were drafted for a drastic curtailment of the powers of the management in the enterprises. A production committee with powers to overrule or veto decisions of the management in many important matters was to be instituted in enterprises meeting certain requirements as to size etc. However, the act finally adopted in 1946 and renewed in 1949 only provided a forum for discussion and exchange of information between management and personnel. These historical developments might be a partial explanation, at least, as to why the practical significance of the protection committee remained small in many enterprises: the management resented the original far-flung project, the organized labour its 'watered-down' realization. However, where all parties were willing to take the production committee at its face value, it could prove its usefulness just as a forum for discussion and mutual information.

333. Depending on the size of the establishment, the production committee consisted of two or three representatives of the employer, one or two representatives of the white-collar employees and three or five representatives of the blue-collar employees. It rested with the management to submit quarterly reports to the committee, and the committee also had to consider any questions raised by the members concerning the financial situation and production of the enterprise. The act furthermore recounted various specific questions for the consideration of the committee.

Despite the resentment and disappointments connected with the establishment of the production committee system, the role of the production committee as a forum for informative and consultative activities has been enhanced and made more precise by way of collective agreements since 1970. The agreement clauses defined the art, extent and timing of information to be given by the management and the employees. It was further stated in agreements applicable in manufacturing – other fields being in general outside the production committee system – that the production committee was to be the central organ to receive and disseminate information. These provisions were, however, superseded by a new Information Agreement, concluded in 1977 between the STK and the SAK and containing no more references to the production committee. On the other hand, the Organization and Methods ('Rationalization', hereinafter 'O' and 'M') Agreement, 1978, still referred, as did its predecessor of 1971, to the production committee as a forum where the periodic O and M plans of every enterprise should be discussed before they were implemented.

334. Besides the production committee system (and the cooperation system for labour protection), systems for workplace participation in specific matters had gradually been established by way of collective agreements. According to the O and M Agreement, 1978, just mentioned, a working party, composed of representatives of the management and the employees, should be set up for each O and M project, and training and information should be given to the employees concerned. (The O and M Agreement, 1971, already contained similar albeit less elaborate provisions.) The Information Agreement, 1977, above, did not provide for any new institutions but referred to existing organs – the shop stewards as well as common organs of the management and the employees – as essential receivers and disseminators of information; special rules were given for the dissemination of information concerning the activities of the common organs. Similarly, the Workplace Catering Agreement, 1976, referred to existing common organs, such as the labour protection committee and the production committee, as organs of cooperation for the purposes of this agreement. The Training Agreement, 1976, provided for common training for purposes of workplace cooperation to be given preferably at workplaces, jointly by the employer and the employee side (without loss of earnings for the employees involved).

B. Development of the Present Cooperation System

335. Since the mid-1960s, plans had been developed for a new statutory system for the participation of employees in decisions affecting their work. Most of the time, the aim was to draft provisions to replace the production committee system with a participation system resembling the codetermination system in the Federal Republic of Germany. According to these plans, there would have been set up a Personnel Council, elected by all the employees without regard to their organizational affiliation (but with specific quotas for white-collar and blue-collar employees), and a Cooperation Committee composed of members appointed by the management and elected by the Personnel Council. The Personnel Council and the Cooperation Committee would have had a decisive power in certain matters. However, in most of the really important matters, a decision would only have been binding if concurred in by a majority in each of the three groups – the management group, the white-collar group and the blue-collar group – in the Cooperation Committee. In the autumn of 1977, however, the confederations of employers and employees and the Council of the State (National Cabinet) reached an agreement on a new basis for the participation system. The nearest model to the new basis can be seen in the Swedish Codetermination Act of 1976. According to the agreement, participation was to be based on the existing negotiation system without any essentially new organs. In contrast to the earlier plans, the legal provisions on participation were to be to a large extent optional only, allowing modifications by means of industry- or craft-wide collective agreements. A Government Bill to carry through the agreed system was presented to the Parliament, passed by Parliament, and enacted in September 1978, to replace the Production Committee Act as of 1 July 1979. The Act has been amended several times, especially to provide for an enhanced negotiation system for collective terminations and for a cooperation system for groups of companies (1990). An amendment of August 1996 includes provisions for international cooperation within Finnish groups of companies which operate in two or more countries (except the United Kingdom) of the EEA.

C. *Scope and Structure*

336. The Act on Cooperation within Undertakings was enacted in 1978 and the Act entered into force on 1 July 1979. The Act on Cooperation within Undertakings was supplemented in 2005 due to the Directive 2002/14/EC of the European Parliament and of the Council establishing a general framework for informing and consulting employees in the European Community – Joint declaration of the European Parliament, the Council and the Commission on employee representation. In 2007, after a tripartite committee work in Finland, an overall reform took place and a new Act on Cooperation within Undertakings was laid down with the intention of creating better more comprehensible legislation. At the same time, the provisions concerning cooperation within Finnish and Community-wide groups of undertakings were separated from the Act on Cooperation within Undertakings and a new Act on Cooperation within Finnish and Community-wide Groups of Undertakings was laid down. It entered into force on 1 July 2007 at the same time as the Act on Cooperation within Undertakings. The present Act is new and came into force at the beginning of 2022. The Act applies to private undertakings normally employing at least twenty persons as parties to an employment relationship. If the undertaking is a non-profit organization, artistic association, scientific society, religious community or other denominational organization or if its purpose is mainly in industrial policy, labour policy, general political or humanitarian, the provisions of the Act shall not apply to decisions or their preparation regarding the purpose of the organization or denomination or other similar objectives. The Act does not apply to offices or public services or to offices and public services of municipalities, federation of municipalities, the Evangelical Lutheran Church, the Orthodox Church or the Province of Aland or its municipalities or federations of municipalities.

Additionally, employees' rights of participation in Finland are laid down in the Act on Employee Involvement in European Companies and European Cooperative Societies which provides the arrangement of employee involvement in European companies and European cooperative societies.

The new Act consists of three entities: (1) continuous dialogue between employer and employees, (2) negotiations in changing circumstances (change negotiations) and (3) employee representative in company administration (administrative representative).

The Act would apply to companies and organizations employing at least twenty persons. The provisions on administrative representatives would apply to companies that employ at least 150 people in Finland. The Act would not apply to central or local government agencies or public bodies.

337. Parties to the cooperation according to the Act are still the employer and the personnel of the undertaking. The practical cooperation takes place mostly between the representatives of the employer and the personnel. However, if change negotiations only concern a single employee or a few individual employees, they can be held directly between the employees in question and the employer. If there is no employee representative, dialogue can be held in a joint meeting of the employees. Negotiating levels are mutually exclusive. If negotiations concerning several employees are held between the employee representative and the employer, negotiations on the same matter should not be held with individual employees. Consequently, negotiations held at different levels are mutually exclusive. The employer's representative is not defined in the Act on Co-operation within undertakings. The Act does not define the employer's representative; instead, the employer must assign to the dialogue or the negotiations a person who is authorized to act as the employer's representative in the matter in question. Primarily a shop steward represents a personnel group. The personnel may consist of several personnel groups with representatives of their own. The personnel group representative is primarily a shop steward elected on the basis of the collective agreement. The representative may also be an elected representative as referred to in Employment Contracts Act (Elected representative). If the employees have not elected a shop steward or an elected representative, even though they are entitled to do so, they can elect from among their own number a specific co-operation representative for a maximum of two years at a time. Ultimately, a representative can also be elected separately for a single negotiation or dialogue meeting. In the absence of a representative, negotiations are conducted with the employees. If a personnel group does not elect even a negotiation-specific representative for themselves, the employer must fulfil their obligations by holding the negotiations together with all the employees belonging to the said personnel group. If a matter subject to cooperation concerns a single employee only, it shall primarily be handled between him and a representative of the employer; but upon demand of the employer or the employee, negotiations upon the matter shall also be conducted between the employer and the personnel representative concerned. If a matter subject to cooperation concerns employees of a department or another similar unit in a general manner, it shall be handled with the personnel representatives for the unit in question. If two or more personnel groups are concerned, a meeting of the employer and of the personnel representatives concerned shall be held, unless the matter is to be handled by the committee mentioned in the preceding paragraph.

D. Continuous Dialogue and Change Negotiations

338. Continuous dialogue helps develop the company and work community. As a result of the reform, the employer and employees or employee representatives should engage in regular dialogue. The dialogue could address, for example, the financial situation of the company or organization, workplace rules and practices, personnel structure and competence needs and well-being at work.

339. The ways to carry out the dialogue in practice will be agreed at workplaces. The dialogue should take place at least on a quarterly basis. In small companies of twenty to twenty-nine employees, the dialogue should be held twice a year. However, if there is no elected employee representative in the company, one dialogue per year is sufficient. A plan for developing the work community is formulated as part of the dialogue.

340. Before the employer makes decisions on matters that have a significant effect on the employees, such as reductions in workforce, the employer must consult employee representatives or the employees. The revised act refers to this process as change negotiations.

The procedure for change negotiations has remained broadly the same as in the previous Act. However, the right of the employee representative to submit proposals and propose alternative solutions are now strengthened. The timing of the opening of negotiations is also specified. Change negotiations refer to negotiations between the employer and the personnel, which should take place when the employer is considering a business decision that, if realized, would essentially change the position of one or more employees. Essential changes that require negotiations already include termination, lay-offs or reduction of a contract of employment into a part-time contract, or unilateral amendment of a substantial term of an employment contract on production or financial grounds. The obligation to negotiate also covers solutions that have a material impact on one or more employees for work tasks, working methods or work, workspaces or arrangements for regular working hours.

Matters to be handled in the change negotiations include the transfer of the workplace to another address or the conversion of the workspaces into an open-plan office.

341. Change negotiations must be initiated when the employer is considering measures that may lead to employment contract terminations, lay-offs or reductions of the employment contract to a part-time contract concerning one or more employees or unilateral changes to essential conditions of the employment contract for financial or production reasons. This refers to the stage at which the employer is already able to identify the planned measure and the associated personnel impacts in a manner that makes it possible to draw up a negotiation proposal and negotiate the questions related to the matter. On the other hand, the measure must be under consideration only, that is, the negotiations must be held and also completed before the employer makes the decision on the measure. When necessary, the employer must be capable of making changes to its plan of measures on the basis of matters that have come up in the negotiations. If the preparations for the measure have proceeded too far, the employer's plan can no longer be actually influenced in the negotiations and the related discussion in the spirit of co-operation cannot be carried out.

342. Personnel impacts may be a consequence of the employer's business decision. Having negotiations only after the business decision has been made may lead to the inability to exert influence on the questions that are associated with the decision. In this case, the negotiations must be held before the business decision is made. If the relation of the business decision to personnel impacts is unclear and, as a result, the impacts cannot be estimated, the negotiations must be started when the employer begins considering changes targeted at the personnel. However, before the change negotiations, there may be preliminary discussion already in connection with the dialogue. Even if the need for the measure being considered by the employer emerged suddenly and no feasible alternatives could be found for it, having change negotiations is still significant. In this case, the negotiations can involve, among other things, discussion on the details of the implementation and means to alleviate personnel impacts.

343. If the employer's business decision can be considered as leading to a major change in the employee's duties or work methods or arrangements of work, work premises or regular working hours, the negotiations must be held before the business decision is made. However, if the business decision leaves room for different personnel impacts, the employer may start the negotiations after the business decision before deciding on personnel impacts. If the relation of a decision within the scope of the employer's power of management to personnel impacts is unclear, the negotiations must be held when potential changes influencing the personnel's position can be estimated and before they are decided.

344. It was stated above that information necessary for handling matters in cooperation shall be furnished by the employer. In addition, the employer shall provide the personnel representatives with regular information not connected with any specific matter under cooperation.

Employee representation in the company administration promotes the flow of information and allows the expertise of the personnel to contribute to the decision-making. In the new act, the employee representative in the administration of a company is referred to as an administrative representative. The provisions on representation in administration are largely in line with the previous legislation, albeit transposed from the Act on Personnel Representation in the Company Administration to the Act on Co-operation within Undertakings. Personnel must be represented in administrative bodies that de facto deal with important business, financial and personnel issues.

E. *Cooperation Agreements*

345. Virtually all provisions of the Cooperation Within Undertakings Act are suppletive in the sense that their contents can be deviated from by means of agreements concluded between national federations of employers and employees. In the Act, such an agreement is not called a collective agreement but is stated to have the legal effects which a collective agreement has under the Collective Agreements Act. This locution has evidently been chosen to confer the said legal effects upon such an agreement and its various provisions even if the agreement contains no employment terms and at the same time to eliminate the general applicability under the Employment Contracts Act; but the locution leaves open whether the agreement has the effects a collective agreement has under the Labour Court Act or whether any (or some) disputes arising under the agreement are to be handled by regular courts. An employer bound by the agreement is entitled to apply its provisions also in regard to such employees which are not themselves bound by the agreement but are members of a personnel group envisaged in it. A national Cooperation Agreement was in 1981 concluded between the Confederation of Finnish Employers (STK) and the confederations of employees. In 1986, this agreement was replaced by a new Agreement on the Promotion of Cooperation and Information Activities in Undertakings, concluded between the same parties and also superseding the Information Agreement, 1977. The 1986 agreement was in 1989 in turn replaced by a new agreement with the same name. Furthermore, the O and M agreement, 1978, was, in 1986, also superseded by a new O and M Agreement, taking account of the new cooperation system. The Training Agreement, 1976, was likewise replaced by a new agreement in 1990. In 1997, the Agreement on the Promotion of Cooperation and Information Activities in Undertakings, 1989, the O and M Agreement, 1986, and the Training Agreement, 1990, were all superseded by the new comprehensive General Agreement. Reference has already been made to local agreements concerning cooperation in the workplace in question as well as to the shop rules adopted and other decisions affecting the employees taken in the cooperation procedure under the Cooperation Within Undertakings Act. Such agreements and decisions are also to be acquiesced in by those employees who either had no vote in the elections for the employee representatives approving the agreements or decisions, or who voted for an unsuccessful candidate.

F. *Supervision and Violations*

346. The observance of the Cooperation Within Undertakings Act is supervised by the Co-operation ombudsman at the Ministry of Employment and the Economy and by the parties to the national (i.e., industry- or craft-wide) collective agreement which shall be applied in the enterprise concerned. An employer or his representative contravening the provisions of the act concerning submission of matters to cooperation procedure, information to be given to employees and personnel representatives, or time off and compensation for personnel representatives, is liable to a fine. An employer, employer's representative, or fellow employee who prevents or tries to prevent the election of an employee's representative for co-operation within a group of companies is likewise liable to a fine, and so is anyone divulging matters to be kept secret according to the act. An employer or employer's representative violating an agreement on national or international cooperation in a Finnish group of companies in an essential manner shall also be fined. If a provision in the act has been (validly) deviated from by means of a nationwide agreement, the normal consequences for violations of collective agreement clauses apply instead of a fine according to the act. Employers' associations and trade unions bound by such an agreement are also, under threat of a compensatory fine, obliged to see to it that their member employers and employees observe the agreement clauses; but it seems that a local trade union is not liable to any adverse consequences for breaches of any duty which such an agreement purports to impose on the union or its representatives, such as shop stewards (acting as such).

347. If an employer decides a matter concerning a collective termination, a lay-off, or a transfer to part-time work in wilful or obviously negligent disregard of the provisions of the Cooperation Within Undertakings Act on the conduct of negotiations and as a result of the decision an employee is dismissed, laid off or transferred to part-time work, the employee is entitled to a pecuniary compensation, amounting to twenty months' salary or wages at most. The disregard of the negotiation rules does not render the decision of the employer invalid, but if the decision was in itself unlawful, the employee is in addition to the pecuniary compensation entitled to a compensation for his actual damages.

IV. Participation in Enterprise Administration

348. The employees had been given a say in the administration of enterprises in the Act on the Representation of the Personnel in the Administration of Enterprises of 1990. From the beginning of 2022, the provisions have been in the Act on Co-operation Within Undertakings. The purpose of the participation is stated in the Act to be the development of the activities of the enterprise, the intensification of cooperation between the enterprise and the personnel, and the enhancement of the influence of the personnel. The act is applicable to Finnish corporate employers (except public bodies) which regularly employ at least 150 persons in Finland.

349. The representation can be arranged by agreement between the employer and at least two of the personnel groups under the Cooperation Within Undertakings Act representing together the majority of the employees. In the absence of such agreement and if so required by two personnel groups representing together the majority of the personnel, the personnel is entitled to elect its representatives to the administration of the enterprise. In this case, the employer is entitled to choose whether the representatives will be elected to the board of directors, to the council of administration (if any) or to the management groups of the different units of the corporation, covering together the activities of the whole corporation, and the number of representatives shall be one-quarter of the other members of the organ in question, but at least one and at most four.

350. The representatives of the personnel have the same position as the other members of the organ in question. They are not, however, entitled to participate in the handling of matters concerning appointment, dismissals, or service conditions of the directors of the undertaking, service conditions of the personnel, or industrial actions. The job security and time off of the representatives of the personnel have been discussed earlier.

V. Personnel Funds

351. The participation of the personnel in the profits of the enterprises is regulated in the Act on Personnel Funds of 2010. Personnel funds are not compulsory. A personnel fund may be erected in a Finnish undertaking or Government agency having at least ten employees, or at least ten employees if no person owns more than one-tenth of the enterprise or of its voting power. The fund is erected, owned and administered by the personnel of the enterprise. Its assets consist primarily of profit premiums paid by the employer according to a profit premium system decided by the employer after having discussed it with the representatives of the personnel according to the Cooperation Within Undertakings Act (or, as the case may be, the Act on Cooperation Within Government Agencies and Institutions, 1988).

352. The assets of the personnel fund are invested either in the employer enterprise (or another enterprise within the same group of companies) even as venture capital or elsewhere in a safe and profitable manner. The share of each member in the fund is divided into a bound part and a free part. Profit premiums paid by the employer are added to the bound part, as well as the gains from the investments of the fund. After five years' membership in the fund, at most 15% – as determined according to the by-laws of the fund – of each member's bound part is annually transferred to the free part, which can be freely disposed of by the member. After the end of a member's employment relationship, the bound part of his share is after certain delays paid out to him (or his heirs, as the case may be).

Chapter 4. Collective Bargaining

§1. General Framework

I. Agreements Network

A. *National Blue-Collar Agreements*

353. The origin and development of the collective bargaining system are discussed in the historical part. The present framework of collective agreements is based on the structure of trade unions and employers' associations. As the recruiting areas of employers' and employees' federations do not, however, always coincide, an employers' federation may have collective agreement relations with several employees' federations, and *vice versa.* For example, the (employers') Federation of the Wood Industry regularly concludes a collective agreement with the Paper (workers') Federation, on paper and pulp mills, and another agreement with the Wood and Special Branches' Federation, on sawmills and plywood factories, etc. However, the Wood and Special Branches' Federation has another collective agreement with the (employers') Federation of the Joinery Industry. But even though the number of collective agreements concluded by any one federation is not limited to one, most of the employers' and employees' federations are not parties to more than a handful of such collective agreements which in principle cover the whole area of the country. The opposite is true of the few craft federations, notably the Finnish Electric Workers' Federation, which has separate collective agreements with quite a number of employers' federations having members employing electricians for maintenance work in their respective plants of different kinds. But even where the system of industrial unions prevails and the maintenance employees, truck drivers, etc., accordingly belong to the same union as the blue-collar employees of the production departments, the industry-wide collective agreement often has no wage provisions applicable to the maintenance employees, etc. Instead, the collective agreement refers to the wage provisions in the industry-wide (or even craft-wide) collective agreements for metal trades, construction work, motor vehicle transport, etc., often incorporating any future changes in the wage provisions in the agreements referred to – as long as the referring agreement itself is in force.

354. The discussion in the preceding paragraph covers the agreements commonly referred to when speaking of the collective agreement for a given industry or craft or in a given firm or for a given group of employees. The collective agreement in this sense is usually concluded for a definite agreement period, and although the agreement regularly provides for an extension of one extra year if notice to terminate the agreement is not served a certain period (usually two months) before the close of the original agreement period, and so on, it is envisaged by both parties (and their members) that notice will in fact be served and negotiations for the collective agreement for the next period begun in due time. There exists, however, another type of agreement concluded between employers' associations and trade unions and regulating relations between associations of employers and employees and their members but in normal usage not called collective agreements (even though they generally are collective agreements in the legal sense of the term). This type comprises the confederation-wide agreements concluded for an indefinite period of time and in fact intended to be in force for several years (although notice to terminate the agreement is sometimes given quite soon after the conclusion of the agreement; the period of notice is usually six months, and a minimum period of agreement – e.g., until the end of 1980, in the Grounds for Dismissals and Lay-offs Agreement, concluded in June 1978 – is sometimes provided for). According to their subject matter, these confederation-wide agreements are called 'The General Agreement', 'The Holiday Pay Agreement', 'The Shop Steward Agreement', etc. The growth of this system of general and specific agreements is described in the historical introduction, and the fundamental provisions of these agreements are discussed in appropriate parts of this monograph.

B. National White-Collar Agreements

355. Until quite recently, a somewhat different framework was used to govern the employment relations of white-collar employees. As regards supervisors and technicians employed by members of the STK, agreement negotiations for each agreement period were in fact conducted on the confederation level between the STK and the Confederation of Technical Employee Organizations in Finland. These resulted in a Basic Agreement signed by both confederations and in a framework for separate, but, especially in manufacturing, very uniform Salary Agreements for each industry, each agreement to be signed by the Federation of Technical Staff (and possibly by one or more other member federations of the Confederation of Technical Employee Organizations in Finland) and by one of the member federations of the STK. However, with regard to office employees other than technicians, not only were the negotiations conducted at the confederation level but they resulted in a single collective agreement – called 'The General Agreement' – signed by the STK and by both the TVK and its member federation, the Finnish Federation of Industrial Employees. From the agreement round of 1994 to 1995, the white-collar agreements are, however, negotiated and concluded on the federation level. As they are based on the earlier agreements, they still are very similar to each other.

356. In relation to employers outside the TT and especially as regards negotiations and agreements with the Employers' Confederation of Service Industries and its member federations, the framework for white-collar employees have already earlier resembled the framework for blue-collar employees except that in many cases two separate agreements are drawn up and signed: a 'collective agreement' and a 'salary agreement', the 'collective agreement' comprising employment terms not directly pertaining to salaries. We accordingly meet agreements which are not cast in the same mould and which are negotiated and concluded between the various member federations of the Employers' Confederation of Service Industries and of the STTK or SAK, as the case may be, e.g., between the Bank Employers' Federation and the Federation of Bank Employees.

357. Most of the provisions in the General Agreement of 1946 between the STK and the SAK did not have their white-collar counterparts – as regards members of the TT and their employees – in any agreement concluded for an indefinite period. Corresponding clauses are instead included in the collective agreement concluded for each agreement period. However, the specific confederation-wide agreements, such as the Job Security and Lay-offs Agreement or the Shop Steward Agreement, do have similar counterparts concerning white-collar employees. Moreover, specific agreements are sometimes signed by two or three confederations of employees in common. Thus, the General Agreement on Labour Protection Cooperation (for production and maintenance departments in manufacturing, had on the employee side been signed both by the SAK and by the Confederation of Technical Employee Organizations in Finland, and the companion agreement for offices of factories, etc., both by the STTK and the TVK. The Employers' Confederation of Service Industries and the TVK not only concluded confederation-wide agreements on specific matters but they also made a General Agreement, resembling the General Agreement of blue-collar employees and concluded for an indefinite period of time.

C. *Local Agreements*

358. In addition to the confederation-wide, industry-wide or craft-wide agreements described in the preceding paragraphs, there are local agreements of various kinds. The prototype for local agreements is a company agreement, covering the employment relationships of an employer not belonging to any employers' association and concluded between the employer and a trade union, which may be either a local trade union or an industry- or craft-wide federation. In most cases, such a company agreement is an accession agreement by which the parties agree to apply the national collective agreement of the industry or craft in question, sometimes with some modifications or additions. Such an accession agreement is often not concluded for any definite period but is drawn up to incorporate all the future agreements of the industry or craft as well, until the accession agreement is terminated by either of its parties. A local agreement may, however, also concern a member of an industry-wide employers' federation, if the business of the employer is of such a special kind that it has not been considered appropriate to include the establishment in the scope of any multi-employer agreement. In such a case, the agreement is often – but not always – negotiated and concluded by the employers' federation. A typical – although at the same time extreme – example consists of the agreements pertaining to the Finnish Broadcasting Company: the employment relationships of the company's employees are governed by a dozen or so collective agreements, all of them pertaining to no other employers but nevertheless concluded between the Employers' Federation of Service Branches (of which the company is a member) and the various industry- or craft-wide employees' federations having members in the service of the company.

359. The aggregate number of collective agreements in force is lower than formerly, due essentially to the falling number of local agreements. This is mainly a result of the establishment in 1970 of the Municipal Agreement Delegation, with the power – and the virtual monopoly – to conclude collective agreements on behalf of the municipalities (communes) and other units of local government. Earlier, the municipal entities had no power to delegate their contracting power to anyone, not even by joining an employers' association, and so each entity had to conclude its collective agreements itself. Another reason for the diminishing significance of local agreements lies in the general applicability of many industry- or craft-wide collective agreements. As an employer is in most cases obliged to apply the employment terms set in an industry- or craft-wide agreement, he can derive no other advantage by remaining outside the employers' federation concerned than an exemption from membership dues. As the employees are entitled to all benefits based on a generally applicable collective agreement, without regard to whether or not their unorganized employer concludes a collective agreement and bearing in mind that a collective agreement concluded with the employer brings forth duties even for the employee side, trade unions now less often try to induce unorganized employers to conclude collective agreements.

360. The discussion of local collective agreements in the two preceding paragraphs refers to independent agreements based directly on the Collective Agreements Act. There also exist, however, local agreements based on the authority of other (in general industry- or craft-wide) collective agreements. An industry- or craft-wide agreement may refer certain questions to be solved by local agreements, or authorize exceptions from certain of its provisions by means of local agreements. Such a local agreement is in general concluded between the management of the enterprise and the chief shop steward and other representatives of the employees, just as in negotiations concerning the application of the collective agreement. The legal nature of a local agreement of this kind is not quite clear: can it be regarded as a collective agreement, or has it the legal effects of an employment contract? Local agreements are also envisaged in the legislation on labour protection cooperation, workplace participation and participation in enterprise administration References to local agreements in the legislation concerning labour protection cooperation and workplace participation have, however, been largely superseded by national agreements and by similar references in these agreements.

II. Making of a Collective Agreement

A. *Preparations*

361. An industry- or craft-wide collective agreement for the next agreement period gets its contents essentially in two ways: the grassroots way and the centralized way. In a typical blue-collar employees' federation, the aspirations of the members concerning the contents of the next collective agreement are discussed in the shop circles and local trade unions in good time before the agreement negotiations are scheduled to begin. After the results of the local discussions have been gathered by the federation officials, the bargaining goals of the federation are discussed and formulated by the competent organs of the federation and presented in writing to the employers' federation concerned. At this stage, the demands presented to the employer side generally still have blanks (or the letter 'x') instead of definite figures in regard to wage increases, etc.

B. Negotiations

362. The confederations have meanwhile begun their negotiations, nowadays often under the auspices of incomes policy. They endeavour to agree on principles for the new collective agreements. If the confederations succeed in this, their agreement usually provides for a general wage increase (e.g., so many pennies per hour, but not less than so much per cent of the current wage) plus a given percentage of the aggregated yearly wages of each agreement field, to be used in wage increases or other benefits as agreed to by the federations concerned. In addition, the agreement of the confederations may provide for augmented fringe benefits, such as lengthened holidays, increased sickness leave with pay, etc. The statutes of the confederations generally provide for a two-week period for the member federations to decide whether or not to accept the general solution: if a decision to reject the solution of the confederations is not announced within the two weeks, the solution is regarded as accepted by the federation. But whether the general solution is accepted or not, the final negotiations with the opposite party are still to come, for in the former case, the principles and numbers included in the general solution shall now be converted into agreement terms. Employee federations naturally endeavour to observe the grassroots aspirations as far as possible; but often they have to be dropped to a large extent, considering that no confederation can support a member federation's demands in excess of the general solution, disregarding whether the general solution had been taken or left by the member federation. In the harsher economic climate of the 1980s, it became, however, more common for several federations to reject the solution of the confederations and to force more favourable wage numbers through a strike, often long. The general solutions reached at the incomes policy negotiations of 1995 and 1997 were, however, protected with a clause providing that the whole solution would fall through if after the federation-level negotiations all the confederations were not able to agree that virtually all negotiations had led to collective agreements in accordance with the solution.

363. In cases where the confederations are not able to agree on a general solution, the next step consists of bargaining at the federation level. Now the federations have freer hands; although in practice the difference may not be so great, as the real economic possibilities must – or at least should – be taken into account in this case, too, and the organs of incomes policy may present their recommendations and persuasions also to the federation-level negotiators. The negotiations are often prolonged as it may be difficult to find the 'end opener', i.e., an employees' federation willing to conclude its agreement before the others; but after an end opener of sufficient importance has been found, the other federations often know that it is futile – or at least very difficult – to try to achieve a substantially better solution, and so the end opener is usually followed closely by several other federations, making the agreement network fairly complete within a period of some weeks.

364. Collective bargaining negotiations are at the confederation and federation levels conducted by the grand and small delegations, etc., mentioned in describing the institutionalized relations at these levels. The official aim of both negotiating parties is generally to agree on a new agreement without needing to terminate the previous agreement by means of notice. In order to facilitate the attainment of this aim, in case the last possible notice day is approaching but a new agreement has not yet been concluded, it is common for the federations to agree to postpone the notice day, usually by one month. Nevertheless, it quite often happens that this additional month, too, passes with no agreement, with the result that the notice to terminate the existing agreement is served. Despite the notice, negotiations continue; and even when no solution is reached before the existing agreement expires, the negotiations are regularly still continued. The work, too, continues despite the end of the agreement period; the slogan 'no contract, no work' is unknown in Finland (although local 'accelerating strikes' may occur – before or after the end of the agreement period – if the employers' side is felt to be retarding the negotiations). But if even the extended negotiations remain fruitless, eventually one of the parties – usually the employees' side – declares the negotiations broken off. Now each of the parties can proceed by other means, e.g., by threatening with an industrial action; but now is also the time for the mediation machinery to start to function.

C. *Approval and Conclusion*

365. The fact that the negotiators of both parties have come to an agreement does not yet imply that a new collective agreement has been concluded. Negotiators often have no authority to accept and sign the result of the bargaining before it has been endorsed by the council or the board of the federation concerned. The bargaining result may also be balloted upon by the members at large. In some employee federations, such balloting follows as a matter of course, before any collective agreement is signed, while most federations institute balloting only as regards the initiation or calling off of a strike. An agreement proposal presented by a conciliator may also be balloted upon, the board or council of the federation recommending its adoption or rejection or declining to make any recommendation. Even a result of negotiations between the bargaining parties may, however, be presented for a ballot with a recommendation to reject it: 'This is the best agreement that can be achieved without a strike; we do not recommend it to be adopted; but it is for you members to decide.' According to the statutes of the blue-collar federations, a majority of two-thirds of votes cast is generally required for the initiation or continuation of a strike. If such a majority is not achieved, the result implies an authority or even a mandate to sign the agreement.

366. The paper eventually signed by the representatives of the parties does not in general comprise a complete collective agreement. Instead, it only relates to the changes made in the collective agreement of the preceding period. A complete agreement text is subsequently compiled by officials of both federations. The compilation is then usually printed and used by the employers, employees, and their organizations as the collective agreement for the period in question.

§2. COLLECTIVE AGREEMENTS LAW

367. The history of Finnish collective agreements law has already been described in brief. So have several aspects of the present law, especially collective agreements as a source of employment terms.

I. Notion

368. For an agreement to be a collective agreement under the Collective Agreements Act (and thus to have the legal effects of a collective agreement), certain requirements as to its parties and its contents must be met. As to the parties, a collective agreement may on the employer side be concluded either by an employers' association or by an employer ('company agreement'. On the employee side, a collective agreement can only be concluded by a trade union. As to the contents, the agreement must set conditions to be observed in employment contracts or otherwise in employment relationships. The agreement may in addition contain other provisions, but if it does not include a single employment term to be observed in employment relationships between an employer and at least some of his employees, it is not a collective agreement. (Accordingly, an agreement purporting to regulate solely relations between associations is not a collective agreement.)

II. Scope

369. The scope of a collective agreement primarily comprises those bound by the agreement under the Collective Agreements Act: the parties, the member associations (employers' associations and trade unions), the member employers and employees, and the parent associations (employers' associations and trade unions), as shown in the figures The effect of a collective agreement is, however, very different on the different categories of those bound by the agreement. The employment terms set in the agreement shall be observed in employment relationships between employers and employees bound by the agreement. The parties to a collective agreement may find themselves, in general, shouldering any obligations they choose. As to the member and parent associations, the Collective Agreements Act confers on them certain rights and duties, notably the peace obligation and the surveillance obligation, immediately upon the conclusion of the collective agreement without any express clause in the agreement. But the collective agreement parties have a very limited competence to adopt agreement clauses which would be binding upon the member associations, and no such competence in regard to the parent associations.

370. A collective agreement often has effects extending outside the sphere of those bound by the agreement. An employer bound by the agreement shall apply the agreement terms upon employees not bound by the agreement ('wild employees'), and in certain cases, the agreement may confer not only rights but also duties on such employees. Certain collective agreements are extended to be applied by employers not bound by the agreement according to the Collective Agreements Act ('wild employers'), but, as a general rule, the employees of such an employer derive rights only and no duties from the agreement, disregarding whether they are bound by the agreement under the Collective Agreements Act. However, the scope of a collective agreement under the Collective Agreements Act – but not its extension to wild employers – can be restricted in the agreement itself; and further restrictions may be brought forth in case several collective agreements purport to regulate the same employment relationship.

III. Parties

371. In order to be able to conclude a collective agreement, an employers' association or a trade union must be a registered association under the Associations Act. Furthermore, in order to qualify as an employers' association or trade union, the association must have the furtherance of employers' or employees' interests in employment relationships as one of its essential objects. The furtherance of employers' or employees' interests, as the case may be, thus need not be the sole object of the association, but it must be one of its essential objects mentioned in its statutes. (According to the Associations Act, every registered association must have statutes, and the required contents of the statutes include the object or objects of the association.). Any employer capable of concluding employment contracts may conclude a company agreement with a trade union, but the employer part of a company agreement can have no 'member associations' or 'member employers' bound by the agreement.

372. There may be more parties than one on either side – or on both sides – of a collective agreement. On the employer side, the agreement may thus be concluded by one or more employers, by one or more employers' associations, or by one or more employers together with one or more employers' associations. On the employee side, the parties, one or more, must all be trade unions. It is also possible for a party, capable of concluding a collective agreement, to accede to an existing agreement, provided that the accession is accepted by all the previous parties to the agreement. These requirements fulfilled, the acceding party comes to a position vis-à-vis the agreement equal to that of the original parties. But if the consent of all previous parties is not acquired – e.g., when an unorganized employer agrees with an employees' federation that the collective agreement concluded by the federation with an employers' federation shall be applied in the employer's enterprise – the operation does not result in a single collective agreement with several parties but in two separate collective agreements with identical contents but different parties.

IV. Form and Interpretation

373. In order to be valid, a collective agreement shall be concluded in writing. This requirement is obviously met when the agreement articles are signed by duly authorized representatives of both parties. But the Collective Agreements Act provides for an alternative manner in which the requirement of written form can be fulfilled: the agreement terms may be entered in a record over the agreement negotiations and the record certified in a manner agreed to by the parties. To comply with this alternative form, it is not necessary that the record be certified in writing by representatives of the parties. For example, if the parties to a conciliation procedure orally agree on employment terms and likewise orally entrust to the conciliator the certification of the record over the procedure, the form requirement is met with the record signed only by the conciliator. An accession to a collective agreement shall be both made in writing and accepted in writing by the former parties to the agreement.

374. Within one month after a collective agreement has been concluded, a copy of it shall be sent to the Ministry of Social Affairs and Health by the employer side. A notification shall also be sent to the ministry within one month if a new association or employer accedes to a collective agreement or if the business of an employer, party to a company agreement, is transferred (whereby the successor *ipso jure* becomes a party to the agreement. The fulfilment of this duty is not a form requirement: an omission does not affect the validity of the agreement, the accession or the succession. The copies and notifications received by the Ministry of Social Affairs and Health are kept and registered by the office of the National Conciliators.

375. The requirement of a written form does not imply that the contents of a collective agreement must be found in a single document. References in a local collective agreement to an industry- or craft-wide agreement and in an industry-wide agreement to the agreement of another industry or craft have already been mentioned. There is no doubt as to the validity of such references. Collective agreements often include references to pieces of legislation: entire statutes or separate provisions in statutes. There has been some doubt as to the effects of such references: whether the statutory provisions referred to receive all the legal effects of collective agreement provisions, some of them only or none at all. The present situation is that the references are construed liberally, so as to place the statutory provisions as far as possible on the same level as the literal contents of the collective agreement. This consequence can, however, be avoided with an express clause to this effect in the collective agreement.

376. The interpretation of collective agreement clauses is not limited to the literal contents of the agreement either. The main emphasis is placed on the common intention of the parties, and the general principles for the interpretation of contracts are also applied in other respects. In the words of Professor Folke Schmidt, these general principles can be expressed in the way that interpretation principles are maxims for negotiators: with the aid of these principles, the party is selected which shall bear the adverse effects of the fact that a contract clause was not clarified sufficiently during the course of the negotiations which led to the conclusion of the contract. One of the most important of these principles or maxims is the rule *contra proferentem*: an ambiguous clause can be interpreted to the disadvantage of the party which proposed the wording (except where the other party should have comprehended the real intent of the proposing party). To assist in the application of a collective agreement, the agreement parties often draw up and publish common advisory remarks to the agreement. Sometimes these remarks are negotiated and agreed upon together with the agreement clauses concerned, and in such a case there is obviously no doubt as to their authority. But even when the remarks are drawn up and published only by the offices of the contracting parties subsequent to the conclusion of the agreement, the remarks are in general accorded a decisive importance in the interpretation of the agreement. The agreement parties also have an interpretation monopoly in the sense that if they agree on an interpretation, this interpretation shall in general be accepted by their member associations, employers and employees, even though it does not in fact correspond to any common intention at the stage when the agreement was originally drawn up and concluded.

V. Period

377. A collective agreement may be concluded for a definite or indefinite period. An agreement concluded for a definite period ceases to have effect as a collective agreement at the close of the stipulated period. An upper length for the agreement period has been provided for in that if the period has been stipulated to exceed four years, on the expiration of the four years, the agreement shall be treated as an agreement concluded for an indefinite period. If no definite agreement period has been stipulated, the agreement is regarded to have been concluded for an indefinite period. Such an agreement is terminated by way of notice. The period of notice may be stipulated in the agreement; but in default of an express stipulation, the notice period shall be three months. To be effective, notice shall be served in writing.

378. The agreement periods in common use have already been mentioned as well as the common – but not universal – stipulation that despite the end of the agreement period, the agreement terms shall be observed until a new agreement has been concluded or the agreement negotiations have broken down. Another common stipulation is that a party giving notice of termination shall enclose proposals for a new agreement; if the stipulation is neglected, the notice is without effect.

VI. Agreement Clauses

379. Clauses in collective agreements are commonly divided into two groups: normative clauses and obligatory clauses. Normative clauses are those referred to in the definition of the collective agreement as concerning conditions to be observed in employment contracts or otherwise in employment relationships. Normative clauses are thus norms for – or contents of – a legal relationship (the employment relationship) other than that (the collective agreement relationship) based on the collective agreement. Normative clauses are, further, one of the distinctive traits without which no agreement can be a collective agreement. Obligatory clauses are such clauses which derive their binding force immediately from the collective agreement itself, without needing another contractual relationship as their substratum. In this sense, the obligatory clauses are like the ordinary clauses in any contract, and like any contract clauses, they can, with some minor exceptions, create rights and duties for the agreement parties only.

A. *Normative Clauses*

1. Individual and Solidary Norms

380. Normative clauses in collective agreements are commonly divided into two categories, individual norms and solidary norms. This distinction is seen to have its statutory basis in the definition of the collective agreement referring separately to conditions to be observed in 'employment contracts' and 'otherwise in employment relationships'. Individual norms are such clauses which really could be entered in employment contracts concluded separately between an employer and each of his individual employees. Individual norms can thus concern such matters as wage rates, working time, sickness leave, annual holidays, termination of employment, etc. Individual norms can create obligations for both the employer and the employee vis-à-vis each other. Solidary norms regulate the relationship between an employer and his employees – or a part of them – as a group. Any clauses with the contents of solidary norms would not normally be entered into an individual employment contract. Solidary norms can only create obligations for the employer vis-à-vis his employees; under the Collective Agreements Act, it is not possible to create solidary obligations for the employees vis-à-vis their employer. The example which earlier was usually given for solidary norms comprised agreement clauses on washing facilities, canteens, etc., to be provided by the employer in the workplace. There is no doubt as to the validity of agreement clauses of this kind. Another type of solidary norms comprises clauses creating obligations for the employer to facilitate the management of the common interest of employees, e.g., to provide facilities for shop stewards. It is difficult to draw a line between valid solidary norms of this kind and clauses purporting to regulate relations between employers and trade unions and hence invalid (except in company agreements). The Labour Court has, however, considered such clauses valid in which the employers have been obliged to allow representatives of the employee federation to enter and inspect the workplaces. The construction is evidence that the employer does not owe this duty to the employees' federation but to his own employees in whose interest the representatives of the federation are presumed to act.

2. General Applicability of Various Kinds of Norms

381. If a collective agreement is generally applicable, it is beyond doubt that all its individual norms – as far as they impose duties on the employer – shall be applied without regard to whether the employer is bound by the agreement by virtue of the Collective Agreements Act or by virtue of the general (extended) applicability only, but it is a disputed question whether and to what extent the general applicability also covers the solidary norms. The prevailing opinion seems to be that such solidary norms which do not presuppose the existence of organized activity on the employee side – such as the clauses on washing facilities, etc. – are applicable also in the general applicability sphere, while the opposite is true in regard to clauses concerning the representation of employees at the workplace or anything dependent on such representation.

3. Employers' Relations with Outsiders

382. An employer's relations with persons not in his service are ultra vires for the collective agreement parties to regulate (except as far as such regulation is now made possible under the Cooperation Within Undertakings Act. Collective agreement clauses purporting to tell employers to whom to sell their products and at what price, etc., are thus invalid. But clauses concerning employment conditions may in fact restrict the employers' freedom of action in relation to other independent contractors. A clause obliging employers to treat all plumbing work of one building project as a single object in piece-work contracts has thus been regarded as valid even though it has, in fact, prevented employers from accepting orders to execute a part only of the plumbing work of a building project as well as from subcontracting such a part to another independent contractor. More recent legislation on the freedom of competition may, however, make such clauses invalid. The Paper and Pulp Agreement used to reserve permanent maintenance tasks in factories for the own employees of the factory and thus to prohibit employers from using outside contractors for such tasks; and the Labour Court earlier upheld this prohibition. In a suit brought by a cleaning firm, however, the Supreme Administrative Court – which is the highest instance in cases concerning the regulation of competition – in 1995 held that the collective agreement clause violated the freedom of competition and was hence invalid. Thereafter, the Labour Court took the same position.

4. Obligatory and Empowering Clauses

383. Some clauses in collective agreements are obligatory – and ultra vires – from one aspect and normative – and valid – from another. For example, as far as clauses regulating the grievance procedure purport to impose duties on the negotiating parties, they do not concern duties of the parties of employment relationships to each other, and from this aspect, such clauses are obligatory and do not bind the negotiating parties (except the collective agreement parties themselves). But if grievance negotiations are in fact conducted according to the clauses and a result is achieved, the result does concern employment conditions, and therefore, the clauses on grievance negotiations can be regarded as normative clauses as far as they empower the negotiators to decide the questions submitted to them under the clauses; and the result itself is binding on the employer and employees concerned as if it had been written in the collective agreement. Similarly, when collective agreement clauses on meetings at workplaces include provisions to be observed in requisitioning meeting space and conducting meetings, such provisions do not impose any duties on employees collectively or their local organizations, but the observance of these provisions is a precondition on the employer's duty under the agreement to provide meeting space.

5. Cooperation Agreements

384. Certain agreements concluded under the Cooperation Within Undertakings Act have the legal effects which collective agreements have under the Collective Agreements Act. This rule seems to signify, *inter alia*, that agreement clauses adopted under this rule are binding on the employers and employees concerned – and perhaps even on the associations concerned – without regard to the classification of agreement clauses under the Collective Agreements Act. Obligatory clauses would thus be binding even on member employers and employees, solidary norms on employees collectively, and all – or some – kinds of agreement clauses perhaps also on member associations.

6. Recommendations

385. In collective agreements, the parties sometimes undertake to recommend a certain course of action to their members. Such a recommendation is sometimes used when it would not be within the competence of the parties to impose a duty on the members to act as envisaged. For example if employees have been dismissed during a strike, the agreement terminating the strike often includes a recommendation for the member employers to reinstate the dismissed employees. As reinstatement could not be a term of any existing employment relationship, a clause obliging employers to reinstate former employees would be an obligatory clause and hence ultra vires for an employers' association to agree to. Recommendations are, however, also used where a normative clause would also be completely valid: the agreement parties have chosen not to make it a contractual duty for the member employers or employees to observe the clause in question. A recommendation can often be regarded as involving not only a duty for the agreement parties to communicate the recommendation to their members but also an engagement to take steps to induce the members to act as recommended.

B. Obligatory Clauses

386. Vis-à-vis each other, collective agreement parties may shoulder any obligations which are valid under the general law of contracts. In a company agreement, the employer may thus undertake the reinstate former employees and parties to collective agreements may commit themselves to observe certain rules in their negotiations. But if an agreement clause would have nothing whatsoever to do with labour relations, it could hardly have the specific legal effects of collective agreement clauses, even if situated in a collective agreement (having at least one normative clause and concluded between parties capable of concluding collective agreements). To take an extreme example, if a clause in a collective agreement provides for a sale of a piece of real estate between the agreement parties, any disputes concerning such a clause could not be heard and tried by the Labour Court.

387. Confederation-wide general and specific agreements regularly include provisions for the member federations as well as for their member employers and employees to observe. Under their statutes, the confederations have, however, no general power to make agreements engaging the member federations and their members. It is, therefore, sometimes stipulated in a confederation-wide agreement that it is only to be applied by member federations and their members in so far as it is so agreed in the (federation-wide) collective agreements concerned. It is, however, also possible under the statutes of the confederations to stipulate in a confederation-wide agreement that it becomes binding on the member federations and their members as far as the federations concerned do not declare within a stated time (not less than two weeks) that they will remain outside the agreement. But it is common also under such an agreement for the member federations (not having filed a declaration of non-acceptance) to incorporate the confederation-wide agreement, by reference, in their collective agreements. Even without such a reference, the normative clauses of the confederation-wide agreement would become binding on the member employers and employees concerned; but an explicit incorporation is needed for the obligatory clauses to become binding on the member federations.

VII. Statutory Effects: Labour Peace and Surveillance

388. An important aspect of Finnish collective agreements law consists of the statutory effects collective agreements have without any explicit base in the agreement text and even in spite of any contrary clause in the agreement. The most significant of these statutory effects are the peace obligation and the surveillance obligation as well as the statutory remedies – to be discussed later – for violations of statutory as well as contractual duties based on collective agreement. The origin of the peace obligation can be seen in the collective agreement as a peace – or truce – treaty in industrial warfare, the employer party undertaking to respect certain minimum wages and other employment terms for a certain period of time against the agreement of the employee party not to use methods of industrial warfare during the same period of time in order to extract more favourable employment terms. But in law, both aspects of the collective agreement concern both sides. The employees, as well as the employers, have to observe the employment terms embodied in the agreement, and both are equally bound to respect industrial peace. The peace obligation comprises two subcategories: the passive and the active peace obligation. The passive peace obligation consists of the duty to refrain from industrial actions directed against the collective agreement. The active peace obligation implies the duty to ensure that members refrain from such actions. The surveillance obligation comprises the duty to ensure that members do not violate any provisions in the collective agreement.

A. Scope

389. The passive peace obligation is incumbent upon all those who are bound by a collective agreement according to the Collective Agreements Act except the individual employees. The passive peace obligation thus encompasses the agreement parties (employers' associations and trade unions as well as, in company agreements, employers), the member associations (employers' associations and trade unions), the member employers, and the parent associations (employers' associations and trade unions). The active peace obligation and the surveillance obligation are incumbent upon all the employers' associations and trade unions bound by the collective agreement except the parent associations. The two obligations thus encompass the employers' associations and trade unions which are parties to the agreement or which are bound by it as member associations. It is to be noted that even though individual employees have no duty to refrain from industrial actions, their trade unions have a duty to see to it that their members do not engage in industrial actions directed against the collective agreement.

390. There is no peace obligation outside the scope of the collective agreement according to the Collective Agreements Act: although a collective agreement may be extended under the Employment Contracts Act to a 'wild employer', the peace obligation is not extended, and thus it is possible even for a trade union bound by the agreement to engage in an industrial action against a wild employer in order to exact more favourable employment terms than those the employer shall observe by virtue of the extended agreement. As to the surveillance duty, the Employment Contracts Act entrusts the supervision of the application of the act not only to the labour protection authorities but also to the parties to the extended collective agreement in question; but despite the words of the statute, the associations hardly have any duties in this respect, nor any other rights than to demand that the labour protection authorities pay due attention to any defects on which the agreement parties inform them.

B. Industrial Action

391. For behaviour to be of a kind which is forbidden under the passive peace obligation and must be suppressed under the active peace obligation, two conditions must be met. It must be an industrial action, and it must be directed against the collective agreement as a whole, or against a provision in it. Neither of these concepts has a statutory definition. The notion of industrial action does not comprise only such overt actions as strikes and lock-outs. Also included are overtime bans, go-slows, blockades, mass resignations, mass dismissals, etc., in short, all concerted actions of employees or actions directed against a group of employees, undertaken in order to exert pressure against the opposite party in labour relations. Even a mere threat to employ industrial action is itself an industrial action if it is, with reason, taken as real by the opposite party. It was earlier a disputed question whether only actions executed in some connection with employment relationships can be regarded as industrial actions or whether, e.g., a boycott instituted against the business operations of an employer by a trade union (urging members and friends to avoid patronizing the employer's enterprise) can be included in the concept. The Labour Court has held for the latter alternative.

C. *Actions Violating the Peace Obligation*

392. When is an industrial action directed against a collective agreement as a whole or against a provision in it? The most obvious case is the use of an industrial action in order to compel the opposite party to a modification of the collective agreement currently in force. But it is not necessary that an express modification is striven for: it suffices that there is an endeavour for the opposite party to be compelled to deviate factually from the agreement terms, e.g., to pay higher, or to acquiesce to lower, wages than those set in the agreement. And the requirement itself need not be against the agreement: wage provisions in collective agreements are in general minimum requirements only, allowing employers to exceed them; but if a demand for a wage rise is supported by force, the peace obligation is violated. Furthermore, it does not help if the party resorting to an industrial action believes itself to be lawfully entitled to the benefits demanded, not even if this belief turns out to be correct: disputes over rights shall be decided by judicial means and not by recourse to force. (But if there is no genuine dispute over rights, e.g., if an employer just lacks the means to pay wages undisputedly due, an action in order to compel the opposite party to honour such obligations is not directed against the collective agreement.) As long as a collective agreement is in force, an action to influence the contents of a future agreement is directed against the corresponding clause – if any – in the existing agreement. Some Labour Court judgments have been regarded to entail that industrial action could be directed against a collective agreement provision not only when it is sought to influence employment conditions embodied in the provision but also when the action as such violates the provision (e.g., that an overtime ban would be directed against an agreement clause on the duty to perform overtime work); but the judgments in question seem open to other interpretations as well.

393. The peace obligation is relative in the sense that if an industrial action has nothing to do with a collective agreement, it does not violate the peace obligation connected with that agreement. The present-day collective agreements are, however, so comprehensive than an industrial action concerned with the participants' own employment terms can hardly ever be considered not to be directed against their collective agreement, as long as 'the' collective agreement for the agreement period is in force but after that agreement has expired, the continuing validity of (confederation-wide) general or specific agreements does not preclude industrial actions not bearing upon the narrower range of matters regulated in such agreements. But during the existence of the comprehensive collective agreement for the agreement period, the possibility to institute lawful industrial actions is essentially limited to actions not connected with own employment terms. There are two main occurrences of such actions: sympathetic actions and political actions.

394. A sympathetic action is an industrial action instituted for the benefit of employers or employees other than those engaged in the action. To qualify for this exemption from the peace obligation, the action must be purely sympathetic. This entails that the action, even if successful, must in no way affect the employment terms of the participants: when the action is over, their employment terms must remain the same as they were before the action. Moreover, even a purely sympathetic action is regarded as directed against the participants' own collective agreement, if the action is instituted for the benefit of such parties which are themselves in breach of the peace obligation. Just as a sympathetic action in this way shares the destiny of the supported action, so does a counteraction share the destiny of the opposed action: e.g., a lock-out instituted as a countermeasure against a strike is considered to be directed against the same agreement provisions – if any – which the strike was directed against.

395. A political action may be a short demonstration to express dissatisfaction with the acts or omissions of any public authorities, domestic or foreign. It may also be of a longer duration, intended not only to show the opinion of the participants but also to exert real pressure on the political decision-makers. According to the prevailing opinion, at least partly corroborated by court decisions, political actions do not violate the peace obligation.

D. *Supervision Duties*

396. The active peace obligation and the surveillance obligation do not involve a guarantee that the members observe the labour peace and the agreement terms, respectively. Utmost care must be taken to ensure that the members behave as required, but if all reasonable steps to this end have been taken and the members nevertheless misbehave, the association is free from responsibility. The reasonable steps include, *inter alia*, that the association keeps organs and officials capable of acting with an efficiency and speed usual in comparable circumstances. A tight inspection scheme is not required, but if complaints are presented from the opposite side that a member is in breach of the labour peace or of the agreement clauses, it is not enough just to trust in the member's assurances that everything is in order; the association must itself ascertain the situation and make its moves on that basis. It goes without saying that the supervision of labour peace is the more exacting duty for the trade unions and the supervision of the observance of agreement terms for the employers' associations. Associations having member associations shall also see to it that the member associations fulfil their own supervision duties. For example, an employees' federation shall ensure not only that the local trade unions concerned and their members do not engage in industrial actions against the collective agreement but also that the local trade unions supervise their members. The surveillance duty of the associations which are parties to the collective agreement is now defined in a clause inserted in the Collective Agreements Act in 1984. Such an association is deemed to have neglected its surveillance duty if a clear and undisputed agreement clause has not been applied in a manner which corresponds to a unanimous opinion of the agreement parties and the wrong application is not rectified swiftly, under the circumstances, after the association became aware of it.

E. *Freedom of Agreement*

397. The statutory peace and surveillance obligations are mandatory. They cannot be curtailed by agreement. The agreement parties themselves may enlarge their own obligations, e.g., by guaranteeing absolutely that their members observe the labour peace or by extending the coverage of the peace obligation to, e.g., sympathetic or political actions. It is not, however, possible for the agreement parties to enlarge the statutory duties of the member associations or member employers in any way or to engage individual employees in any personal responsibility for the observance of labour peace. Agreement clauses concerning the peace or surveillance obligation have no effect in the sphere of general (extended) application of a collective agreement.

VIII. Violations and Remedies

398. There is no official supervision of the observance of duties based on collective agreements except as far as the general (extended) application of certain collective agreements is supervised by the labour protection authorities. Instead, the obligations based on collective agreements are in principle enforced like any contractual duties: the wronged side may ask for the fulfilment of the neglected obligation or for another remedy. The remedies are, however, not quite the same as for ordinary contracts.

A. *Compensatory Fine*

399. The most important remedy is the compensatory fine, to be paid by the violator to the wronged party. Such a fine is inflicted upon an employer or employee who wittingly violates the provisions of a collective agreement or who with reason should have known that he violates such provisions, and upon an association – except a parent association – or employer which intentionally or negligently violates the statutory duties: the peace obligation or the surveillance obligation. All the circumstances of the case should be taken into account, in particular, the extent of the damage and the degree of guilt shown.

400. Statutory compensatory fines for violations of collective agreement clauses can only be inflicted on employers and employees, never on employers' associations or trade unions, not even in cases where the agreement clauses themselves are binding on the associations. It has been a disputed question whether a statutory compensatory fine can be inflicted on an employer for a violation of employment terms (normative clauses) only or also for a violation of obligatory clauses (where, as in the case of a company agreement, such clauses are binding on the employer). The answer of the Labour Court is that a compensatory fine can be inflicted if the obligatory clause can only be violated by an employer and not by an employers' association (e.g., a clause providing for reinstatement), but not if the clause could be violated by an employers' association as well (e.g., a clause extending the statutory peace obligation. The compensatory fines are not extended to the sphere of the general (extended) applicability of collective agreements. Obligations based on general applicability are enforced like any obligations based on employment contracts between individual employers and employees.

401. A compensatory fine for a breach of the peace obligation or the surveillance obligation is imposed in lieu of any damages. The amount of the compensatory fine is not limited to the actual damage (if any), but no compensation can be granted in excess of the compensatory fine (limited by the statutory maximum), no matter how big the actual damages are. Direct damage caused in connection with an industrial action (e.g., by letting a blast furnace cool down in an irregular manner) or with another violation of collective agreement duties may, however, give rise to a compensation claim within the individual employment relationship concerned.

402. It is possible to modify the statutory provision on compensatory fines by agreement. It is thus possible to lower the statutory maxima, increase the statutory maxima for violations of agreement terms, replace compensatory fines with compensation for actual damages, remove the compensatory fines for some or all kinds of violations, etc. It is not, however, possible to provide for an elevation of the statutory maximum for a violation of the peace or surveillance obligation, except in so far as to provide for compensation of the actual damages in excess of the maximum. It is possible to provide for a compensatory fine or another remedy for a violation of an obligatory clause, but such a fine or remedy can only be recovered from a party to the agreement.

B. Rescission

403. A collective agreement can be rescinded if the agreement has been violated to such a degree that those bound by the agreement on the opposite side cannot reasonably be required to continue to be bound by the agreement. Unlike other contractual relationships, a collective agreement, however, cannot be rescinded with a unilateral declaration by the wronged party to the opposite party but only by a court order, issued upon an action brought by the wronged party at the Labour Court. In deciding whether a collective agreement shall be declared rescinded, any violation of the duties of a parent association shall also be taken into account, even though no compensatory fine can be recovered from such an association. The statutory provisions on rescission cannot be modified by agreement: even when the remedy of a compensatory fine has been totally suppressed, the remedy of rescission is always available in the eventuality of very grave breaches. Actions for rescission are, however, extremely rare, since the interests of the wronged party seldom require a mutual release from the agreement duties (and since the suppression of compensatory fines by agreement is also very rare).

404. By virtue of the court order, the collective agreement is terminated with an immediate effect on the agreement parties concerned and in regard to members, etc., deriving their position from those parties. If the agreement had more parties than one on either side or on both sides, the rescission order has no immediate effect on relationships between other agreement parties than the successful plaintiff and the losing defendant. Such a plaintiff is, however, entitled to terminate the agreement in relation to any or all parties of the same agreement side as the defendant. All parties on the same agreement side as the plaintiff are also entitled to terminate the agreement in relation to the losing defendant as well as to any or all parties on the same agreement side as the defendant. Notice to terminate the agreement can only be served within two weeks after the rescission order was rendered, and it takes effect immediately. There is no corresponding right to serve notice in the opposite direction. All derivative relationships, concerning members, etc., follow the destiny of the relationship between the agreement parties concerned.

Chapter 5. Industrial Action

405. It is customary to refer to the 'rules of the game' played in the industrial relations playground. The current Finnish rules allow the use of methods intended to coerce or induce the opposite party to concessions, but only under certain important restrictions, notably the peace obligation under the Collective Agreements Act and the provisions of the Mediation in Labour Disputes Act on notice and deferment of labour stoppages. It used to be common to take a moral view of the rules of the game, considering their observance to be required for fair play, but just as in sports, the attitude has been gaining ground (but not the whole ground) that the rules can be violated if the risk of getting caught and penalized is small enough in comparison with the gain foreseen. This development was for a long time accentuated by the erosion of the real value of the main penalty involved, the compensatory fine under the Collective Agreements Act.

§1. Kinds of Industrial Action

406. Industrial actions are classified on several grounds. An action involving a total cessation of work (of all or some employees) is either a strike or a lock-out. A strike may be effected either by vacating the workplace or by remaining there without doing work (sit-down strike). As already mentioned, industrial actions short of a total cessation of work, such as overtime bans, go-slows, blockades and mere threats to institute a strike, a lock-out, or any other industrial action, can violate the peace obligation just as strikes and lock-outs. The same would apply to work-ins, where the employees continue to work despite the employer's order to stop working (although the conformity of the only such known case with the peace obligation was never investigated). The distinction between total cessations of work and other methods of industrial action is, however, material under the Mediation in Labour Disputes Act: a notice over a contemplated industrial action need only be given concerning 'stoppages of work', and only such actions can be deferred for another fortnight. An overtime ban, e.g., may thus be begun without any notice either to the opposite party or to a conciliator; nor can such an action be ordered to be deferred.

407. A legal industrial action is an action undertaken in conformity with the 'rules of the game'. An action violating the peace obligation is an illegal industrial action. The term 'wildcat strike' has no precise denotation, but typically this expression is used for an illegal strike, undertaken at a local level by a group of employees without the consent of their union. In the distinction between legal and illegal action, it is unclear where to place actions not violating the peace obligation under the Collective Agreements Act but begun contrary to the provisions on notice or deferment in the Mediation in Labour Disputes Act. It is often contended that these provisions are rules of order only and that while it is a misdemeanour to omit the notice or to disregard a deferment, such an omission does not make the action itself illegal. However, the Employment Contracts Act makes the employer's right to dismiss employees on strike as well as the right of a locked-out employee to rescind his employment contract dependent also on whether or not the said provisions of the Mediation in Labour Disputes Act have been complied with. A strike undertaken neither in violation of the peace obligation under the Collective Agreements Act or a collective agreement nor in disregard of the notice or deferment provisions of the Mediation in Labour Disputes Act is never a valid ground for dismissal, but a strike not fulfilling these conditions may, depending upon the circumstances in the actual case, be regarded as a 'serious ground' entitling the employer to rescind the employee's contract of employment. And while an employee need not refer to any specific ground in order to give notice to terminate an employment contract concluded for an indefinite period, a lock-out may be regarded as a 'serious ground' permitting him to rescind his contract – without regard to whether it has been concluded for a definite or for an indefinite period – with immediate effect only if the lock-out has been undertaken in violation of the peace obligation or in disregard of the notice or deferment provisions of the Mediation in Labour Disputes Act. As industrial actions short of a complete stoppage of work are not within the purview of the notice and deferment provisions of the Mediation in Labour Disputes Act, such actions may only be used as a ground for dismissal – or as a ground for an employee to rescind his contract with an immediate effect, as the case may be – if they are undertaken in violation of the peace obligation under the Collective Agreements Act or under the provisions of a collective agreement and if, in addition, they can in the circumstances be regarded as 'serious grounds'.

408. The distinction between legal and illegal industrial actions does not coincide with the well-known distinction between disputes over rights and disputes over interests. As long as a comprehensive collective agreement is in force, the peace obligation covers virtually – but not quite – all disputes over rights as well as virtually – but not quite – all disputes over interests. In fact, many industrial actions violating the peace obligation arise in connection with disputes over interests: a typical wildcat strike is undertaken to back a wage demand exceeding the wage rates in the current collective agreement (and without even asserting any legal right to the wage rise). And when no collective agreement is in force, industrial actions – provided that the provisions on notice and deferment in the Mediation in Labour Disputes Act are observed as far as they are applicable – may be undertaken in disputes over rights as well as in disputes over interests, with the possible exception of disputes over claims based (directly and not solely because of the after-effect) on the provisions of an expired collective agreement.

§2. Statistics

409. Finland is a rather – but not exceptionally – strike-prone country. However, the impact of industrial actions varies greatly from year to year, as Table 8 shows. The number of industrial actions in 2016 was sixty-nine. This was less than in 2015. The number of industrial actions was then 163. Working days lost in 2016 amounted to 6,584.

Table 8 Impact of Industrial Action

Year	Industrial Actions	Employees Involved, Thousands	Working Days Lost		
			Number Thousands	Per Action	Per 1,000 Employed Persons
1971	838	403	2,711	3,235	1,250
1972	849	240	473	557	217
1973	1,009	678	2,497	2,475	1,127
1974	1,788	371	435	243	191
1975	1,530	215	284	186	128
1976	3,282	513	1,326	404	613
1977	1,673	744	2,375	1,419	1,124
1978	1,237	165	132	107	63
1979	1,753	229	243	139	108
1980	2,238	413	1,606	717	690
1981	1,612	493	659	409	283
1982	1,240	168	208	167	87
1983	1,940	422	720	371	301
1984	1,710	563	1,527	893	633
1985	848	171	174	206	72
1986	1,225	603	2,789	2,276	1,147
1987	802	99	131	163	54
1988	1,353	244	179	133	74
1989	629	158	204	325	83
1990	455	245	935	2,055	379
1991	284	167	458	1,614	196
1992	168	104	76	453	35
1993	126	23	17	137	8
1994	171	71	525	3,074	260
1995	112	127	869	7,763	414
1996	94	43	20	213	9
1997	91	28	103	1,139	48

410. In 2020, there were 108 industrial actions. About 19,000 employees were involved and working days lost about 176,000. As can be seen, it is not so much the number of industrial actions as the number of days lost that varies from year to year.

The years with the largest amounts of days lost are characterized by vast industry-wide conflicts, in 1971, a national metal workers' strike, in 1977, a national technicians' strike, and in 1986 a Government officials' strike. However, the number of days lost has been exceptionally low in years like 1975, 1978, 1982 or 1985, when very few collective agreements expired and the peace obligation accordingly covered most workplaces throughout the year.

In such a year, most industrial actions are wildcat strikes comprising one workplace or a part of it only and lasting but some hours or a couple of days. In fact, every one of the 1,237 registered conflicts in 1978 occurred in a workplace covered by an existing collective agreement, and not one was undertaken with the consent of the national federation concerned. The still lower numbers in 1992 and 1993 than those just mentioned were due to these years' deep depression – which continued even afterwards but was no more able to restrain the readiness for industrial action to the same extent. The almost equally low numbers of 1996 and 1997, again, reflect the exceptionally tight incomes policy which was adopted in 1995. The figures given in the preceding table cover all kinds of industrial actions, whether undertaken by employers or employees and whether involving a complete work stoppage or not. An overwhelming majority of registered conflicts consist, however, of strikes. (Overtime bans and go-slows are, however, only registered in the statistics if they are reported by both parties; such an action reported by the employer side but denied by the employee side remains thus outside the statistics).

411. In the following, statistical figures are given on the impact of industrial actions in different industries. These figures like the preceding ones are based on the detailed labour conflict statistics compiled annually by Statistics Finland (*see* Table 9).

Table 9 Conflicts and Hours Lost

	Number of Conflicts				*Working Hours Lost, Thousands*		
Year	*1994*	*1995*	*1996*	*1997*	*1994*	*1995*	*1996*
Agriculture and forestry	–	–	1	–	–	–	0
Manufacture of consumption goods	6	10	2	7	3,776	9	0
Manufacture of wood and paper products; printing and publishing	52	22	8	25	183	32	8
Metal industries and mining	52	45	48	48	77	51	17
Other manufacturing; gas, electricity and water	46	7	10	3	139	4	7
Construction	2	3	–	–	0	19	–
Wholesale and retail trade	1	2	1	–	0	3	5

	Number of Conflicts				*Working Hours Lost, Thousands*		
Year	*1994*	*1995*	*1996*	*1997*	*1994*	*1995*	*1996*
Restaurants and hotels	–	–	–	–	–	–	–
Transport and communications	14	15	15	2	17	88	24
Financing and insurance	–	2	9	4	–	136	45
Public administration, safety services	–	1	–	2	–	1,113	77
Social and related community services	–	1	–	–	–	5,500	–
Other services	2	3	–	–	92	0	1
Total	173	112	94	91	4,206	6,955	161

§3. Limitations on Industrial Actions

412. President Urho Kekkonen said in a speech at the celebration of the seventieth anniversary of the SAK in 1977 that strike was by now an outmoded weapon in industrial relations. The speech did not contain any suggestion of legal measures to curtail the freedom of industrial action. Such measures have, however, been discussed publicly from time to time, especially after such actions as the technicians' strike in 1977, the hospital nurses' and municipal fire departments' strikes in 1995 and the air controllers' strike in 1999 which caused inconvenience and even danger to the general public (e.g., by disturbing railway traffic and the delivery of electric current). It is in this context often contended that 'small key groups' should not be allowed to create difficulties for the society at large and that it should therefore be possible to enjoin such industrial actions and to refer the wage or other disputes involved to compulsory arbitration. On occasion – especially when threats of general strikes during the depression of the early 1990s prevented the National Government from economic measures diminishing unemployment benefits – the legality of political strikes (cf. paragraph 376, *supra*) has also been questioned. Such discussions and suggestions have, however, remained without result. It is true that on one occasion, the incomes policy solution agreed to by the 'most representative confederations' of employers and employees was by virtue of a special enactment extended to cover the whole labour market despite the fact that it was not accepted by two confederations; but even this sole occasion was probably more a shortcut in negotiations than a real curtailment of the freedom of industrial action. Apart from this sole occasion – and from some not very far-reaching special rules concerning public officials and hence outside the scope of this monograph – the only legal protection of essential services in the event of an industrial action lies in the provisions of the Mediation in Labour Disputes Act allowing a proclaimed stoppage work to be deferred for a fortnight in case where the stoppage is deemed to affect essential functions of the society or to prejudice the general interest to a considerable extent.

Selected Bibliography

Books and Articles

Anttila, Outi, *Kohti tosiasiallista tasa-arvoa? Sukupuolisyrjinnän kiellot oikeudellisen pluralismin aikana* (with an English summary. *Towards Actual Equality?*). Helsinki. Suomalainen Lakimiesyhdistys, 2013.

Bruun, Niklas, *New Forms and Aspects of Atypical Employment Relationships in Finland*, in *XI Congreso internacional del derecho del trabajo y la seguridad social*, Caracas 1988, tema II, Vol. II, pp. 5–26.

Bruun, Niklas, *Some Aspects of Labour Law Research in Finland and Sweden*, in *Labour Law Research in Twelve Countries*, Stockholm, The Swedish Centre for Working Life, 1986, pp. 31–45.

Bruun, Niklas, *The Autonomy of Collective Agreements Työoikeudellisen Yhdistyksen vuosikirja*, 2001–2002.

Bruun, Niklas, Ruth Nielsen and Dennis Töllborg, *Corporate Labour Law in a European and Nordic Perspective*, in *The future of the Nordic model of labour relations*, Copenhagen, NORD, 1993, pp. 165–240.

Bruun, Niklas, Boel Flodgren, Marit Halvorsen, Håkan Hydén and Ruth Nielsen, *The Nordic Labour Relations Model, Labour Law and Trade Unions in the Nordic Countries –Today and Tomorrow*, Aldershot, Dartmouth, 1992.

Esko, Timo, *Lainvalinta ja kansainväliset työsuhteet* (with an English summary: *Choice of Law in International Employment Relationships*), Helsinki, Suomalainen Lakimiesyhdistys, 1985.

Esko, Timo, *The Law Applicable to International Labour Relations*, Helsinki, Institutum Iurisprudentiae Comparativae Universitatis Helsingiensis, 1982.

Hellsten, Jari, *From Internal Market Regulation to European Labour Law*, Helsinki, 2007.

Huttunen, Mikko, *Sportsmen and the Categories of Persons in the Legislation of the European Union Concerning the Free Movement of Persons*, *Tyooikeudellisen Yhdistyksen vuosikirja*, Helsinki, 1995.

Kairinen, Martti, *Perussuhdeteoriasta työoikeuden yleisten oppien osana* (with a German summary: *Über die Grundverhältnistheorie als Teil der allgemeinen Lehren des Arbeitsrechts*), Helsinki, Suomalainen Lakimiesyhdistys, 1979.

Koskinen, Pirkko K., *Työntekijöiden osallistumisesta päätöksentekoon yrityksessä* (with an English summary: *The Co-decision in an Industrial Enterprise*), Porvoo, Werner Söderström, 1973.

Selected Bibliography

Koskinen, Pirkko K., *Flexibilisation of Working Life*, in Finnish national reports to the XVth Congress of the International Academy of Comparative Law (Studia iuridica helsingiensia, Vol. 16), Helsinki, Finnish Lawyers' Publishing, 1998, pp. 143–161.

Koskinen, Pirkko K., *Finnish Law on the Supervision of Safety at Work and Its Sanctions, Scandinavian Studies in Law*, Vol. 24 (1980), pp. 219–232.

Koskinen, Seppo, *Työtaistelu ja työsopimuksen purkaminen* (with an English summary: *Industrial Action and Discharge of the Employment Contract*), Helsinki, Finnish Lawyers' Publishing, 1989.

Lampi, Heimo and Antti Suviranta, *Arbitration and the Role of Courts: The Administration of Justice in Labour Law, National report, International Society for Labour Law and Social Security*, 9th International Congress, Reports and Proceedings, Heidelberg 1978, Vol. II, pp. 118–131.

Lamponen, Helena, *The Principle on Employee Protection in a Merger and a Transfer of an Undertaking*, Helsinki, Yliopistopaino, 2008.

Lamponen, Helena and Jaana Paanetoja, *European Work Councils Finland*, Kluwer 2015.

Liinamaa, Keijo, *Wages Policy: The Role of the State and of the Organizations of Employers and Employees, Rapport National*, in *Actes du VIIe congrès international de droit du travail et de la sécurité sociale*, Varsovie 1973, Vol. III, pp. 169–179.

Modeen, Tore, *The Freedom of the Worker to Organize in Finland, Beiträge zum ausländischen öffentlichen Recht und Völkerrecht*, Vol. 75, part 1 (1980), pp. 223–239.

Murto, Jari, *Ryhmänormit yrityksessä: tutkimus työntekijäryhmiä koskevien normien asemasta* (with an English summary: *So Called Group Norms in Companies*), Helsinki, Suomalainen Lakimiesyhdistys, 2015.

Orasmaa, Pekka, *Labour Courts and Industrial Action, Finland*, in *Proceedings of the third meeting of European labour court judges* (Labour-Management relations series, No. 77), Geneva, ILO, 1993, pp. 19–24.

Paanetoja, Jaana, *Työsuhteista työtä vai työtoimintaa?* (with an English summary: *Working under an Employment Contract vs. Work Activity?* A research on the juridical nature of the work done by the disabled), Helsinki, Suomalainen Lakimiesyhdistys, 2013.

Paanetoja, Jaana, *The Broadening Interpretation of Worker in the European Union*, in. *Development on Labour Law from a Comparative Perspective*, eds. Izabela Florczak and Zbigniew Góral, University of Lódz, Poland, 2015, pp. 25–42.

Pekkanen, Raimo, *Sekatyyppinen työsopimus* (with a German summary: *Der gemischttypische Arbeitsvertrag*), Helsinki, Suomen Lakimiesliiton Kustannus Oy, 1966.

Pelkonen, Jorma and Olli Huopaniemi, *Preparation of the Case for Hearing by the Court*, in *Proceedings of the second meeting of European labour court judges* (Labour-management relations series, No. 70), Geneva, ILO, 1989, pp. 15–17.

Saloheimo, Jorma, *Hallintopakosta työsuojelun valvonnassa* (with a German summary: *Der Verwaltungszwang in der Gewerbeaufsicht*), Helsinki, Suomalainen Lakimiesyhdistys, 1987.

Saloheimo, Jorma, *Flexibility in Working Time*, in The Finnish national reports to the XIIIth Congress of the International Academy of Comparative Law (Studia iuridica helsingiensia, Vol. 14), Helsinki 1990, pp. 64–80.

Sarkko, Kaarlo, *Työrauhavelvollisuudesta* (with an English summary: *The Labour-peace Obligation*), Helsinki, Suomalainen Lakimiesyhdistys, 1969.

Sarkko, Kaarlo, *Codification of Labour Law, National Report*, in *International Society ..., 9th International* Congress, Vol. II, pp. 841–843.

Sarkko, Kaarlo, *The Employee's Responsibility for Industrial Actions, Scandinavian Studies in Law*, Vol. 16 (1972), pp. 253–281.

Sarkko, Kaarlo, *Worker Participation in Decisions Within Undertakings*, in *International Society ..., 10th International Congress*, Vol. 1, pp. 176–180.

Schmidt, Folke, *Law and Industrial Peace, the Scandinavian Approach, Scandinavian Studies in Law*, Vol. 17 (1973), pp. 253–274.

Sigeman, Tore, *Damages and Bot, Remedies for Breach of Collective Agreements in Nordic Law, Scandinavian Studies in Law*, Vol. 29 (1985), pp. 185–212.

Suviranta, Antti, *Acerca del alcance y la imagen del derecho del trabajo*, in *La proteccion del trabajo en el mundo moderno, Obra-homenaje al profesor emérito Dr. Alfredo J. Ruprecht*, Tijuana 1987, pp. 90–94.

Suviranta, Antti, *Discussion on Methods of Comparative Labour Law*, in *XI Congreso internacional ...*, tema III, Vol. II, pp. 477–486, 489–490.

Suviranta, Antti, *Il diritto del lavoro in Finlandia e in Norvegia*, in Giuliano Mazzoni, ed., *Enciclopedia giuridica del lavoro*, Padua 1981, Vol. 15, pp. 57–100.

Suviranta, Antti, *Inflationsbewältigung im finnischen Zivil- und Arbeitsrecht, Arbeiten zur Rechtsvergleichung*, Vol. 78 (1978), pp. 41–47.

Suviranta, Antti, *Invisible Clauses in Collective Agreements, Scandinavian Studies in Law*, Vol. 9 (1965), pp. 177–215.

Suviranta, Antti, *Les grandes tendances du droit du travail à l'époque contemporaine, Pays Scandinaves, Revue Internationale de Droit Comparé*, Vol. 19 (1967), pp. 89–107.

Suviranta, Antti, *On the Influence of International Labour Standards on Finnish Labour Law, Kansainoikeus, Ius Gentium*, Vol. 3 (1986), pp. 123–129.

Suviranta, Antti, *The Neutral and Public Interests in Resolving Labour Disputes in Finland, Comparative Labor Law Journal*, Vol. 13 (1992), pp. 421–437.

Suviranta, Antti, *The Role of Neutrals in the Resolution of Interest Disputes in Finland, Comparative Labor Law Journal*, Vol. 10 (1989), pp. 310–323.

Suviranta, Antti, *The Role of Neutrals in the Solution of Shop Floor Disputes in Finland, Comparative Labor Law Journal*, Vol. 9 (1987), pp. 55–67.

Suviranta, Antti, *The Scandinavian Labour Councils*, in *In memoriam Sir Otto Kahn-Freund*, Munich 1980, pp. 687–700.

Suviranta, Antti, *Worker privacy in Finland, Comparative Labor Law Journal*, Vol. 17 (1995), pp. 45–60.

Suviranta, Antti, *Workplace participation in safety and health matters in Scandinavia*, in *Studia z prawa pracy, Dla uszczenia 50-lecia dzialalnosci naukowej Profesora Doktora Waclawa Szuberta*, Warsaw 1988, pp. 335–344.

Sädevirta, Markus, *A Comparative Study of the Regulation Governing the Use of Fixed-Term Contracts in Three EU Member States*, Helsinki, 2013.

Selected Bibliography

Tiitinen, Kari-Pekka, *Työ- ja virkaehtosopimusten neuvottelulausekkeista* (with a German summary: 'Über die Verhandlungsklauseln bei Tarifverträgen und Diensttarifverträgen'), Helsinki, Suomalainen Lakimiesyhdistys, 1979.

Tiitinen, Kari-Pekka, *Procedures and structures of collective bargaining at the enterprise and plant levels in Finland*, in *XI Congreso internacional,* tema I, Vol. I, pp. 427–452.

Tiitinen, Kari-Pekka and Ilkka Ruponen, *Mediation of the Collective Interest Disputes*, Helsinki, Finnish Labour Law Society, 1999.

Ylhäinen, Marjo, *Työoikeus ja prekaari yhteiskunta* (with an English summary: *Labour Law and the Precarisation of Society*, Helsinki, 2015.

Court Reports

Those decisions of the Supreme Court and the Supreme Administrative Court which are deemed to have significance as precedents are published in semiannual publications of the respective courts. Decisions and advisory opinions of the Labour Court are published in like manner. Each case is published in its own language, Finnish or Swedish, but the registers of the publications and to some extent the headlines of the cases are in both languages. Summaries of the decisions (and advisory opinions) which will be published are also stored in the Finlex database system. The advisory opinions of the Labour Council are also regularly published.

Legislation

All new legislation – Acts of Parliament as well as subordinate legislation, regulations adopted by organs lower than the Ministries, however, partially excluded – are currently published in the collections *Suomen Säädöskokoelma* (Finnish) and *Finlands Författningssamling* (Swedish). International treaties concluded by Finland are, however, published in the separate Treaty Series (*Sopimussarja, Fördragsserie*) of the said collections in Finnish and Swedish as well as in the (other) official language(s) of the treaty in question. A very comprehensive collection of the legislation currently in force is published in Finnish annually under the name *Suomen Laki* ('The Law of Finland') in three volumes. The contents of the collection is stored in a database system ('Finlex'), administered by the Ministry of Justice and available to an increasing number of subscribers. A Swedish edition, *Finlands Lag*, comprising a large selection from the Finnish edition, is published, with intervals of about two years. In addition to these general collections, there are special collections of labour legislation, suitable also for display on working sites in compliance with legal requirements. English translations of some labour legislation have been published and are found on the database Finlex.

Index

The numbers here refer to paragraph numbers.

Index

Index

www.ingramcontent.com/pod-product-compliance
Lightning Source LLC
Chambersburg PA
CBHW071447230926
51846CB00001B/369
* 9 7 8 9 4 0 3 5 3 4 7 6 3 *